M000228626

THE GREAT NORTH KOREAN FAMINE

Andrew S. Natsios

THE GREAT NORTH KOREAN FAMINE

ANDREW S. NATSIOS

UNITED STATES INSTITUTE OF PEACE PRESS
Washington, D.C.

The views expressed in this book are those of the author alone. They do not necessarily reflect views of the United States Institute of Peace.

UNITED STATES INSTITUTE OF PEACE
1200 17th Street NW, Suite 200
Washington, DC 20036-3011

© 2001 by the Endowment of the United States Institute of Peace. All rights reserved.

First published 2001

Printed in the United States of America

The paper used in this publication meets the minimum requirements of American National Standards for Information Science—Permanence of Paper for Printed Library Materials, ANSI Z39.48-1984.

Library of Congress Cataloging-in-Publication Data
Natsios, Andrew S.
    The great North Korean famine / Andrew S. Natsios.
      p. cm.
    Includes bibliographical references and index.
    ISBN 1-929223-34-X (cloth) — ISBN 1-929223-33-1 (paper)
    1. Famines—Korea (North) 2. Food supply—Korea (North) 3. Korea (North)— Politics and government. I. Title

HC470.2.Z9 F36 2001
363.8'095193—dc21   2001039667

For my wife,
Elizabeth,
and our children,
Emily, Alexander, and Philip

CONTENTS

Part III: The Consequences

FOREWORD

The Great North Korean Famine is a powerfully argued account of perhaps the greatest humanitarian disaster of the 1990s, one that took the lives of millions and blighted the lives of millions more. Andrew Natsios has written a provocative analysis of international reaction to the North Korean famine, reflecting the author's own involvement in the events he describes: as vice president of World Vision, one of the largest nongovernmental organizations (NGOs) in the field of international disaster assistance, Natsios played a prominent role in persuading a skeptical world that the famine was real and in trying to prompt governments and NGOs to launch a timely and adequate humanitarian response.

Natsios's narrative is in many ways a personal account, illuminated and animated by the author's firsthand experiences and recollections. It draws together a considerable body of evidence and argues its case with scholarly care. While some may disagree with his assessment of the extent of the famine and of what the West should or could have done about it, no observer of North Korea or analyst of the humanitarian relief community can lightly dismiss its conclusions or ignore the impressive source material that Natsios has marshaled.

Moreover, this book also raises issues pertinent to other humanitarian crises. Natsios's approach stresses the importance of seeing such disasters from multiple perspectives—political, economic, diplomatic, international, governmental, and nongovernmental—and from the "bottom up" as well as the "top down." This approach allows him to identify interconnections between often-conflicting perspectives and to retrace the steps that led to calamity. For instance, while bad weather, poor agricultural practices, and a precipitous decline in food subsidies from the Soviet Union and China were among the most immediate causes of the North Korean famine, the chief culprit, argues Natsios, was the country's political system. Dictatorial and omnipresent, the regime held rigidly to a self-destructive agricultural system and impoverishing industrial policies while walling itself off from the rest of the world. When its food supply failed, it had no foreign exchange with which to buy food and no friends from whom to ask for food. The regime then made the situation far worse by deciding for political reasons to triage one area of the country and to reduce rations to farmers nationwide. "Most analyses of the North Korean famine," writes Natsios, "have been conducted using the disciplines of public health, nutrition, national agricultural production, and food aid distribution. But famines at their core are principally economic and political phenomena with public health and nutritional consequences, not vice versa."

The most controversial question this volume asks, however, is not "Who or what caused the famine?" but "Who failed to stop it?" In answering this latter question, Natsios criticizes humanitarian aid officials and agencies who failed to act upon the evidence of starvation that even the obsessively secretive North Korean regime could not entirely disguise. He censures, too, the governments of South Korea and Japan, which could have done much more to help their impoverished neighbor. Finally, he condemns American policymakers, who first denied the existence of a North Korean famine and then responded inadequately, Natsios argues, possibly at the cost of hundreds of thousands of lives. In so acting, the Clinton administration was responding to pressure from a powerful chorus of interest groups and politicians who were demanding that no U.S. food aid be sent until North Korea agreed to behave more responsibly on the international stage and until the regime could demonstrate that the aid would not be diverted from starving citizens to its military. Even so, says Natsios, the administration should have put political and strategic considerations aside in favor of the moral obligation to feed the hungry. Natsios cites the doctrine adopted by Ronald Reagan midway through his tenure as president that "a hungry child knows no politics," a policy that continued under the administration of George Bush senior, of which the author was a part, serving as director of the Office of Foreign Disaster Assistance.

Natsios wrote this book while he was a senior fellow at the United States Institute of Peace in 1998–99, immediately after leaving World Vision. He is now again in government, serving as administrator of the United States Agency for International Development under George W. Bush. An appointee under Republican administrations and formerly a longtime Republican member of the Massachusetts legislature, Natsios is highly critical of decision making within the Clinton administration, but he is also critical of people of all political standpoints who opposed sending aid to North Korea.

This volume confronts the reader with the rending question of how to balance moral values against political, diplomatic, and geostrategic interests. This is an issue that any president or prime minister confronts in deciding whether to send food to the hungry people of a hostile state, to deploy troops to halt genocide or ethnic cleansing in an unstable and dangerous region, or to dispatch diplomats to negotiate a peace settlement with war criminals. It is also a question that is of great concern to the United States Institute of Peace, whose congressional mandate is to explore the causes of international conflict and the means by which such conflict can be prevented, managed, or resolved. Directly or indirectly, much of the work supported by the Institute addresses this tension between the schools of realism and idealism, and assesses the complex relationships between morality, expediency, and effectiveness. What may seem to be the most economically or politically expedient policy, for example, may turn out to be a singularly ineffective or counterproductive way of pursuing national interests. And what may seem to be the correct moral course may in fact lead one into deeper and darker moral dilemmas while achieving little or nothing of substance.

Many aspects of this book resonate with other Institute-funded research. To take just a few examples from work published by the Institute in the past two years: *The Great North Korean Famine* complements Scott Snyder's study of North Korean negotiating behavior, *Negotiating on the Edge*, which also offers insights into the North Korean worldview and the idiosyncratic ways that the leaders of the "Hermit Kingdom" deal with what they see as a threatening international environment. Some of the same broad questions about foreign aid raised here by Andrew Natsios are addressed in Rex Brynen's book, *A Very Political Economy: Peacebuilding and Foreign Aid in the West Bank and Gaza*. The relationship between

NGOs, intergovernmental organizations (IGOs), and governments, which is central to *The Great North Korean Famine*, is likewise the focus of the *Guide to IGOs, NGOs, and the Military in Peace and Relief Operations*, a handbook written by Pamela Aall, Lt. Col. Daniel Miltenberger, and Thomas G. Weiss. The multiauthor volume *Turbulent Peace: The Challenges of Managing International Conflict*, edited by Chester Crocker, Fen Hampson, and Pamela Aall, offers numerous perspectives not only on the role of NGOs and IGOs in international humanitarian operations but also on the wisdom or otherwise of subordinating moral to political considerations in the making and conduct of foreign policy.

In short, *The Great North Korean Famine* furthers the Institute's goal of providing policymakers, practitioners, and other concerned citizens with informative, carefully argued, and thought-provoking analyses of issues critical to international peacemaking and stability. Andrew Natsios's passionate volume is sure to enhance our knowledge of North Korea— which may again be facing a food crisis—and of the dynamics of famine and disaster relief while stimulating debate on issues central to the making of foreign policy within a democracy.

RICHARD H. SOLOMON, PRESIDENT
UNITED STATES INSTITUTE OF PEACE

INTRODUCTION

WRITING A BOOK ABOUT AN EVENT AS TERRIBLE AS A FAMINE is not an easy task. Writing it as current history is unfolding complicates the task even more. This book on the North Korean famine of 1995–99 should be written a decade or two from now, if by then the character of the North Korea regime has changed. Only then will scholars and analysts have more complete information about what happened. Most of the lasting works on great famines were written well after the events they record. Cecil Woodham-Smith wrote her extraordinary history of the Irish potato famine more than one hundred years after it ended. Robert Conquest wrote his chronicle of Joseph Stalin's forced collectivization of Ukraine fifty-five years after it was over. And Jasper Becker wrote his account of the Chinese famine forty years after the Great Leap Forward. Undoubtedly some more authoritative work on the North Korean famine will be written at some point in the future, but I did not want to wait. The story needs to be told now. Political and economic conditions have not much changed, and although the famine ended by mid-1998, it could recur. The political and security consequences of the famine will be felt for decades. It is better to look at these recent events now, even without knowing the full story, if doing so could have the effect of improving future policy responses toward North Korea or other countries in similar circumstances.

While I was conducting initial research for this manuscript in 1997 and 1998, refugees were streaming across the border into China to escape the catastrophe. Newly dug mass graves for the victims lined the mountainsides. Gangs of abandoned children orphaned by the famine roamed city streets in search of food. And a destitute class of human refuse wandered the streets of the large cities, impoverished by the famine. My task was complicated by my own participation in the events I have recorded, as I worked for one of the nongovernmental organizations (NGOs) that responded to the famine both through advocacy efforts aimed at changing U.S. government policy and by designing programs to assist the victims. For two years I sat through countless meetings on North Korea that took place in Congress, in the executive branch, at United Nations (UN) agencies, and among my NGO colleagues. I have tried to detach myself from the events I am writing about, but I know that detachment may not be entirely possible. Having worked as a relief manager in most of the famines of the 1990s, and having seen them up close, I know what they are about. Nothing can prepare the Western mind for the scenes associated with famines; few Westerners can fully comprehend the absolute terror the very word engenders in countries that have been ravaged by them.

When Jasper Becker interviewed survivors of the Chinese famine of 1958–62, which killed 30 million people, he later described the terrible sadness in their faces—even though the famine had occurred forty years earlier. The consequences of famine in Bangladesh may be observed by the words used in Bengali to describe their nuanced severity. *Akal* describes bad times in which food is scarce, *durvickha* describes a food crisis in which alms are scarce, and *mananthor* describes an event of epoch-changing magnitude against which other historical events are measured in the collective memory of the survivors—a great famine.[1] Traditional societies often measure time by its proximity to or distance from such famines. People in these societies, who do not otherwise know the year of their birth, can describe with great precision their age at the time of a great famine because its horrors were so terrible.[2]

For the North Korean people, what occurred between 1995 and 1999 was a great famine. Used in this context, however, the word "great" has no nobility attached to it; rather, it describes an event that will scar its survivors for the remainder of their lives.

During the occupation, the German army stripped Greece of its food supply—inadequate in a good year but well below normal because of the disruption of the German invasion—to provision General Erwin Rommel's army in North Africa. The famine that followed between 1941 and 1943 killed 500,000 Greeks. One of the victims was my father's uncle,

Demetrios Karadimas. A village doctor found his emaciated body in a field, where he had apparently been trying to eat grass to survive. He was buried in a mass grave, one of the dark motifs of famines across the centuries. While I was growing up, my father more than once told me the story of his uncle's death and of the terrible suffering in Greece during famine. Famines are woven indelibly into the fabric of family history as well.

It is fashionable today, in an effort to minimize or dismiss great events, to engage in intellectual deconstruction when dealing with any sacred subject. One school of famine deconstruction argues that people die all the time, and in poor countries sometimes quite prematurely, even without famines. This argument, which is generally made by people who have never been through famines, trivializes them. Premature deaths are tragic anywhere but deaths from famine are a different matter. During famines, entire families are completely wiped out; whole villages and city neighborhoods are deserted because everyone has died or moved to escape certain death. Only genocide, perhaps, resembles famine in the panic and terror that its approach engenders, and in the pain and disfigurement it inflicts on its victims. Genocide, however, can be perpetrated relatively quickly; starving takes a very long and painful time. The Rwandan genocide was over in five months; the North Korean famine wreaked its havoc over four long and horrifying years.

In writing each page of this book I have kept the political and military context of the famine constantly in mind. Having served on active duty as an officer in the Persian Gulf War and in a state legislature for a dozen years, I recognize that both political and military perspectives are important. The grave dangers posed by the unpredictable behavior of North Korea toward South Korea, the U.S. troops there, and the region generally must not be trivialized. Pyongyang's behavior was and is a real and present danger, despite the recent rapprochement between North and South, but it should never be taken out of an overall moral framework constraining policy. Political and military issues have dominated the debate over how to deal with North Korea, as indeed they should. In the 1990s, however, the humanitarian imperative was given short shrift at a terrible cost in lives, as diplomats and military officers misunderstood the trauma through which the country was passing. More important, political and military analysis devoid of a real understanding of the consequences of a great famine may produce deeply flawed policy.

North Korea holds the distinction, even compared to its former Eastern bloc allies, of being the most controlled and reclusive society on earth. This is one reason why it was so difficult to see physical evidence of the famine. Discerning what was actually happening in such a society was no easy matter. Visual observations by humanitarian aid workers who visited or worked in the country formed the basis of much of the reporting on the famine. Although those visits provided important anecdotal information, neither they nor the data provided by the North Korean government about the food situation constitute conclusive evidence of anything, for they presented conditions as the central authorities wished them to appear to the outside world rather than as they were.

Famines can be observed through at least five different lenses, but two have unfortunately nearly completely dominated contemporary analysis, not just of the North Korean crisis but of most other famines as well. I say "unfortunately" because these two lenses—aggregated agricultural production figures and public health measurements of malnutrition, morbidity, and mortality—were those least useful in analyzing a totalitarian system that exercised nearly complete control over its population. This control distorted or obscured the view of what was really happening in North Korean society. Yet those two lenses are the ones through which humanitarian agencies and donor governments often viewed the North Korean famine.

I have chosen to analyze the North Korean famine using three other lenses that are much more appropriate to the context. The first of these tools of famine analysis, called famine indicators, involves observation of the subtle behavior of the population to cope with their diminishing access to food, which threatens their survival. The North Korean regime did not understand that the appearance of these indicators, some proudly advertised by the central government, were de facto evidence of the presence of famine. I have taken advantage of the regime's ignorance.

The second tool is the analytical model developed by the great Indian economist of famine, Amartya Sen, who argued that famines are caused by an unfavorable relationship between a family's income and resources and the price of food on the markets. According to Sen's model, which won him the Nobel Prize for economics, if a family's ability to purchase or grow food declines rapidly at the same time that food prices increase dramatically on markets, the family will eventually starve.

The third tool I employ to observe the famine is political analysis. All famines occur in a political context. Some government nearly always presides over the crisis—it may exacerbate or even cause the famine, perhaps to rid itself of some unwanted population; it may instead be paralyzed and unable to act; or it may make decisions that unintentionally transform a modest shortage into a catastrophe. The political objectives of the state just before and during a famine determine its outcome, and thus to understand the famine fully these objectives must also be studied.

In addition to using these five lenses, this book examines the famine's historical context, the testimony of its survivors, the role of great-power diplomacy, the political crisis within North Korea, the perspective of humanitarian aid agencies, and the reaction within the United States. My goal in doing so is to provide an extraordinarily complex account that emphasizes the tragedy's many layers.

My introduction to North Korea came because of my position in World Vision and as cochairman of the Disaster Response Committee at InterAction. One of the largest NGOs in the world, World Vision was founded in Korea just as the war began in 1950; InterAction is a consortium of 150 U.S.-based NGOs working in the developing world. Perhaps the richest source of information for this book has come from nearly one thousand messages I received over the InterAction e-mail network during the three-year period from 1996 through 1998. These messages concerned my work in World Vision and with other NGOs working in North Korea. Many of these e-mails were shared in confidence, and their public disclosure would likely embarrass their authors and anger the North Korean government. The North Koreans were so concerned about NGOs exchanging information with one another about what they saw that government officials reportedly insisted on agreements with some NGOs prohibiting this exchange. I have used these e-mails as background information to ensure that my theories and time lines are accurate, but I have not violated the confidence of the organizations that produced them; I quote from the messages only if I have received consent for their use. Some NGO reports are quoted directly, but, to protect their authors from potential retribution, unless they were public documents to begin with, I have omitted their specific source.

Nine other sources provide valuable anecdotal and empirical evidence about North Korea's food crisis: Scott Snyder's United States

Institute of Peace Special Reports, *A Coming Crisis on the Korean Penin-sula?* and *North Korea's Decline and China's Strategic Dilemmas;* defector inter-views; books and public statements of the preeminent defector Hwang Jong Yop, including *North Korea: Truth or Lies?* and *Theses;* research by scholars of North Korea; four studies based on refugee interviews (two large surveys and two smaller NGO surveys); U.S. newspaper interviews with refugees in China, particularly the February 11, 1999, articles by John Pomfret of the *Washington Post;* interviews with Korean Chinese and Han Chinese who have traveled into North Korea as merchants or to visit relatives; official North Korean government documents and pub-lications, no matter how contrived the documents are; and the speeches of Kim Jong Il, particularly a December 1996 speech that provides excep-tional insight into the dynamics of the famine. I visited North Korea in June 1997 and the Chinese border with North Korea in September 1998 and interviewed twenty food refugees and merchants. I interviewed twenty-three staff members of the UN World Food Program and the UN Food and Agriculture Organization, as well as staff of foreign policy agencies of the U.S. government. Many asked that our interviews be kept in confidence because of the sensitivity of what they shared with me, a confidence I have respected unless they agreed to full disclosure.

Two journalists stand out among those who reported on the famine. Jasper Becker, a British journalist and reporter for the *South China Morn-ing Post* stationed in Beijing, wrote twenty articles over a four-and-a-half-year period based on interviews with dozens of food refugees, border officials, and merchants. He provided the most in-depth reporting on what was happening, in part because his border reports were informed by his own research and writing on the Chinese famine of 1958–62, con-tained in his book *Hungry Ghosts.* The photographic and written accounts of the famine by Hilary Mackenzie, a Canadian journalist with unusual internal access, also provide a powerful description of the tragedy.

I have attempted to cross-check information from at least three independent sources before concluding it is true. All these sources, taken exclusively, have limitations, but combined and woven together they provide a reasonably accurate record of what has happened.

One source—the refugee interviews mentioned earlier—stands out above all others and has allowed a glimpse into the terrible pathology of the famine and its impact on people and their communities. The

refugees painfully describe conditions in their home villages and neighborhoods, deaths in their families and *bans* (the lowest unit of Korean
society, equivalent to twenty to forty families), and their journeys to
China. They recount the deaths of their companions along the way, the
separation of parents and children in the chaos of their movement, their
capture at the border, and their imprisonment and escape. These accounts
are by far the richest and most powerful of my sources. One should be
skeptical about their estimates of total deaths for large cities, about self-
diagnosis of disease epidemics they report, and about whether their
remarkably blunt and angry political views represent general opinion in
the country. Unless the refugees were public officials or medical doctors
in a position to gather the data they present, the accuracy of their information cannot be confirmed. Their testimony on what they and their
families experienced, however, including what happened in their own villages and neighborhoods, what they themselves witnessed, and how they
survived—testimony that unmistakably parallels the historical pattern of
other famines—must be taken seriously, particularly since 2,300 of these
accounts exist.

One British reporter interviewed me in January 1999 about the
famine and my experience on the Chinese border, asking probing questions with a slight air of doubt in her voice. At the conclusion of the
interview she admitted to me that she had been deeply skeptical of these
border reports until she traveled there and interviewed refugees herself.
She was shocked by what she heard, but she believed the testimony. She
had no doubt there was a terrible famine under way. Since my own trip
to North Korea in June 1997, I have argued with my NGO and UN colleagues that it is impossible to get a complete picture of the famine from
information taken inside the country. One must travel across the border
to confront its terrifying face. I am convinced that no account of what
happened between 1995 and 1999 in North Korea can be accurate or
authoritative without considering the evidence from the food refugees,
corroborated by defector information.

The description of the famine in this book takes a very different view
of North Korea than most scholarship, because it looks up from the murky
and often unseen bottom of society through to the top. It is ultimately
written from a grassroots perspective, whereas most books—regardless
of their focus—view North Korea from the top down and are written

from the elite level. Perhaps the single exception to this is Robert A. Scalapino and Chong-Sik Lee's *Communism in Korea,* which makes extensive use of defector testimony. Both views are certainly needed; what happens at the bottom affects what is going on in Pyongyang, even if it is difficult for outsiders to discern and even though this totalitarian society holds the entire population captive. Totalitarian regimes—mindful, perhaps, of how most of these regimes ended in the twentieth century—fear their own people more than outsiders may understand.

This book is not primarily an account of the international aid effort to end the famine; however, a full understanding of why the famine occurred and how it ended is impossible without understanding the humanitarian mistakes made in responding to it and how diplomatic interests exacerbated these mistakes.

For his assistance to me while I researched this book, I am indebted to the Venerable Pomnyun, a South Korean Buddhist monk. Pomnyun founded an NGO, the Korean Buddhist Sharing Movement (KBSM), which works along the Chinese border with North Korea collecting information from refugees and helping them to survive their ordeal. From the summer of 1997, Pomnyun led the crusade to draw the attention of a skeptical world and aid community to the severity of the famine. He has been attacked, ridiculed, and harassed in his own country; ignored in Europe; and greeted with polite skepticism in Washington. Pomnyun refused to give up, though, and he stubbornly continued his courageous work. As with most pioneers, he was finally successful through sheer persistence; he knew he was right even if others would not listen initially. He was my host and guide along the border region in September 1998, at considerable personal risk to himself and the KBSM staff. We tirelessly debated our respective theories about the famine and reached some agreement on some central findings. Pomnyun will undoubtedly disagree with some of the political judgments I express here, and he bears no responsibility for them. He has been patient with my unending and sometimes overly aggressive questions, as well as with our debates about what was really happening. Without the information he and his staff collected on the border, I would not have been able to create the many layers of evidence necessary to confirm some of my findings. I have come to know people of many different religious faiths in my decades of relief work across the globe, but Pomnyun is the first Buddhist I can count among my good friends and colleagues. He is an extraordinary symbol of his faith.

I also have many other individuals to thank for their support and assistance. I thank Bob Seiple and Ken Casey, president and senior vice president, respectively, of World Vision during my time there, for their support and leadership in the NGO advocacy effort. Dick Solomon, Sally Blair, Bill Drennan, Patrick Cronin, Joe Klaits, Scott Snyder, and Young Chung, my research assistant, were friends and colleagues at the United States Institute of Peace, which supported my research and writing. Professor Youngsuk Park of Boston University deserves thanks for her painstaking translations of KBSM refugee interviews. Davis Bookhart, from Tufts University's Feinstein International Famine Center, and Kate Almquist, who has been my chief of staff in several jobs, helped me with the footnotes and references. Don Oberdorfer and Nicholas Eberstadt read the initial manuscript and made many helpful suggestions. I would like to thank Nigel Quinney, the United States Institute of Peace editor whose persistence and critical comment improved the manuscript. Many of my friends and colleagues at World Vision and in the NGO community in general will undoubtedly disagree with some of my research and findings. My views were not the norm in the NGO community, and certainly what I have written does not reflect World Vision or NGO views on the North Korean crisis. The great risk of my candor in this book may be more harassment and obstruction by the North Korean government for UN agencies and NGOs trying to help address the crisis in that country. I thought the risk less compelling than the terrible facts of what happened, and I therefore determined that the events needed to be recorded to instruct responses to other famines.

Most important, I thank my wife, Elizabeth, for her patience and encouragement in the writing of this book. She translated some critically important documents from their original French into English.

Finally, I would also like to thank the Smith Richardson Foundation for its encouragement through a grant to support the research for this book.

THE GREAT NORTH KOREAN FAMINE

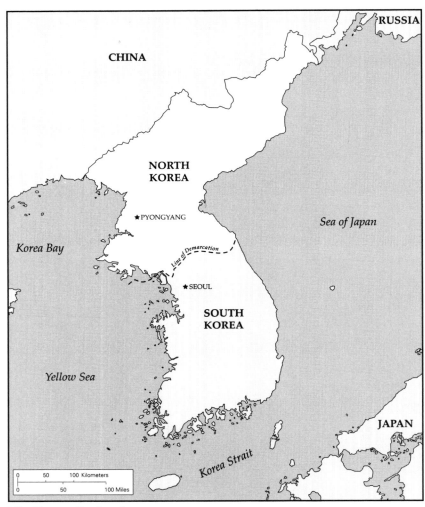

The Korean Peninsula

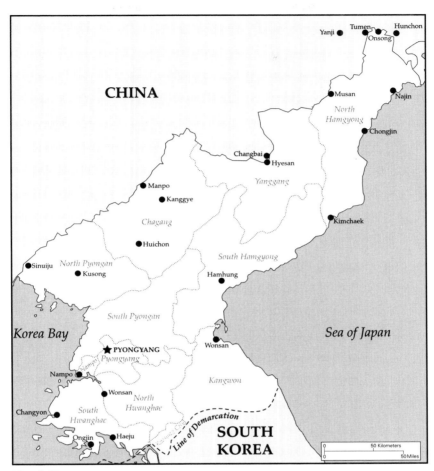

North Korea

ROOTS OF THE CRISIS

I N SEPTEMBER 1995 THE NORTH KOREAN GOVERNMENT, in a rare admission of vulnerability, announced to the outside world that severe flooding had devastated its agricultural regions and that the subsequent crop failure had caused widespread food shortages. It appealed for help to the World Food Program (WFP)—the food agency of the United Nations—and to donor governments.

Appeals for help from countries struck by natural disaster typically elicit outpourings of international assistance without much hesitancy. The complication of this particular appeal was that it was for North Korea, and nothing about North Korea is typical. Pyongyang's acknowledgment of the crisis had an ideological cast: official propaganda drew an unmistakable connection between the famine and Kim Il Sung's guerrilla resistance to Japanese occupation in the late 1930s, calling both the "arduous march." In fact, ideology was one of North Korea's greatest problems in its appeal for help. By 1995 North Korea was, with Cuba, one of two remaining Eastern bloc countries that steadfastly refused to acknowledge the bankruptcy of the great socialist experiment that had begun with the Russian revolution of 1917. As it entered its greatest crisis since the Korean War, North Korea could count on one hand its remaining allies. To varying degrees, all of its fellow Eastern bloc members had embraced market capitalism and many constitutional democratic polities as well. North Korea stubbornly refused to make any systemic accommodation to the new economic and political order in the world, and this refusal was at the root of the crisis it faced in the autumn of 1995.

North Korea's appeal for help was rare for several reasons. Pyong-yang had spent five decades making unrelenting rhetorical attacks against its principal enemies, the United States and South Korea, with which it had never signed a permanent peace agreement after the Korean War. Its standard propaganda warned of the threat of imminent invasion by these enemies, and the request for help could have been misinterpreted as a sign of military weakness. The acceptance of humanitarian food aid would be a radical departure from the governing philosophy of *juche,* a neo-Confucian permutation of marxism demanding radical self-sufficiency. Kim Il Sung, who ruled from the end of the Japanese occupation until his death in 1994, had imposed *juche* on the country, and it had continued as the governing ideology of the North Korean regime under Kim's son and successor, Kim Jong Il. For the regime to accept international charity was an ideological heresy from the start—an admission of failure that would cause the regime to "lose face." The very fact of the appeal meant that something was seriously amiss in the hermit kingdom. North Korea watchers took note.

In response to the request for help, the WFP, in keeping with estab-lished practice, took two actions. First it sent a team of technical experts with the UN Food and Agricultural Organization (FAO) to conduct an assessment of the general state of agriculture and the extent of the autumn 1995 harvest. Then it issued an appeal to traditional donor governments, the three largest being the United States, Canada, and the member-states of the European Union, for that portion of the food deficit that it believed it could raise from these donors. The WFP did not ask for the full amount that was needed, as it believed from informal consultation that donor governments were unenthusiastic about providing assistance to this pariah state. The languid prose of the agricultural assessment pub-lished by the WFP and the FAO in December 1995 technically acknowl-edged the alarming condition of the agricultural economy, but its dry statistics conveyed no sense of drama or alarm. Yet, the reported food deficit amounted to nearly 50 percent of the food requirements of the population, a greater deficit than the one that caused the 1985 Ethiopian famine that killed a million people.

These appeals for help were the first evidence to the outside world that the North Koreans might be facing a famine. Famine experts would likely have recognized the warning signs that had begun to appear in the summer of 1994 had they been granted free access to the country, but they were not. It was not until February 1996 that a British journalist provided anecdotal evidence that famine might be sweeping the country. After a week of interviewing North Korean refugees in China, Jasper Becker wrote that a famine was waging a grim assault on those most vulnerable to starvation: children under five, the elderly, nursing mothers, pregnant women, and sick and disabled people.

The possibility of famine in an industrialized country with a relatively advanced standard of living—by communist standards—and a high level of literacy was indeed unusual. Except for the Ukrainian famine of 1932–33—which Joseph Stalin deliberately contrived to collectivize the farms and destroy the middle-class farmers, called *kulaks*, who actively opposed his forced collectivization—no peacetime famine has occurred in a relatively advanced society. Famines have more recently been associated with Africa, but Asia has experienced four since World War II. The Bengali famine of 1943 left two million dead; the Chinese famine of 1958–1962 left thirty million dead; and the Bangladeshi famine of 1974 left one and a half million dead. In the fourth, the Cambodian famine contrived by the Khmer Rouge as part of its holocaust against the urban and educated population in the late 1970s, the number of famine victims is unknown. The Chinese famine was not only the worst in Asia in the twentieth century, but also the worst in recorded world history measured by the total number of deaths.[1]

Amartya Sen, the Nobel Prize–winning economist of famine, and his colleague Jean Dreze have argued that no country with a democratic government has experienced a famine for two reasons. The first, which is intuitively obvious, is that the people who are dying have the ballot box as a means of expressing their panic and anger; moreover, in a democratic system a free press will publicize the crisis, forcing a government response.[2] North Koreans had neither a free press nor a democratic system of governance to deal with the impending disaster. In fact, no government in the world has been more reclusive, more suspicious of contact with the outside world, more isolated, and more devoted to absolute control and secrecy than North Korea's. The totalitarian nature of the North Korean regime—combined with a complex set of international political complications—transformed a manageable problem into an unimaginable nightmare.

A HISTORY OF FAMINE IN KOREA

Over the centuries, the poor peasants of the Korean peninsula have been intimately acquainted with famine and epidemics. During half a dozen periods—some of them decades' long—the peasants have suffered from widespread famine stimulated alternately by war or natural disaster, by confiscatory levels of taxation or outright expropriation of the peasant harvest by rapacious landlords or royal officials. Most peasants lived on the edge of absolute destitution much of the time, with no savings or assets accumulated to get them through to the next harvest in the event of a manmade or natural disaster. During such crises, many peasants starved in their homes, while others left their farms in search of food, dying along the way.[3]

Famine and war devastated the Korean peninsula between 1592 and 1598 when the Japanese feudal lord Hideyoshi Toyotomi, who had just ended internecine feudal conflicts and united Japan, led an invasion force of 158,000 men in conquering and occupying the south. The Chinese emperor, to whom Korean dynasties had for many years paid tribute, sent 150,000 troops to Korea to stop the Japanese invasion. In the following seven years a series of battles, followed by unsuccessful peace negotiations and more warfare, devastated the country. The Chinese and Japanese armies battled each other and, alternately, the Korean regular army, while guerrilla bands rose up across the country to fight the Japanese army behind their lines. Under these conditions agricultural and administrative systems fell into chaos. Whatever food was grown by the peasantry was confiscated either by the commanders to feed their troops or by landlords and local officials who used the chaos to exact even higher rents. Hordes of wandering poor people, displaced by the war and with no means of support, filled the countryside and succumbed to disease, starvation, or the frigid cold of the arctic winters. In fact, it was this weather, as much as local resistance, that ultimately defeated the Japanese invasion.[4]

The latter part of the Yi dynasty witnessed one disaster after another, with drought-induced famines accompanied by epidemics that spread across the country. These crises climaxed with the particularly calamitous famine of 1671, in which three hundred thousand Koreans starved to death, even more than had died during the Japanese invasion.

Japanese historian Takashi Hatada reported, "At the time of this famine, starving people openly broke into graves and ripped off the clothes from dead bodies, and babies were abandoned on roads and thrown into irrigation ditches."[5]

The reign of King Yongjio is generally regarded as the renaissance of Korean cultural history, but the political order and economic prosperity enjoyed by the aristocracy and merchant classes disguised widespread starvation and suffering among the peasantry. During 1748–49 a famine and accompanying epidemics killed five hundred thousand people, and the "spectacle of starving people eating corpses was common."[6]

The nineteenth century was worse than the eighteenth century. A series of major floods, followed by epidemics and famine, struck the country between 1810 and 1832, causing enormous suffering. The population declined by nearly a million as a result of these disasters. The dynastic chronicles record that in 1812 the number of starving people on the royal census reached 900,000 in Pyongan province, 520,000 in Hwanghae province, 170,000 in Kangwon province, and 400,000 in Hamgyong province.[7] Measures taken by the central government to deal with this large number of destitute people were largely ineffective, as the oppressive economic system that produced this human disaster remained unchanged. The poor peasantry, organized and led by disgruntled provincial and local officials who had been passed over for appointments, periodically rose in unsuccessful rebellions throughout the century.[8] One such rebellion, in the ancient province of Cholla in 1862, drove the entire country into chaos.[9] A description of the period is worth repeating, as it so resembles refugee reports from the Chinese border during the great famine of the 1990s:

> The governor-inspector of Cholla Province reported that many persons were deserting their homes, that in extreme cases there were not even ten families remaining in a township, and that fertile fields had become wasteland. . . . [T]he number of peasants who left their homes and became wanderers rose enormously. . . . First they became beggars, then they obtained food by selling their daughters, then they abandoned their sons. Many died on the road. Some went to the mountains with the idea of carrying on fire-field agriculture, that is, clearing an area for planting by burning off the vegetation. . . . Organized uprisings, however, did occur, and robber bands grew up from the chronically starving, sick and homeless people.[10]

The corrupt and incompetent royal bureaucracy refused to address these problems, and it largely ignored calls for systemic reforms. Japan then absorbed Korea into its new empire in 1905, and between 1919 and 1939 the Japanese colonial administrators moved to modernize Korean agriculture. Little of the surplus created by these reforms stayed in Korea, however; most of it was destined for Japan, where local production was inadequate for the burgeoning population. Once again, Korean peasants were left with a diminishing proportion of their harvest. Japanese and local landlords commonly extracted anywhere from 50 percent to 90 percent of a peasant's harvest in rents.[11] This caused sporadic localized famine conditions to reappear in the 1930s. The peasants once again abandoned their farms and cultivated fire fields in the mountains, choosing to grow sweet potatoes, millet, and corn on the steep hillsides rather than till their fields only to have the harvest confiscated. In 1931, 27,000 families lived on mountain fire fields; by 1939 this number had risen to 340,000 families.[12]

Not surprisingly, in the 1990s the North Korean peasantry once again turned to these fire fields for their survival, as the central government confiscated larger and larger portions of the harvest to feed the starving cities during the great famine.

THE COLLAPSE OF THE EASTERN BLOC ECONOMIC SYSTEM

North Korea reacted angrily to the conversion of China and Russia to different varieties of market capitalism in the 1980s and 1990s, accusing both of betraying socialism and the communist revolution. Kim Il Sung had kept close personal relations with the communist leaders of East Germany and Romania and reacted with some horror at their demise. Erich Honecker was arrested, tried, and eventually exiled, while a firing squad executed President Nicolae Ceausescu and his wife in December 1989 during a successful coup disguised as a popular revolt.[13] Both men had considered escaping to North Korea.

North Korea had long been part of the Soviet economic system, sustained by barter arrangements among its members. As North Korean food production began to decline steeply in the 1980s, the Soviet Union and China increased food subsidies to make up for these increasing deficits. The North Korean industrial economy would produce goods, otherwise unmarketable in the competitive international economy, which the Soviets took in payment for these food subsidies. As North Korea had no petroleum resources of its own, Russia and China met the country's oil requirements.[14] When the greater Soviet economic system collapsed in 1990–91, driven by Mikhail Gorbachev's political reforms and Boris Yeltsin's privatization revolution, the North Koreans lost their food and oil subsidies simultaneously. Soviet petroleum subsidies to North Korea dropped precipitously from 506,000 metric tons (MT) in 1989 to 30,000 MT in 1992. Given North Korea's limited level of foreign exchange and the absence of any indigenous supply of oil, this drop more than any other marked the beginning of the collapse of the country's industrial sector.[15] Although the floods of August 1995 marked the official beginning of the great North Korean famine, food shortages began well before the official date of the appeal for help.

Pyongyang couched its request for food aid in what became a tiring refrain in all its public pronouncements on the crisis; it claimed the famine was caused by natural disaster. Like Soviet officials in the 1980s —who had regularly claimed that World War II was why the country lagged far behind the West—the regime refused to admit to any ideological or systemic problems. When Westerners working to alleviate the famine suggested to North Korean officials that the famine was directly attributable to their agricultural and economic policies, the officials energetically countered that the real cause of the country's problems was the Korean War. North Korea had pursued the same form of collective farming as the Soviet Union and the People's Republic of China, but the Soviets and the Chinese had recently abandoned the practice. In North Korea, the only vestiges of private agricultural production were the secret agricultural plots up in the mountains and the small household vegetable plots from which each family was allowed to keep what it grew.

Even before the floods, North Korea was at an agricultural disadvantage, as only about 15 percent to 20 percent of its land is arable. North Korea ranks near the bottom of the international scale on one of the critical indicators of the ability of a country to feed its own people without importing food: arable land per person. Only ten poor countries have lower ratios than does North Korea.[16] Moreover, only a few nations with poor ratios have become wealthy despite this agricultural limitation:

Israel, Iceland, Japan, Singapore, the Netherlands, oil-rich Arab countries, Switzerland, and, most interestingly, South Korea. The arable-land-to-population ratio for the United States, for example, is five times higher than China's and six times higher than North Korea's. The central and western regions are mountainous, and potatoes and corn are grown there, but seldom enough to produce much of a surplus. Only the southwestern coastal plain and a few smaller areas along the border with China produce surpluses of rice and corn, and then only in good years.

An industrialized society whose arable land has a limited carrying capacity can avoid hunger by exporting products and importing the food it cannot produce itself. In a traditional agrarian economy, however, the amount of tillable land determines whether the mass of peasantry is prosperous or destitute. North Korea at its birth in the 1940s supported itself even with limited arable land because its population, still primarily agricultural, was fairly small. The rapid industrialization of the 1960s and 1970s and the country's integration into the greater Soviet economic system permitted the growth of the population far beyond what the land could support, as the country traded its industrial products for Soviet grain at heavily subsidized "friendship" prices. When this symbiotic economic arrangement collapsed in the 1990s, North Korea plunged into an economic crisis that could lead only to famine over the longer term. North Korea could not produce enough food to feed its now burgeoning population, and, with the collapse of its industrial capacity, neither could it export products.

Kim Il Sung, obsessed with national self-sufficiency, ordered the cultivation of corn on hillsides so steep that heavy rains carried off soils and dumped them into the country's river system. According to UN agronomists, the soil deposition into the waterways raised the river bottoms to such a degree that they are no long capable of absorbing the water from heavy rains or the spring thaw. The result is annual flooding that seems to be increasing in severity each year, destroying more and more of the neighboring agricultural land. In June 1997, on my first trip to North Korea, I traveled along one of the rivers that had experienced heavy flooding; the contiguous hills and countryside were torn apart by soil erosion from these regressive agricultural policies.

Kim Il Sung's involvement in agricultural development was not limited to determining where corn and rice should be planted, though.

Marxist-Leninist ideology demanded that private farms be confiscated and formed into collectives. Forced collectivization was accomplished between 1945 and 1953, though with a minimal loss of life compared to that during the Chinese and Soviet collectivizations, in which millions died. In North Korea, the central authorities invited anyone opposed to forced collectivization to leave the country and move to South Korea, an offer five million people chose to accept.[17] Between 1960 and 1970, in a series of celebrated speeches, Kim Il Sung announced the framework for the agricultural development of the country based on four principles: mechanization, chemicalization, irrigation, and electrification—principles right out of Lenin's prescriptions for Russian agriculture. In addition to these more operational initiatives, Kim also described in his speeches the Chongsan-ri method of agriculture. This method took its name from that of a small agricultural collective west of Pyongyang where Kim spent fifteen days talking with farmers and making marxist-based corrections to the way they were cultivating their crops. These corrections added an ideological dimension to an already highly centralized system of control over agricultural practice. The Korean Workers Party Central Committee formally approved the four principles and the Chongsan-ri system on February 25, 1964, after which the practices—handed down as they were from the Great Leader himself—were etched in proverbial stone.[18]

Since the mid-1960s, the regime has pursued these agricultural policies with great energy and ideological fervor and with no reference to market-driven economic incentives. It has consistently subordinated economics and science to political ideology, with disastrous result. Pyongyang's policies were designed to create a salaried farming proletariat employed on collective and state farms—the rural counterparts of the industrial proletariat in the cities, another ideal direct from Lenin's ideological handbook.[19] Kim had no desire to create a Jeffersonian ideal of a nation of independent yeoman farmers who owned their own land and houses. Kim's dream was a nation of factory farms with proletarian workers who owned nothing and were permanently tied to the land.

Mechanization, chemicalization, irrigation, and electrification were all inspired by the belief that modern technology and marxist-driven "science" could help the state realize its utopian dreams. It was in irrigation that the North Koreans were most successful. But if the increases in the North Korean harvest during the 1960s and 1970s were based on progress in these four areas, they also explain why the harvest was so poor in the 1990s. By the 1990s chemicalization—the production of fertilizer, pesticides, and herbicides—had declined steeply. Fertilizer production, for example, declined to 217,000 MT in 1995 and only 81,000 MT in 1997, but 350,000 MT were required.[20] Agricultural mechanization also declined: Most farm work was done by human and animal labor, as the country's tractor and trucking fleet had rusted into mechanical oblivion. Irrigation also had its problems, in part because of electrical failures: The electrical grid needed to pump water was offline much of the time.[21] One FAO irrigation study, which found that the unreliable electrical grid had adversely affected the rice crop in many areas, proposed to convert the electrically driven irrigation system north of Pyongyang to a gravity-fed system.[22]

While chemical inputs do have their place in improving harvests, their gross overuse can damage soils over time, as appears to have happened in North Korea. International agronomists with a wide knowledge of the farming system say they have never seen such excessive use of chemical fertilizer anywhere else in the world.[23] This, of course, was when chemical fertilizer was available. During the boom harvest years one agronomist suggested that the North Koreans were growing corn and rice in more fertilizer than soil, which, though an exaggeration, is not far from reality. For a time in the 1960s and 1970s, agricultural chemicalization appears to have resulted in steadily growing harvests each year, though it is difficult to separate government propaganda from reality in published statistics. Beginning in the mid-1980s, however, the production curve began a steady, apparently inexorable decline. After the economic decline of the manufacturing sector accelerated in late 1980s and early 1990s, fertilizer and pesticide production dropped substantially (as did fertilizer consumption—see figure 1).

Western agriculture has long employed several means to improve harvests, such as inter-cropping, crop rotation, double cropping, leaving fields fallow periodically, and using improved seed varieties that have disease and pest resistance bred into them. Such means are combined with the more moderate use of chemical inputs. Only recently has a modest experiment in double cropping been attempted in North Korea, and then over the adamant opposition of senior figures in the regime. This experiment, more than anything else, illustrates the destructive effects that

Figure 1. Consumption of NPK Fertilizer in North Korea, 1989–98 (in thousands of nutrient tonnes)

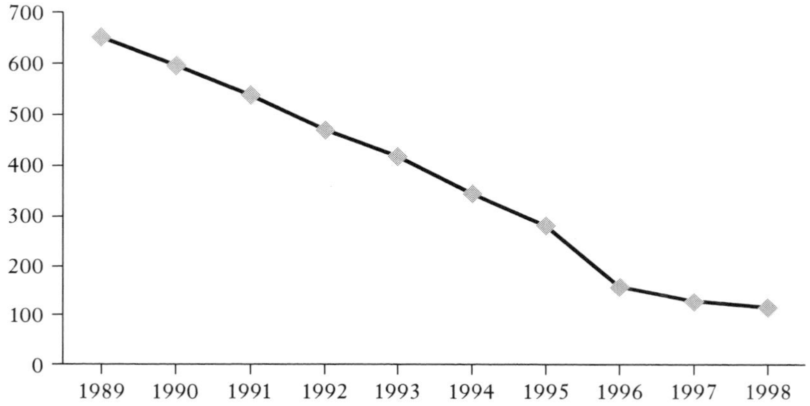

Source: FAO, Global Information and Early Warning System.

political ideology had on the agricultural system. Double cropping is a common practice in most agricultural systems, used to increase harvest production by planting two crops a year. North Korean Ministry of Agriculture policy in the late 1940s and 1950s was to encourage double cropping, but at some point the policy was abandoned because the short growing season meant one or sometimes both crops would not reach maturity.[24] Between then and now, however, Western agronomists have bred early maturing seed varieties, making double cropping feasible in most places. But during this same period of time, the policy against double cropping became a rigid part of *juche* agricultural policy: unchanging and unchangeable. The North Koreans did not know about genetic advances in seed quality because they were so isolated from the outside world, and even if they had known of them, they would have been unable to change the policy. Once again, politics—not science or economics—drove policy; witness Kim Il Sung's instruction in his infamous speech of February 1960 on agricultural policy to "put politics in command" on the farms.[25]

The story one defector told me is illustrative. While attending a UN meeting in Rome, the North Korean deputy minister of agriculture toured some Italian farms and noticed the farmers spreading maize seed in the fields for the spring planting. The North Korean practice was to plant maize seed in beds in the early spring, and later to hand-transplant the germinated plants to the fields. Pyongyang tried to justify this practice —which is followed nowhere else in the world—by citing the short growing season. The deputy minister met with Kim Il Sung and told him of the Italian practice and recommended an experiment be performed in North Korea using the same technique. Kim approved and the deputy minister then went to the minister to implement the experiment. But the minister instantly fired his deputy for having violated a prime directive of *juche* agriculture. The deputy minister fought for a month to be reinstated and was successful only after getting a message about his situation to the Great Leader himself. The minister had not realized that Kim had given his approval; rather, he was following the principles of *juche:* Take no risks, make no changes, and consider no innovations.[26]

One way in which North Korean agricultural scientists increased rice production was to combine improved seed varieties with extraordinarily heavy use of chemical fertilizer and unusually close planting of rice seedlings in the paddies.[27] Chinese agronomists familiar with the North Korean system claim that the practice is counterproductive; although the fields look good from a distance, they produce less rice per hectare. The damage to production is even more acute if the close planting is continued after the heavy use of chemical fertilizer has been curtailed, which of course happened in the mid-1990s.[28] The drop in production and the exhaustion of the soils both increased dramatically. This may be one reason why agricultural authorities ordered many collective farms of the southwest to revert to traditional, hearty rice varieties not requiring chemical fertilizer and to abandon improved varieties that did.[29]

NORTH KOREAN FINANCES

If the North Korean government had had budget reserves despite its agricultural and industrial dysfunction, it could have bought grain from the international markets to make up for what it could not produce. It would have helped my analysis to have a balance sheet on North Korean finances and currency reserves. Estimating the economic and budgetary condition of the central government, however, involves more conjecture than is required to quantify any other part of this elusive famine. The

North Korean government stopped paying its debts to Western countries in 1976 and to Eastern bloc countries in 1994, effectively declaring bankruptcy.[30] This prevented it from borrowing money on international markets. Yet, early in 1999 it apparently had enough foreign exchange to afford a shipment of Mercedes-Benz cars, and in the summer of 1998 it purchased a shipment of bicycles for its population.[31] It is possible that the goods were purchased not for the population but to be smuggled into China, although the bicycles were used domestically by residents of major cities.

By the late 1990s, the North Korean military machine, though still formidable in size and in brute destructive power, had been steadily decaying for a decade, particularly in comparison with the South Korean military, which had been modernizing itself using the revenues generated by South Korea's robust economy. From the mid-1990s, North Korea had been approaching Asian arms manufacturers in India, Russia, and China to modernize its weapons system in an effort to keep up with its southern competitor. But the North Koreans insisted that they be allowed to buy on credit, which few countries or businesses would accept.[32]

Given that the regime's central political objective was the preservation of its political and economic system, the insistence on credit arrangements to purchase weapons suggested it had exhausted its foreign exchange and gold reserves. If the central government had currency reserves, it would certainly have been spending them to modernize its deteriorating military power. Although it made some purchases on the international arms markets during the famine, they appear to have been limited.

Perhaps the only goods North Korea produces that remain marketable outside its borders are weapons—surface-to-air missiles, land mines, and small arms—and mineral ore. But even North Korean commercial exports of weapons showed a precipitous decline from their high point in the 1980s, when they averaged $250 million a year, to an average of $50 million a year for the period between 1990 and 1995, according to a South Korean report. This decline was attributed to the same maladies paralyzing industrial output generally: increasing transportation problems and a lack of raw materials and energy.[33]

Pyongyang has ordered North Korean embassies to find their own revenue to support embassy operations, which in many cases has led them into the black market and other illicit activities.[34] Credible sources report that the North Korean regime has engaged in the illicit drug trade to earn foreign currency of $85 million a year.[35] Although countries from the developing world do sometimes have trouble supporting their embassies abroad, given their budget constraints back home, it is fair to say that Pyongyang's instruction to its diplomats suggested a near-empty treasury. In an attempt to reduce their isolation from the rest of the world, the North Koreans had been trying to establish diplomatic relations with developing countries since the 1960s. In the summer of 1997 several North Korean operatives were attempting to pass around envelopes of U.S. dollars to Kenyan officials in Nairobi in order to gain diplomatic recognition.[36] But as embassy after embassy closed because of the economic crisis, Pyongyang abandoned its effort to compete with South Korea in establishing diplomatic relations with these countries. Instead, plans were under way in the fall of 1998 to close all DPRK embassies around the world except those at the United Nations and in the capitals of North Korea's remaining allies and adversaries.[37]

One way that the mountainous provinces in the northeast dealt with the economic collapse was by engaging in commercial trade, usually through barter, as the North Korean currency is not easily exchanged. Perhaps the most self-destructive barter arrangements for food have been undertaken across the Chinese border. Villagers in the northeast region have been cutting down their remaining forests for lumber to barter for Chinese corn, an arrangement that will only increase soil erosion and deposition in the deteriorating river system. Every visitor to the border area has reported convoys of scrap metal and industrial machinery crossing from North Korea as factory managers and local officials desperate for something to trade for Chinese food are disassembling what remains of the country's industrial infrastructure. Relief workers have provided credible reports of arrangements to barter North Korean mineral ore, fertilizer, and fish for corn in China.[38] By the summer of 1998, however, much of the tradable material from North Korea had been exhausted and these commercial transactions had diminished to a trickle in some border areas.[39]

For much of the past several decades the North Korean regime has received remittances directly from an association of ethnic Koreans living in Japan who run gambling parlors to raise money for their relatives in the North. These remittances have declined dramatically from perhaps as much as $2 billion to less than $100 million, according to both Nicholas Eberstadt and Marcus Noland, practiced North Korea watchers.[40]

One of the central government's efforts to increase both investment in the country and foreign earnings is the Najin–Sonbong Free Trade and Economic Zone: North Korea's only passing, if suspicious, nod to Western capitalism, located in the most remote area in the country. In 1997 Pyongyang announced the enactment of a series of policy reforms designed to encourage private investment, but they applied only to the zone, not to the entire country. Not surprisingly, the news disappointed the international financial community. But the regime's decision on both the location of the zone and the extent of the reforms appears to be consistent with the principle of keeping its one experiment in Western capitalism as far away from the capital city as possible.

Within the regime, ideological hostility toward the zone is palpable. Some Western analysts have incorrectly interpreted the experiment as a precursor to economic reforms, when it is in fact nothing but a means for increasing foreign exchange earnings. Kim Jong Il toured the zone in 1998 and was appalled to see eight commercial billboards overshadowing banners with his father's slogans. The next morning the eight offending billboards were cut down; the name of the zone had the word "free" deleted from it; and the zone director, a prominent party official and advocate of trade liberalization, was removed from his post. He has not been seen since.[41]

Pyongyang's persistent efforts to have U.S. economic sanctions lifted were directly related to its hopes for the Najin–Sonbong trade zone as a source of revenue to revive the country's economic system. North Koreans believed the sanctions impaired their ability to obtain foreign capital for new enterprises in the zone. They understood that the United States had provided capital and a huge market for Asian goods and had thus been a major factor in the Asian economic miracle. But the sanctions regime excluded North Korea from both U.S. capital and U.S. markets. They believed few businesspeople, regardless of nationality, would make a major investment in new enterprises in which U.S. capital and markets were precluded from participating. Although this was true up to a point, what the North Koreans failed to understand was that much U.S. investment had been curtailed since the 1997 Asian economic crisis.

Indeed, although the U.S. sanctions regime ended in 2000, North Korea has still failed to attract any significant capital flows.

The zone has attracted more promises than actual investment. The region is so remote, the infrastructure so wretched, the investment climate so unfriendly, the prospects for the country's future so dim, and the essential market reforms needed to make it successful so unlikely, little investment will be made unless North Korea embarks on a greater degree of systemic reform than it has been willing to consider.[42] Najin–Sonbong remains an anemic capitalist island in a sea of exhausted Stalinism.

This macroeconomic analysis of the situation facing North Korea from 1992 forward suggested a looming famine, but it did not prove that one was in progress. The financial balance sheet for North Korea is, at best, ambiguous. In place of authoritative data on the condition of the economy are ranges of estimates from high to low for every important resource, whether foreign remittances, food imports, grain harvest, or oil and grain subsidies. Such data are, finally, unsatisfying. Even at their most optimistic end, however, the figures tell us that North Korea was in serious economic trouble, enough to cause a famine if the allocation of sharply declining economic resources should miss the poorest families.

To deal with famine, vulnerable people develop coping mechanisms that can keep them alive up to a point. When these coping mechanisms are exhausted, people die. Western aid organizations did not know how well developed these mechanisms were in a society accustomed to having the state provide for every need. Nor did we know how effective the totalitarian state would be in supplementing the population's coping mechanisms, or for how many years people could cope before the looming famine would finally strike them down. In my own experience, famines seldom peak with mass starvation during the first year of a war, economic downturn, or crop failure; rather, one's instincts for survival prevail. By the second or third year of a crisis, however, deaths begin to mount as people can no longer cope. Starvation takes a long time. Given that the country's economic nightmare had begun well before 1995, it is likely that coping mechanisms were already severely strained before the flooding that summer led to the downturn in harvest production.

Complicating any efforts to deal with the foreboding economic news was the fact that the transition of political power in North Korea following Kim Il Sung's death in 1994 was proceeding at a snail's pace. In the first attempt at dynastic succession in a communist regime, power was being transferred to Kim Jong Il after a period of mourning required by Confucian tradition. Although Kim Jong Il was undoubtedly in control of the military, party, and internal security apparatus, his expected formal ascension to power in the summer of 1998 did not take place. Instead, the national party congress named him the head of the national defense commission. The address at the congress had traditionally been given by Kim Il Sung, the head of state, and this year was no different. The Great Leader, dead for four years, remained head of state as a speech he had given at an earlier party congress was rebroadcast to the delegates.

The eventual succession in 1999 ensured the continued legitimacy of the state at a time of national crisis. Without Kim Jong Il as an inheritor of his father's legacy, what remained of the political system might well have completely unraveled. The father's unrivaled political power and popular support might have allowed him to orchestrate the massive transformation of ideology needed to convert the rigid Soviet centralized economic system into a more Chinese-style market system, but he died before the crisis reached a catastrophic stage. The son enjoyed neither his father's popularity nor his absolute hold on power, and he was remarkably unwilling to take the risk of systemic reform.

The economic downturn set a dark and somber stage for the famine, but it did not cause it. Other invisible forces were at work, as will be explored later. Knowing that a massive gap exists between the food needs of the population and the harvest supplemented by food imports does not say much about exactly who is dying, where they are dying, and why they are dying. Not everyone suffers equally in a famine, and in fact some prosper because of prevailing economic forces. Only carefully constructed microeconomic analysis provides this insight. Most families were doing what they could to cope with their deteriorating diet, as rations coming from the public distribution system continued to decline. The WFP's later characterization of the situation as a "famine in slow motion" was quite descriptive of the period before 1994. But forces at work at the local level drove the political leadership to a series of disastrous decisions, plunging the country into one of the most severe famines since the Chinese famine during the Great Leap Forward.

To determine what actually happened at the local level, one must look beyond the national data at the internal economic forces that drove the famine and the politics of the central government's food allocation decisions.

One North Korean refugee interviewed in China along the border with North Korea in January 1998 described the situation well. He explained that the party cadres told the population to prepare for a period of suffering in 1996 and 1997. The food crisis, he said, was comparable to being thrown into a well; if you could at least see the sunlight above, you survived the famine. When the same party leadership told the population to prepare for an even greater period of suffering in 1998, it was like having a cover put over the well. At that point the refugee knew it was time to leave the country, before the grim reaper made an encore appearance in North Korea.[43]

INSIDE NORTH KOREA: PREFAMINE INDICATORS

A S THE MYSTERY SURROUNDING THE CRISIS INCREASED, so did my interest in visiting North Korea to see the famine for myself, but each time I applied for a visa the North Korean Foreign Ministry denied my application. "Later," they would say; "now is not the right time." With no other explanation than this I wondered if I would ever get there. Finally, in May 1997, I received a visa along with other senior officials of World Vision, the nongovernmental organization (NGO) for which I then worked. Getting into the country was nearly as difficult as getting a visa, though. Given the modest demand to travel there, few airlines have regularly scheduled flights into the country. From Beijing we took one of the twice-weekly flights to Pyongyang.

We arrived in North Korea in time for the planting of the annual rice crop, and we watched the process from the window of our Mercedes cars as we were driven from the airport to our downtown hotel. Perhaps a third of the workers in the rice paddies wore military uniforms, as did the relatively few people on the streets. For a city of 2.7 million, the streets of Pyongyang seemed rather empty during the middle of the day. They had none of the bustle and crowds of people one sees in other Asian cities. The only traffic on the streets other than our two Mercedes cars was an occasional, if overpacked, bus moving at a snail's pace down avenues as wide as those of Paris or London. Young women dressed in police uniforms directed nonexistent traffic at each intersection, making sharply executed turns in synchronized rhythm in a robot-like dance. These traffic police replaced traffic lights, which were turned off to save scarce electricity.

23

Unlike Moscow or Beijing, Pyongyang displays no evidence of the past in its design and architecture. The central icon in Pyongyang is Kim Il Sung. His image, name, and memory dominate much of the architecture, public places, and institutions of the city. Children of the elite aspire to attend Kim Il Sung University. They drive down Kim Il Sung Avenue, sing songs about the Great Leader, and attend sporting events at Kim Il Sung stadium. Visitors to the Kim Il Sung mausoleum, where the Great Leader's body lies in state, are greeted by a massive gold-plated statue of Kim Il Sung with his hand outstretched—a statue that reportedly cost $851 million.[1]

Our group's first meeting was a dinner with Mr. Jong, the vice director of the Flood Control and Rehabilitation Commission that oversaw the relief effort and relations with the NGOs and UN agencies. Jong treated us to an opulent banquet that made my colleagues and me uncomfortable, given what we suspected was happening among the mass of people. During the dinner conversation, he described with unusual candor the food crisis and what they were doing about it. He made three points I was to spend the next two years trying to prove or disprove. First, he said, the epicenter of the famine was in the urban rather than the rural areas, as the peasants could harvest wild foods or grow food on their private plots. Second, the government had imported 370,000 MT of grain commercially during 1996–97. And third, the northern regions of the country, which could barter for food with China, were much better off than the south, which was geographically isolated.

Only on occasion were we given the unprocessed truth, and telling the difference between it and the official explanations of conditions was not an easy task, even for North Korea watchers who knew the language and had traveled to the country many times before. The expatriate NGO and UN staff members whom I met at the airport displayed a level of cynicism, anger, and frustration I had never seen in any other emergency anywhere in the world. Many argued that there was no emergency, that no one was dying, and that the international community should not be there. They said they were tired of the daily diet of manipulation, deceit, and propaganda fed to them by the authorities. I left the country only a week later feeling much the same. Such reactions had been common among Westerners visiting the Eastern bloc during the Cold War, often because of a clash of cultures and ideology; the same reasoning could be applied to Western reactions to North Korea. Its society had been insular for centuries even before the arrival of communism; the most apt description of the country—the Hermit Kingdom—refers not only to its communist period but also to its dynastic period.

The North Korean reaction to the outside world gradually changed during the course of the emergency. NGO visa applications in early 1996 required two to three months for processing, whereas I received the visa for my June 1997 visit in just two weeks. In early 1996 no more than a half-dozen expatriate relief workers were granted longer-term—usually six-month—residency visas; since mid-1997, more than one hundred such visas have been granted annually. According to a U.S. diplomat familiar with North Korea, the State Department believed the North Korean reluctance to allow more expatriates into the country reflected an absence of English-speaking translators as much as an aversion to more outsiders. Both reasons are likely the case.

During a visit to Sariwon, an industrial city south of Pyongyang, one incident seemed to characterize my entire trip. At one point I walked ahead of the delegation, turned a corner, and stepped off the narrow cobblestone street into an alleyway that was not on our itinerary. Several local people subsequently walked down the same alleyway, but as soon as they saw me they turned back, ran into their homes, and shut their doors. I thought perhaps I had frightened them, but on reflection I realized that nowhere in the world had my presence ever elicited such a reaction. Quite the opposite, I have usually been greeted with either great warmth or intense curiosity. Only later did North Korean refugees explain to me that contact with foreigners was a crime with a severe penalty.

THE SEARCH FOR EVIDENCE OF FAMINE

It did not take long after our arrival to realize that a government as controlled as North Korea's would not let us see stark evidence of a famine. I therefore decided to try to find subtle evidence that the authorities might not have thought to disguise. The past century and a half of research on famines has yielded an extensive body of scholarship, including indicators of the onset and continued existence of a famine. Unfortunately, this information has not necessarily been well used operationally, but an experienced relief manager would recognize from experience the following classic famine indicators.

Market-based indicators include increases in the cost of seeds, number of seed shortages, or consumption of seed stock as a food source by families. Farmers generally keep 10 percent of their crop as seed for the next planting, but they will eat this supply if they do not expect to survive until the next harvest. Another market indicator is the widespread sale of land and homes at abnormally low prices, to provide cash to buy food. During the onset of a famine one may notice an increased sale of domesticated animals and a decrease in their average market prices. Farming families sell their animals before they die, but when this is done en masse the market becomes glutted and the price of animals declines. The price of food staples may also rise owing to shortages, which in turn may cause a rise in the ratio of staple grain prices to prevailing wages. Often, the cause of famine is not food shortage but the inability of poor families to afford the drastically increased prices. Finally, as these prices rise, dealers may hoard more grain stocks with the goal of selling them later when prices have peaked.

Non-market-based indicators include the consumption of wild foods that are not normally part of the family diet. These foods are harvested from the countryside as a coping mechanism, and in places where famine is common, farmers and peasants are generally well versed in which foods are edible when necessary. Similarly, the overconsumption of domesticated farm animals often indicates a famine's onset. Starving individuals may mix staple grains with inedible material such as sawdust or powered corn cob, to extend the stock of the edible food. In the marketplace, families may be forced to sell family possessions—jewelry, ornaments, bedding material, and household goods—to get cash to buy food. All of this could be precipitated by a prolonged drought or other natural disaster that would cause a crop failure, as a dramatic decline in crop production diminishes family income and simultaneously causes steep rises in grain prices.[2]

These prefamine market indicators appear as a famine begins and indicate that a famine is under way. As a famine accelerates in its intensity and then surges to a climax, overt indicators, sometimes called trailing indicators, become more apparent. It was just these indicators of crisis that the North Korean regime so assiduously sought to disguise while the famine continued.

In any famine, trailing indicators include increased death rates from starvation and related diseases, and the mass migration of people in search of food or employment. Others include increased rates of abnormally slow growth in children, called stunting, and nutritional disorders and vitamin and protein deficiencies such an edema, kwashiorkor, and wasting. Birth rates also decline as malnourished women become infertile, poor nutrition leads to increased miscarriages, and women choose not to have children they cannot feed.[3]

Some prefamine indicators are visible only in economic systems where markets are legal and functional. Under a marxist economic order, markets disappear or—more likely—trading is simply driven underground and is less visible to outsiders. The North Korean central government sanctioned local markets in the 1940s on a small scale, but it has refused to allow expatriates to see them in operation. The German consul in Pyongyang, while traveling with a diplomatic delegation to one of the affected provinces, wandered from the group into one of these local markets, was promptly arrested by the security forces, and spent a night in prison. According to a U.S. diplomat, prior to his arrest the consul had been a leading advocate of famine relief in an otherwise skeptical diplomatic corps, but his enthusiasm reportedly did not improve as a result of his encounter with the prison system. Not wanting to repeat the consul's experience, I studiously avoided any unscheduled excursions into the marketplace. But given that the market drives six of the ten prefamine indicators, my search had to focus on the remaining four that might be discernable to an experienced eye.

Trying to gather evidence in Pyongyang was no easy matter, though. We entered and exited the city by the same streets, presumably to minimize our observation of the city. While we met with senior officials from ministry after ministry, all of the meetings took place in our hotel; we never entered a single government office. During our trips outside the capital I repeatedly asked to stop in villages to speak with people at random. Our hosts politely turned aside each of my requests with arguments that people would be frightened, that it would not be a useful expenditure of our time, or that time was needed to prepare for such a stop. The one time they did allow us to speak to a family in its home came on our last trip into the field, in Sariwon. After we left a center for orphaned children we stopped at a home on our walk back to our car.

We videotaped the conversation, so I later learned that the translation given by our Foreign Ministry translators was in fact accurate. I doubt the stop was spontaneous, however, and I suspect the home was of a trusted party member, but I have no way of confirming this.

Beyond access and spontaneity, the other barrier to the collection of information was language. The Foreign Ministry made it clear early in the crisis that it did not want expatriate Korean speakers in any delegation. Although the authorities eased this restriction later, when I was there we had no way of determining how accurately our conversations were translated. Having had local translators accompany me into famines before under politically sensitive circumstances, I knew how important language was when trying to get an accurate view of conditions. On an assessment trip I made to rural Angola during the civil war in 1990, five-minute conversations between a translator asking my question and an internally displaced person answering it would be translated into one English sentence; clearly, something was lost in such translations. This same phenomenon occurred during several of the conversations on this trip; I questioned the completeness of the translation because the volume of Korean words did not nearly match the volume of translated English words. Part of the conversation must have been overlooked, though whether it happened deliberately I could not discern. When one NGO recruited a Korean-speaking food monitor to oversee the distribution of 75,000 MT of U.S. government food aid, the World Food Program feared the North Korean authorities' reaction when they discovered his language ability. Inexplicably, however, the North Koreans raised no serious objections.

Our first trip outside Pyongyang was to Huichon, an industrial city of four hundred thousand people about a hundred miles northeast of the capital. Huichon provided evidence to support the regime's claim that the flooding of 1995 and 1996—and not systemic collapse—caused the food crisis, as the city was supposed to have been particularly hard hit. To get there we first traveled on a newly built four-lane divided highway that abruptly ended half-way to the city; ours were the sole vehicles on the road. After the highway we traveled on a narrow, uneven country road full of potholes and deteriorating shoulders. The dichotomy between the modern highway and this dilapidated road provided evidence for a general development principle in North Korea: the further from the capital one travels, the poorer, less developed, and more run-down virtually every aspect of the economic and public works infrastructure becomes. Whereas I saw small herds of goats and cows on the immediate outskirts of the capital, we saw virtually no sign of a bird or animal population, wild or domesticated, after we left the capital proper. During our eight hours outside the city I saw one pig and also nine oxen being used for plowing in preparation for the spring planting. No ducks, chickens, geese, sheep, dogs, or wild animals were to be seen, even though the entire area between the two cities was an intensively cultivated agricultural area. This lack of fauna is quite unusual in rural Asia, even in the poorest areas. The absence of animals outside metropolitan Pyongyang thus suggested the presence of one famine indicator: the consumption of domesticated animals.

As we drove through the downtown area of Huichon, it struck me that the crowds of people on the streets were nearly all young. No one appeared to be elderly or even middle aged; only a few appeared over fifty. They all appeared well dressed, well nourished, and healthy for a city that had been devastated by massive flooding just a year earlier. I could see no smoke exiting any of the smokestacks of the factories in the city, nor did there appear to be any activity inside the buildings. Our hosts said the silence in the factories was a function of the economy's decline. They had neither the fuel nor the raw materials for production. When I asked about the absence of the elderly on the streets, quite unusual for an Asian society, to my surprise our hosts admitted that they were giving their food rations to their grandchildren and were thus too weak to move around. This behavior was predictable in a society still governed by Confucian principles, which teach that continuity of the family bloodline is of paramount importance. Data from the Korean Buddhist Sharing Movement (KBSM) confirmed this statement; people over sixty had the highest mortality rates among refugee families and villages.[4] Nevertheless, although the elderly were absent from both the country-side and Huichon, they represented one out of ten people I saw on the streets of Pyongyang one afternoon as I walked through the neighbor-hood near my hotel.

We visited two schools in Huichon, a kindergarten and a middle school. In the kindergarten in a class of eighteen children, five showed unmistakable signs of acute malnutrition—swelling around the face, dis-coloration of the hair, and skin lesions. I asked the children to pull up the sleeves of their shirts so I could see their upper arm circumference; such data would provide evidence of wasting—a loss of weight caused by severely deteriorating nutrition. Systematically measuring the children was prohibited, so it was difficult to determine how many of the children were moderately or acutely malnourished, but all their upper arms appeared to be quite thin, five or six severely so. When I asked to see another class of children in the same school, we were told they had all gone home. As we left, however, I turned and looked up at the second floor of the school and noticed crowds of children at the windows excitedly pointing down at us, clearly unaware that their appearance was embarrassing our hosts. The school administrators had likely been instructed to select an unrepresentative group of children, but it was unclear whether what we saw had understated or overstated the severity of the crisis.

Along the road to Huichon, I had counted hundreds of people, mostly women, digging up wild plants and placing them in bags. Traditional Korean cuisine does value some wild plants, such as mushrooms and acorns, just as French cuisine uses wild mushrooms and dandelions. It was difficult to tell in a speeding car what exactly was being harvested off the countryside, but the sheer number of people engaged in this task was astonishing and the fact that they were doing this work all along the route was remarkable. When a group of North Korean agronomists visited the United States at the invitation of the NGOs and some agri-businesses in the summer of 1997, we took them to the Midwest to see our agricultural research centers and visit a typical American farm. At one of the farms, as we left a cornfield, we walked through an unkempt and obviously uncultivated patch of weeds and brambles. One of the North Koreans asked me which of the weeds were edible and which were not. I replied that I did not know, because we would never eat them, to which he replied in an unguarded moment of candor, "In my country all of these weeds would be eaten unless they were poisonous." A year later, I was to hear similar statements in refugee interviews conducted by the KBSM in China. Journalists and relief workers alike reported this massive foraging campaign from the time the relief effort began. The harvesting of wild foods I witnessed in the North Korean countryside did not appear to be a matter of fine dining, but rather a coping mechanism for survival, a striking warning of famine.

Perhaps more than in any other crisis in the post–Cold War era, NGOs systematically shared their own internal assessments and trip reports. Retired ambassador Jim Bishop, who ran the disaster response division of InterAction, a Washington, D.C.–based consortium of more than 150 U.S.-based humanitarian NGOs, coordinated this exchange. The similarity of the language and observations in these field reports is remarkable given how assiduously the authorities were trying to disguise conditions. Here is one report from a smaller NGO with good access to areas outside the capital:

> The gap between conditions in Pyongyang city and the rest of the country appears to be significantly widening. While life seems to go on fairly normally in Pyongyang, conditions in cities, towns and rural areas in the rest of the country appear grim with clear signs of human and material breakdown. . . . Recent visitors to nurseries in parts of the country report an alarming increase in the number of severely malnourished children. While it is not easy to ascertain the status of elderly who live at home, there are widespread reports of severe health problems and premature deaths in this group. . . . Our own observations support the more pessimistic assessment. At one cooperative farm we visited, which has access to food resources unavailable in the urban areas, from one-third to one-half of the children are too sick or weak to attend the kindergarten or nurseries. Even among those in attendance, many show obvious signs of malnutrition, with a number of severe cases. Elsewhere we were told that the number of miscarriages was very high this year and the health of nursing mothers and their infants is in serious jeopardy.[5]

AN INTRODUCTION TO THE POLITICS OF FAMINE

Upon our return to Pyongyang we asked to see some of the children's centers that other aid workers had mentioned to us. Our hosts had chosen not to take us to the one in Huichon that other NGOs had visited. Instead we visited one in Pyongyang and another in Sariwon. The precise purpose of these children's centers, one of which exists in every province and large city, remains somewhat of a mystery. Staff members told us that families with twins, triplets, or quadruplets must institutionalize their newborn children because official policy says a mother and father cannot care for that number of infants properly. The children of athletes and musicians who travel a great deal are institutionalized, as are the children of families without the means to care for them because of unemployment, illness, or the death of one or both parents. NGO and UN staff suspected that children orphaned or abandoned because of the famine were also institutionalized, which would have explained the sudden rise in the population of the centers beginning in 1995.

The staffs of the centers seemed to care a great deal for the children, but they knew little about treating malnutrition, various feeding regimes, vitamin deficiencies, or baseline measurements of the children during treatment. Most of the children in the centers were suffering from some level of moderate or acute malnutrition; many were in terrible condition. In the rooms with the most severe but readily apparent cases, our hosts would not allow us to take photographs. By the autumn of 1997 UN officials were warning NGOs to send no more medicine or food to the children's centers because the children appeared to be in the same condition then as they had been a year earlier. Supplies had poured into the centers, along with training for staff members in how to treat malnutrition at different levels of severity, but neither the training nor the commodities appeared to be having any effect. The authorities did not allow any expatriate health officers to be permanently posted to the children's centers, so it was impossible to determine why the children continued to be in such terrible condition.

Aid agencies sympathetic to the regime claimed that while the staff members of the children's centers had received a great deal of training, they would revert to old dysfunctional treatments as soon as the trainers from NGOs and the United Nations Children's Fund had left. In one center I asked the manager to show me what they were feeding the children: nonfat dry milk from a donor. Although nutritious, nonfat dry milk does not provide the fat that malnourished children need. Some of the more jaded relief workers argued that the North Koreans kept the children malnourished to keep the commodity donations flowing, though the products were obviously not being used for these children. A less pessimistic explanation may be that, in marxist economic systems, workers frequently take commodities from their workplace as a supplement to their meager salaries; in North Korea, these salaries had been cut or eliminated entirely as the economy began a tailspin. As the children's center workers' own children may also have been malnourished, the caregivers probably did not think twice about such wage supplements.

That night in Pyongyang, I retired to my hotel room early but was awakened at 10 p.m. by a call from Ambassador Kim Soo Man, who asked me to meet him in the cafe downstairs. We sat at a table I presumed was equipped with hidden microphones, and he proceeded to grill me on my political views: What did I think of his president? What about the North Korean political and economic system? What was my real reason for joining this delegation? He began answering his own questions in a tone of measured hostility. I opposed his system and his president, didn't I? I was here for political reasons, just like the U.S. government, wasn't I? I almost told him exactly what I did think of his political system, but I knew if I did, our relief effort would either be shut down or so constrained as to become dysfunctional. Instead, I replied that my political views on his system and his president were irrelevant and that we were here to save innocent people's lives, not to impose any political or diplomatic agenda. I reminded him of the article I had written for the *Washington Post*—which I knew he had read—attacking the Clinton administration for politicizing the relief effort.

I then turned the tables on him and accused North Korea of doing the same thing that South Korea and the U.S. government had done. Although the Clinton administration had said North Korea would be fed if it cooperated in the normalization of relations with South Korea, the North Koreans were now making the inverse proposition—demanding food aid before they would negotiate seriously. This, I reminded him, was just as destructive a demand as the U.S. position. Both diplomatic positions would ensure the starvation of his people by placing political conditions on aid. These conditions would inevitably slow down the commitments of food aid by donor governments, for if the U.S. government reversed its position and sent aid it would appear to be reacting to the North Korean demand. His government was making it harder for the U.S. government to reverse its position on the conditionality of food aid. Time, I reminded him, was the great enemy in all famine relief efforts, and we were dangerously beyond the date when food aid should have been shipped by donor governments. The hungriest time would be in the months preceding the autumn harvest. He replied that the reports of his government's negotiating position were wrong, that it had made no such demand, and that the international news media relished making his country look bad. I chose not to answer him even though I knew the reports of Pyongyang's negotiating position were accurate. The conversation ended. Politics and diplomacy, like it or not, were inextricably linked to the relief effort, thus ensuring that the unfolding catastrophe would not be stopped. The clash among the understandable diplomatic interests of the donor and North Korean governments was fast approaching checkmate, with terrible consequences for the common people.

Our trip to Sariwon, an industrial city in the southwestern rice-growing region, provided a repetition of the scenes we had witnessed in Huichon, but with two remarkable exceptions. During the staff presentations at the children's centers, I noticed one of our hosts slip quietly out the back door of the room. I stepped back, close to the doorway, to watch his movements. Around the corner in the hall I could see him transferring children from a back wing of the center into rooms closer to the front of the facility. After the staff presentation, our delegation was escorted into one of those rooms, full of one- to three-year-old children, most of whom suffered from some level of malnutrition. Half were at the acute stage. They were lethargic, neither crying nor smiling. Some of their faces were swollen with edema, some of the children's hair had changed color, others had only patches of hair left on their head, and still others had skin lesions on their emaciated arms or legs caused by kwashiorkor, a protein deficiency. The children were in terrible condition. I stepped away from the delegation discreetly and wandered into the wing of the center we were not going to be visiting. I quickly peered through the window of each closed door into three different rooms. While a quick glance was hardly a scientifically verifiable way of determining nutritional conditions, I did not see any visibly malnourished children in any one of the three rooms that were off-limits, each of which held at least ten children. Our hosts appeared to be transferring all of the worst cases into the rooms we were visiting, leaving the healthy children in the back wing. This confirmed that what we had seen had been carefully arranged, and at the worst, if my brief glance was to be trusted, it exaggerated the severity of crisis among this population of children.

Following the children's center visit we made an officially spontaneous but carefully orchestrated stop at a local high school, something I had been requesting each day. The children, assembled in military-style formation in their schoolyard with marxist banners and flags rippling in the wind, appeared to be in exceptionally good physical condition. Their physical health, the appearance of their clothing, and their grooming appeared much better than those of people on the street. They wore uniforms of short-sleeved shirts, shorts, and skirts, so their nutritional condition was easy to assess even en masse. I counted about fourteen hundred students, of whom perhaps two or three looked underfed. The contrast to what we had just witnessed in the children's center was astonishing. We had moved from a famine that appeared more pathetic than Sudan's or Somalia's to a school three blocks away with children whose condition was comparable to those in South Korea or Japan. I turned to one of our hosts and asked whether this was typical of the schools in Sariwon. He turned, smiled, and shook his head. No, he said, this was the best school in the city. I presumed, but could not confirm, that it was the school for the children of the party cadres. If the nutritional condition of these students reflected conditions in the country, the relief program should have been shut down and every relief worker sent home. Was this a North Korean Potemkin village?

Upon our return to Pyongyang we began a series of conversations, filled with *juche* and marxist ideology, with senior ministry officials. I had asked to meet with the vice ministers of health and agriculture, who turned out to be the senior Communist Party operatives. They were, respectively, the principal party ideologue and the political officer responsible for ensuring party control over the technical managers in the ministries. They knew little about the technical work of their ministries. I asked our hosts why we were meeting ministry political officers, instead of the professionals we had asked to see. They replied that we had asked to see these officials by rank, so they were complying with our request. The officials quoted some wildly exaggerated statistics on morbidity and mortality rates and agricultural production—the child mortality rates were lower than American and European levels. I commented that, if these numbers were accurate, the members of the international community should leave on the next plane and take their humanitarian aid with them, for there was no crisis in the country. They whispered in subdued tones that politics had influenced the compilation of the data and that the numbers were quite old and therefore no longer particularly relevant. When I tried to get the vice minister of agriculture to comment on any changes needed to increase crop production, he immediately replied that no changes were needed nor would they be considered. He then repeated the mantra that the U.S. sanctions regime and natural disasters were to blame for the current famine.

REASSESSING THE SITUATION

As I boarded the plane from Pyongyang to Beijing, I alternated between conflicting reactions to our guided tour of the nearly invisible North Korean famine. The carefully staged scenes, fictitious statistics, and contrived conversations made me skeptical and suspicious of what I saw. There appeared to be a hidden reality behind the outward appearance of nearly everything; the difficulty lay in trying to uncover it. The North Korean system had succeeded in converting the aid workers, a group of advocates who had initially come to help the country avoid the abyss, into adversaries who doubted whether there was a true emergency. Nearly the entire expatriate humanitarian aid community passed their off-hours exchanging theories about what was really happening. Even if it had tried, the North Korean regime could not have designed a more effective strategy to make its people's strongest sympathizers into angry skeptics.

After my anger subsided and I carefully compared what I had seen with the table of classic famine indicators, however, the weight of evidence pointed clearly to famine—the harvesting of wild foods, the rising rates of acute malnutrition among vulnerable populations, the consumption of domesticated animals, the sale of family possessions and even homes, two floods followed by a drought that reduced already declining harvests, and some evidence of mass population movements. Moreover, at the macroeconomic level a huge gap existed between the amount of food the population needed to survive and what the country actually produced— a gap that had not been filled with donor food aid. Finally, the collapse of industry had increased urban unemployment and reduced or ended the average family's entitlement to food from the faltering public distribution system. However skillfully disguised by the internal security apparatus, a famine appeared to be sweeping across the country.

3

THE HIDDEN FAMINE

TWO NORTH KOREAS EXIST SIDE BY SIDE. The first is the North Korea of Pyongyang—of gay parades with colorful marxist banners, and of bright, well-fed, and smiling children of the political elite, dressed in clean uniforms and attending well-appointed cadre schools. It is the North Korea of grand boulevards, massive palaces, and mausoleums—glistening monuments to Kim Il Sung, the Great Leader. It is the North Korea of model collective farms, model hospitals, and model schools. This country does exist—for the party elites, the cadres, and the military leadership, most of whom live in Pyongyang.

The illusory North Korea of Pyongyang is maintained at high cost: it is purged annually of sick, deformed, and handicapped people as well as of those who have misbehaved. Pyongyang receives a much higher grain ration, and residency is regarded as a great reward for good behavior and faithfulness. North Korea analyst Don Oberdorfer wrote of a population cleansing campaign in the capital: "[A]ccording to foreign diplomats, the population was periodically screened, and the sick, elderly, or disabled, along with anyone deemed politically unreliable, were evicted from the capital."[1] Indeed, a Russian diplomat who had lived in the city for many years told me that each year the central government would exile ten thousand troublemakers from the capital to the countryside, replacing them with ten thousand people from the provinces as a reward for their loyalty to the regime. Similarly, a 1988 human rights report by Asian Watch reported that the capital's dwarfs and other visibly disabled people were periodically rounded up and exiled to a remote city in the Northeast. An NGO operating in the Northeast came upon a city with

37

an unusually high portion of disabled people and dwarfs, which seemed to confirm this report.

The other North Korea is where all these people live in exile, to protect Pyongyang's glistening façade of marxist paradise. It is a North Korea of abandoned factories gutted of machinery to be sold in China for food, of detention camps for displaced people, of deserted schools, and of cannibalized apartment complexes. It is a North Korea with gangs of filthy, malnourished orphans abandoned on city streets, wandering beggars stealing food from the burgeoning farmers markets, and train stations clogged with dying people desperately trying to force themselves on decrepit, overcrowded trains in hopes of escaping to China. This is the soft underbelly of North Korea. It is the hidden face of the famine: tragically real but well hidden from outsiders.

From the summer of 1997 through 1998, the UN Children's Fund (UNICEF), the WFP, and most NGO reports on North Korea described a country long on the edge of a precipice, but which had avoided calamity and was on the road to recovery. These reports acknowledged that Pyongyang's official image was a carefully designed façade, but they universally failed to describe the face of the hidden famine. In the summer of 1998 the streets of the capital were filled with new bicycles imported from Japan, and new shops and stores were opening up. Most children under age seven appeared relatively healthy and well fed compared to the year before.

Even the Russians, longtime and shrewd observers of the politics of the Korean peninsula, doubted the reports of famine:

> Most Russians economists . . . disagree with Western reports that two million DPRK citizens have died during the last three years of famine. Moreover, they insist that "famine" is not the correct term to describe the situation in the DPRK. It is rather a "shortage of food," a phenomenon that has always existed in the country, but [one which] in recent years has gotten pronounced due to a number of factors: natural calamities, the obsolescence of farm equipment and the irrigation system, deficiencies in the Stalinist agricultural model, the overall crisis of the economy, and termination of food supplies from the former "socialist" states. These economists suspect that North Korean authorities will deliberately exaggerate their hardships in order to get more international food aid.[2]

As noted in the preceding chapter, during my trip to North Korea in June 1997, I happened to see a group of high school–age students in school uniform, practicing for some sort of parade. They looked healthy, well fed, well clothed, and clean; they showed no evidence of stunting, no gaunt look from poor nutrition, and they were brimming with enthusiasm. Perhaps, I thought, these were cadre children. A year later, celebrations were held in Pyongyang with hundreds of thousands of school children and soldiers marching in endless parades, all to celebrate the ascension of Kim Jong Il, the Dear Leader, to dynastic power. Reading the eyewitness accounts of these imperial events made it hard to believe that a grotesque famine was consuming the flower of North Korean youth in the mountains to the east of the city.

Yet, during the same time period in the same country, reports from starving refugees who fled to China described a horrific scene: mass starvation, widespread clinical depression, mass suicides of ravaged families, refugees pouring across the border into China, desperate people roaming the countryside in search of food, and even reports of cannibalism. According to one NGO report from the area, Chinese observers in Manchuria and Han merchants along the border were placing bets on how much longer the regime could last before the final collapse.[3] One refugee told her story to interviewers from the KBSM:

> It has been about five years since we received a regular food ration from the government. In each household, there are about two or three people who die of starvation or diseases, and dead bodies of homeless wanderers are a common sight everywhere. No one comes to retrieve the bodies; they are left to rot like dead dogs. In the midst of these inhumane circumstances, there was an instance where a person was executed after he killed another person to eat the flesh. In the markets, I can't even buy a bowl of noodles because you can feel the *kochibis* [internally displaced people] watching you, waiting to snatch it away—still, how can we blame them? This is not an unusual sight; it happens everywhere. Ill patients and weak elders who cannot move only drink water. Moreover, electricity and water are often cut off due to lack of resources.[4]

It is difficult to believe that both of these North Koreas could exist simultaneously. Had the people been dying, surely the NGOs and UN agencies would have seen it, but they did not. And yet, utterly compelling information proves the widespread existence of famine conditions. To understand how and why such a famine could remain hidden from public view, one need only read the text of a December 1996 speech by Kim

Jong Il: "[T]he People's Army is not being properly supplied with food. Seeing that we face temporary difficulties, the enemies rave that our social- ism will fall as well, and they are looking for every possible chance to invade us. If they knew we did not have military provisions, the U.S. imperialists might immediately raid us."[5] This extraordinary admission is instructive. When the North Korean leader expresses his fear that the West—and by implication the South Koreans—might invade if they knew that even soldiers were suffering, the famine is transformed from a nutritional crisis into a national security matter. If famine was ravaging the country, as Kim implied, one could expect the central government would try to disguise the devastation.

Aid workers thought otherwise. But then, in a country of twenty- three million people living in an area the size of Mississippi, how accurate an impression could one hundred expatriate humanitarian aid workers expect to obtain? These workers, myself included, could not speak Korean, had no intimate economic or geographical knowledge of the country, and were taken on carefully supervised field trips where the citizens being visited were told ahead of time when to expect them. They were accom- panied by carefully chosen government translators and transported along routes determined by central government authorities under a totalitarian political system with nearly complete control over the population. No humanitarian aid worker had ever worked in a country whose popula- tion had lived under fifty years of Orwellian control of every aspect of their lives, overseen by a secret police apparatus nearly unmatched in its per- vasive control. It is not surprising that the aid workers were confused by what they saw. I admit to having regularly had paralyzing doubts about the elaborate explanation I had constructed to explain to myself the con- ditions and events in North Korea. It seemed some days that I was a pris- oner in Plato's mythological cave, forced to stare at a shadow of what was real and missing the reality itself because the regime had so skillfully dis- guised it.

As one NGO official wrote upon his return from a trip to North Korea in the spring of 1998:

> We don't know what the true reality is in North Korea—despite
> reading background material, visiting there 10 days and talking with
> UNDP [the United Nations Development Program], UNICEF, and
> other NGOs. We have a glimpse of the situation. It's one where

> North Korea is out on a limb all by itself and has a lack of trust with
> nearly any nation. I can identify with a recent visitor to North Korea
> when he said he couldn't sleep—not due to jet lag, but because of
> the difficulty in sorting through the ever-present and strong ideo-
> logical message. . . . A Norwegian UNICEF official told us that he
> had served in Uganda after Obote took over, worked in Afghanistan,
> and worked in Zaire, but "this is the most difficult location—not
> because of physical safety, but because of a sense of not knowing
> what is going on."[6]

UN reports even as late as December 1998 complain of a lack of information:

> Although the humanitarian organizations working in the DPRK are
> trying to gather as much information as possible, the data available
> are far less than normally required in justifying a humanitarian
> operation of the present magnitude. . . . Monitors were not permit-
> ted to conduct unscheduled, unsupervised visits. The lack of access
> —that was not pre-determined—to conduct assessments, moni-
> toring, and impact analysis, combined with the lack of adequate
> data, results in conclusions that were based more on observation
> and inference than [on] statistical information.[7]

THE ROLE OF *JUCHE* IDEOLOGY

The regime had others reasons to fear public disclosure of the severity of
the food crisis. For the previous thirty years, North Korea had spent considerable political capital and resources promoting its own version of
Marxist–Leninist ideology. *Juche*, which roughly translated means self-
reliance, had become the governing ideology of the state. In many respects
juche was an idiosyncratic state ideology only tangentially resembling
orthodox marxist doctrine, and in some profound ways it contradicted it.
Marxism at its root was antinationalist, though one would be hard-pressed
to find an Eastern bloc country that adopted this element of its doctrine
in anything other than its rhetoric. *Juche*, however, grew out of North
Korean nationalist sentiments that sought to separate the country's culture and history from nearly forty years of oppressive Japanese colonial
rule that ended only after World War II. *Juche* requires an autarkic economic system; it even posits, in direct contradiction to marxism, the
existence of a god. Despite the rhetoric of the party leadership, *juche*

reflects the deep Confucian roots of Korean culture more than Marxist–
Leninist doctrine.[8]

Doug Coutts, the WFP director in North Korea during the first
half of 1998, remarked to me as he ended his brief six-month tour that
every day that the humanitarian relief program functioned, it directly
challenged the legitimacy and relevance of *juche* ideology. The food aid
program was an ideological scandal for the North Koreans, because it
served as tangible evidence of the failure of their agricultural and economic
system and as an international advertisement of the country's mendicant
status. Having a hundred aid workers driving around the country monitoring food aid deliveries and distributions only further enraged the old-
order party ideologues, as it implied that the central government could
not be trusted to dispense food aid fairly.

Asians instinctively abhor "losing face" in front of other people or
other countries. Five decades of totalitarian rule had not changed North
Koreans' abhorrence of public embarrassment; in fact, it had exacerbated
it. The photographs of their starving children and emaciated elderly people on television screens across the world made the North Korean elite
cower with social embarrassment or become infuriated that their enemies, the donor governments, were holding them up to international
ridicule. When I have spoken publicly about the severity of the famine,
even without the use of photographs or videotapes, North Korean diplomats have asked me to stop talking so negatively about their country. They
say I ought to find something complimentary to tell the world. Though
some have reacted with anger or resentment, many have asked more in
an embarrassed or hurt tone of voice that I be more sympathetic to their
country's hurt pride.

From the start of the relief effort, the North Koreans made clear
they intended to distribute all food aid through the existing state distribution system. They would brook no interference by aid agencies. Until
late 1998, the government prohibited the customary morbidity and
mortality tracking systems as well as scientifically defensible nutritional
assessments; they prevented expatriate staff from surveying farmers markets to determine food stock levels and to track food price changes. In fact,
they prohibited all of the traditional monitoring systems used by humanitarian relief agencies to target food aid by determining the severity of a
food crisis in a particular region or area. These prohibitions against using

diagnostic tools reflected the central authorities' abiding obsession with maintaining absolute control of the population and the supply system, but it also had the effect of precluding any of the aid agencies from knowing how and where the famine was most severe. This knowledge might have led the agencies to dispute the central government's decisions on how aid should be allocated, thus leading the government not only to lose face but also to lose control. Disguising the famine, then, provided a political benefit to the regime: it allowed the central government to maintain complete control over how, where, and when food aid would be distributed.

THE HISTORICAL CONTEXT OF NORTH KOREAN ISOLATIONISM AND PUBLIC CONTROL

Seen in the context of Korean history, the current regime's isolation, intense xenophobia, secretiveness, and resistance to outside ideas and influence of the current regime are no anomaly. Rather, it is South Korea that made a remarkable departure from five centuries of isolationism to open itself to the outside world by adopting democratic capitalism and liberal international economic policies. In some ways, the threat the North feels from the South is not primarily military: it is the South as a vanguard of modernization that most threatens the totalitarianism of the North.

For centuries, dynastic Korea maintained a foreign policy of utter isolation from the outside world, save for its subordinate relationship to China, which it regarded as its cultural parent. Dynastic Korea enthusiastically adopted the Chinese Confucian worldview more thoroughly than any other Asian society, as Koreans regarded Chinese culture as superior to all others. North Korea continues to maintain this dependent and subordinate relationship even now.

In 1592 and again in 1597 the Japanese warlord Hideyoshi Toyotomi, who had just united Japan after a period of feudal anarchy, sent massive invasion forces to conquer Korea. The great Korean admiral Yi Sun-shin turned back the Japanese invasion by destroying Japanese supply lines. Between naval battles, which in the 1597 invasion destroyed three hundred Japanese ships, and the ferocious fighting on the ground, the destruction visited upon Korea was enormous.[9] The Korean kingdom thereafter pursued a policy of isolation, most aggressively during the nineteenth century. While Western attempts at that time to open China and Japan to trade had been successful, they failed completely in Korea. One American merchant ship, the *General Sherman*, trying to follow Commodore Matthew Perry's successful opening of Japan, was burned and the crew killed by provincial governor Pak Kyu-su's forces when the U.S. ship opened fire on a hostile crowd that had gathered on the shore to protest the ship's presence. European diplomats, merchants, and missionaries all suffered unfortunate experiences in attempting to open Korea. When Roman Catholic missionaries made some progress in converting women and the poor to Christianity, the central government massacred the Christian population because it was seen as a foreign threat.[10]

Like all twentieth-century totalitarian systems, North Korea controlled—and still controls—information for political purposes; several officials told me that was a routine practice in their system that they did not find particularly unusual. Embarrassing information is simply not reported, or if so it is altered. North Korea seems to have gone much further than other totalitarian regimes in withholding general information from the outside world. Nicholas Eberstadt and Judith Banister, in their 1992 book on North Korean demography, describe this practice:

> North Korea . . . is different from other countries for which demographic data are currently scarce. Unlike some countries in sub-Saharan Africa, North Korea has a population that is neither predominantly illiterate nor largely nomadic—nor is the country's administrative apparatus rudimentary. In contrast to such places as Afghanistan and Cambodia, North Korea is not presently in the process of recovering from a period of protracted turmoil and chaos. The unavailability of statistics reflects the longstanding determination by the political leadership of the closed nation to control —or withhold—information about the country. Basic statistical information about the DPRK appears to be withheld not only from international organizations in which it has membership, but also from fraternal Marxist–Leninist governments.[11]

The development of the state security system in North Korea following the end of Japanese colonial rule in 1945 provides some clues on why and how the recent famine was so systematically disguised from the outside world. The institutional outline of the totalitarian state apparatus that has governed the country since its independence began to take shape between 1945 and 1950 as Kim Il Sung established his authority over the Korean state developing north of the thirty-eighth parallel. It is commonly believed that a distinct break was made with the Japanese colonial past and that the Kim government purged all officials, something that the North Koreans accuse the South Korean government of failing to do. But this was not quite true. Kim retained many of the Korean police the Japanese colonizers had employed, and through them the Japanese police system and ethos found their way into the nascent security apparatus. North Korea seems to have combined the most intrusive elements of the Japanese colonial police and the feared Soviet KGB in designing its system. This new police force was given "broad social duties strikingly similar to those of prewar Japan, not to mention colonial Korea. . . . [T]here is an unbroken continuum from the internal discipline of the individual to the external defense of the nation."[12] Thus the police not only enforced criminal laws and the government's social policy, but also saw themselves as defending the sanctity of the state through the reeducation of the wayward individual and the rooting out of reactionary elements by "thought struggle" leading to "thought unification" at the collective level."[13] All of this the police did in the name of protecting society from external enemies, a duty it shared with the military:

> The extraordinary power of the Ministry of Public Security can be seen by outlining the range of responsibilities with which it is charged: the maintenance of law and order; protection against "anti-state" and "anti-revolutionary" activities; surveillance of all individuals, citizens and foreign visitors alike, including demands for identification papers and, when required, detailed background checks; general crime prevention; the guarding of all state properties; traffic control and fire prevention; census activities and control of movement from one area to another within the state; the operation of registration offices handling births, deaths, and marriages; preservation of confidential documents; the regular observation of blacklisted persons; the operation and management of all prisons and labor camps; the guarding of railroads; control over all ships entering or leaving North Korea; and the operation of an air defense system.[14]

Security police nurtured in a culture this intrusive with duties this broad did not need any encouragement from Pyongyang to control every aspect of the famine relief effort, every expatriate worker, and everything these foreigners saw. Their duty was to protect their society from what they perceived as dangerous foreign influences; the relief workers, after all, came from democratic capitalist countries that the police had been taught for five decades were their archenemies. Ample NGO evidence suggests that the very presence of a hundred foreigners traversing the country, trying to impose their humanitarian standards on the distribution of food and medicines, drove the secret police to distraction in a way that nothing in fifty years had ever done. Kim Jong Il's fear that the South Koreans and Americans might discover his country's secret famine and expose the North to potential attack, combined with this secret police culture obsessed with protecting and controlling society from the external and internal threats, created a pervasive institutional rationale to disguise the famine.

The central authorities desperately needed foreign food aid, but they did not want to show their internal weaknesses to the outside world. They had three choices: fix the system causing the crisis, let the population starve, or accept international aid while restricting the world's observation of their collapsing society. They could not fix their system without endangering the control of the central government over the country, so they rejected reform. But they could not choose mass starvation for fear that it would cause unrest. Thus, they accepted international aid, the least dangerous option, while trying to mitigate its adverse consequences. That the central authorities had abundant reason to disguise the severity of the famine, there should be no doubt. But what evidence exists that they actually executed such an elaborate ruse?

A CAMPAIGN OF SECRECY

I asked British journalist Jasper Becker and the Buddhist monk Pomnyun, both of whom had interviewed refugees crossing the border, why relief workers could find no direct evidence of famine within the country itself. Reports from inside North Korea mentioned nothing about emaciated people wandering around begging for food, the odor of putrefied bodies decomposing in unmistakable mass graves, or streets littered with corpses of people who had no relatives left alive to bury them. Anyone who has witnessed the horror of other famines has chilling memories of such hellish scenes. How could there be a famine without any visible evidence? I suggested to Pomnyun that he ask some of the more observant refugees this very question. Their explanation, corroborated by Médecins Sans Frontières (MSF, also known by the English name, Doctors Without

Borders) and Becker's interviews, provided a fascinating insight into the North Korean regime.

Before expatriate relief workers entered a city or rural area to do their work, the local authorities swept the streets of any evidence of famine. Beggars, emaciated people, abandoned children, trash or debris, and dead bodies were removed from the streets. People were told to stay indoors if they did not have presentable clothing to wear. One relief worker who spoke Korean watched a truck drive through a village just before the arrival of a visiting NGO delegation, announcing over a loud-speaker that people should get off the streets. Only party members were permitted outside their homes to take their ration of food aid while the NGO food monitors were in the city. Put simply, the authorities had created one giant Potemkin village, designed to impress visitors but bearing little resemblance to the dark reality facing the population. Orchestrating these contrived visits by expatriate relief workers must have been very time-consuming for the authorities, which helps to explain why the government granted only a small number of NGO visas.

One Korean Chinese retiree visiting relatives in the North reported the following scene from a trip to one city in May 1998:

> The streets were unusually clean. There used to be plenty of home-less people hanging around, but this time I could not see a single person on the street. Street officers whistled and shouted to the people hiding behind buildings. North Korean street police were busy forcefully removing people from the street. They kept saying, "Put your head down." While I was wondering why the street was so clean and calm, vehicles marked with the Chinese and South Korean Red Cross were passing through the street on which I stood. It was when I saw the vehicles that I realized why the street was so clean and calm. The police did not get me away from the street because they were aware that I was not North Korean by my appearance.
>
> Some homeless people slept in and around the buildings to avoid wind. Some children I met were severely suffering from chronic illness and malnutrition. Their spines and wrists were bent, their necks were too thin to support their heads, their eyes were not correctly focused, their hair was dry and stiff, they so rarely smiled and laughed that their lips would not open easily without bleeding, and eye infection was widespread. I saw a boy with an unusually protruded nose. I asked why it was so blown up. The child answered,

"I placed a candy wrapper in my nose. Smelling candy all the time,
I expected to lessen starvation." There were plenty of stray children
in the open spaces between buildings. I saw one who was already
blind because of malnutrition.

I also saw a child who was being stabbed by a corn-cake vendor
in the market place. I made the vendor stop beating the child and
asked the reason for her anger. The vendor replied that she lost two
of her five children because of starvation. She continued, "This corn
cake is thus a life for me. The child tried to steal my life away from
me. So I became unconsciously mad and began to beat the boy."[15]

Another Korean-speaking expatriate aid worker visiting a provincial
city in February 1997 reported that at 5 a.m. one day the public address
system, which could be heard everywhere in the city, announced that
expatriate aid workers would be visiting the city that day. Unless people
had presentable shoes and clothing and appeared to be in good health,
the announcer continued, they should stay off the streets. One refugee
said in a videotaped interview that speaking to any foreigner, even for a
simple request such as a match or cigarette, was a political crime punishable by imprisonment.[16]

When I finally visited the border between North Korea and China
in September 1998 I asked refugee after refugee why no visible sign of
famine existed within North Korea. One former university professor
said, "It is humiliating to speak about our troubles in front of foreigners.
It hurts my pride in my country." He was amused by my naïveté about
the North Korean system. "We are not allowed to meet any foreigners," he
said. "Charity groups have a political motivation, according to the authorities. The real motivation of the charities is to collapse communism and
change North Korea from Red to Yellow. The foreigners will never see
the famine because North is the first paradise on earth. How can the officials show the famine to the world?"[17]

One woman from the Tumen River city of Musan, which was built
around steel mills now silent because of the industrial collapse, told me
what happened when UN aid officials came to the city. "The head of our
ban [a political district roughly equivalent to "neighborhood" or "local
community"] told us that UN officials would be in the city that day and
we were prohibited from leaving our homes the entire day. Absolutely
no one was to be on the streets from our ban." Another refugee told me,
"We must clean up and clear the village streets several days in advance of

the arrival of the foreigners. The government does not want to be dishonored." If true conditions were known, the government would be.

John Pomfret of the *Washington Post* interviewed one refugee from a village near the South Korea border who had traveled to China to escape the famine. He wrote,

> One man from near Mt. Kumgang, a popular tourist destination in the southern part of North Korea, countered that just before a group of foreigners would come to his village, the authorities would turn on the public address system in town and order people to stay indoors. "These people live here but they don't see us," he said. "We are the invisible people."[18]

The North Korean attitude toward the outside world can best be summarized in a story from a historic meeting between Deng Xiaoping and Kim Il Sung in Dalian, China. When Deng showed Kim the extraordinary economic miracle under way in China, which he attributed to the "small window opening to the West" that China had allowed, Kim reportedly replied, "When you open a window to the West, flies come in." Deng replied, "We can use a screen to prevent undesirable elements from coming in the country." Kim's response: "It would have to be a steel screen."[19]

HISTORICAL PRECEDENTS: TOTALITARIAN FAMINES OF THE TWENTIETH CENTURY

Had this been the first successful attempt by a totalitarian regime in the twentieth century to disguise a famine of this magnitude from the outside world, one might wonder how the North Korean government had succeeded in such an implausible task where others had failed. But in all four of the century's previous totalitarian famines—in Soviet Ukraine (1930–33), the People's Republic of China (1958–62), Ethiopia (1984–85), and Cambodia (1975)—exactly the same pattern of government behavior was apparent.

Dekulakization and the Ukrainian Famine

Robert Conquest, the great scholar of the dekulakization and forced collectivization in the Soviet Union that killed 14.5 million people nationwide between 1929 and 1933, described in painstaking detail the lengths to which Joseph Stalin went to disguise the consequences of his policies in Ukraine. Between August and September 1933, the French Socialist leader Edouard Herriot, who twice served as his country's prime minister, visited the Soviet Union; he spent five days of the trip in Ukraine. Conquest wrote of the trip:

> A visitor to Kiev describes the preparations for Herriot. The day before his arrival the population was required to work from 2 a.m. cleaning the streets and decorating the houses. Food-distribution centers were closed. Queues were prohibited. Homeless children, beggars, and starving people disappeared. A local inhabitant adds that shop windows were filled with food, but the police dispersed or arrested even local citizens who pressed too close (and the purchase of food was forbidden). The streets were washed. . . . At Kharkov he was taken to a model children's settlement. . . . Certain villages were set aside to show to foreigners. These were model collectives . . . where all peasants were picked Communists and *Komsomols*. These were well housed and well fed. The cattle were in good condition.[20]

Herriot announced that no famine existed and "blamed reports of such on elements pursuing anti-Soviet policy."[21] *Pravda* announced that Herriot "categorically denied the lies of the bourgeois press about a famine in the Soviet Union."[22] Conquest provides other examples:

> On another occasion a delegation of Americans, English and Germans came to Kharkov. A major round up of peasant beggars preceded it. They were taken off in lorries and simply dumped in a barren field some way out of town. A Turkish mission, on its way home, was scheduled to eat at the junction of Lozova. In anticipation of their stay, the dead and dying were loaded in trucks, and removed to an unknown fate. The others were marched eighteen miles away and forbidden to return. The station was cleaned up, and smart "waitresses" and "public" were brought in.[23]

The Great Leap Forward and the Chinese Famine

Mao Zedong launched the Great Leap Forward in 1958 after having begun forced collectivization of agriculture in 1956. Mao designed the Great Leap Forward to accelerate China's achievement of the marxist utopian paradise through, alongside other initiatives in the industrial sector, "innovative" agricultural practices. Mao borrowed these practices from Stalin's notorious minister of agriculture, Trofim Denisovitch Lysenko, and other pseudo-agronomists.[24] To pander to Mao's ego, the sycophants in the party structure kept information on the famine's devastation from Mao. Indeed, they insisted that his policies were responsible for such a massive increase in production that food, forcibly requisitioned from the starving peasantry, was exported.

During this period, refugees escaping into Hong Kong with stories of famine were dismissed as "biased, rarely accurate, usually interested in painting an adverse picture," according to *The Times* of London.[25] Jasper Becker devotes an entire chapter in his book on the Chinese famine to the story of leftist Western political leaders who admired the radical egalitarianism of Mao's China. China scholars also dismissed reports of the famine as baseless, anticommunist propaganda. While a few journalists such as Joseph Alsop and newspapers such as the *New York Times* accurately reported the Chinese catastrophe, most chose to ignore the evidence. This dismissal of compelling evidence reflected the nearly absolute control the Chinese government—like the Soviet government before it—exercised over any outside visits; foreigners saw only what the security apparatus wanted them to see. And, as previously stated, the authorities' success at disguising the famine in China was not limited to foreigners, but extended to Mao himself. When he visited rural areas, party bureaucrats hid evidence of the famine and provided him with fictitious reports of increased grain production, when production was actually dropping precipitously.[26] Only in 1960 did Mao hear from senior officials like Marshal Peng Dehaui how devastating the famine had become.[27] Even so, it was not until 1962 that he abandoned his schemes, changed policies, and allowed agricultural production to increase. Thirty million people lay dead in the wake of his ideological catastrophe.

Ethiopian Resettlement and Famine under Mengistsu

Another hidden famine killed several hundred thousand people in Ethiopia in 1972–73, precipitating a coup by military officers in 1974 that unseated Emperor Haile Selassie. The subsequent famine of 1984–85, which killed one million people, was reportedly a consequence of drought-induced crop failure. But as Robert Kaplan reported in his book on the famine, the forced resettlement schemes of the central government were a major factor contributing to the disaster. Colonel Mengistu Haile Mariam's marxist regime attempted to resettle hundreds of thousands of people from the Amharic and Tigrayan highlands—people who coincidentally supported the rebel movement seeking to overthrow the regime—to more fertile lowlands. The regime also tried to move family compounds in the highlands into planned villages, ostensibly to improve the "efficiency" of the farms, but in fact the scheme had precisely the opposite effect. The marxist agricultural system prohibited the trading of food across provincial lines, so surpluses from one region could not be moved to another suffering a deficit.

The central government's responsibility for the 1985 famine was never made clear in journalistic reporting. Cultural Survival, a Cambridge, Massachusetts–based organization formed by Harvard University academics to conduct research and publicize reports on endangered ethnic groups in the developing world,[28] interviewed thousands of refugees streaming across the Ethiopian border into Sudan to escape the brutal resettlement program. Perhaps as many as one hundred thousand people had died by July 1985 because of this campaign, according to the Cultural Survival report:

> Some of the resettled people were undoubtedly malnourished as a result of declining agricultural production in their homelands, but many had not experienced famine until they were captured for resettlement. . . . Perhaps it is more important to note that the settlers received minuscule amounts of food for as long as a month before they arrived in the resettlement camps and then were expected to work 11 hours each day for six and a half days each week.[29]

Yet, international relief agencies summarily dismissed the testimonies of the Ethiopian refugees reporting these conditions, because they contradicted the information provided by the central government. NGOs, dependent on central government approval to conduct their relief work in the country, claimed they had seen no evidence of these policies being carried out or no evidence of the high death rates.

The Cambodian Famine and the Killing Fields of the Khmer Rouge

The Cambodian "killing fields" was the fourth great totalitarian famine of the twentieth century—or the fifth, if one includes V. I. Lenin's abortive attempt to collectivize agriculture in the early 1920s, which killed millions. Although the 1976–79 killing fields period in Cambodia was not a famine in the traditional sense, the Khmer Rouge did use starvation as one of several means of execution of the urban elites they were attempting to liquidate. Sichan Siv was a Cambodian national who assisted American foreign service officer Charles Twining in interviewing Cambodian refugees escaping the Khmer Rouge atrocities.[30] He said that perhaps as many as a third of the victims of the atrocities actually died of deliberately planned starvation. The Khmer Rouge worked the victims to death in the countryside and provided such meager rations as to ensure their ultimate death. To increase the death rates further, the communist cadres prohibited these victims from scavenging for food from the countryside, which was rich in wild foods that could have sustained them through the terror.[31]

What is most relevant for the purposes of this study is the international reaction to the refugee reports that leaked out of Cambodia beginning in 1977. In *The Quality of Mercy*, a classic book on the humanitarian relief effort following the Vietnamese invasion that ended the Khmer Rouge nightmare, William Shawcross records this reaction in some detail. Some of the critics refused to believe the apocalyptic refugee reports because they described events that could only be called demonic; even tyrants do not do the kinds of things the Khmer Rouge were being accused of doing. Other critics, such as the left-wing professor Noam Chomsky, dismissed the reports for ideological reasons. Chomsky declared that "from the moment of the Khmer Rouge victory in 1975 the Western press colluded with Western and anti-Communist Asian governments, notably Thailand, to produce a 'vast and unprecedented' campaign of propaganda against the Khmer Rouge."[32] Other academics and journalists on the left took the same view, associating the attacks on the communists with the Vietnam War.

RECOGNIZING THE CENTURY'S FIFTH GREAT TOTALITARIAN FAMINE

All of the totalitarian famines of the twentieth century, without exception, were invisible to the visiting outsider. By definition, every totalitarian government intrinsically seeks control over all elements of the society it governs, including the face it shows to the outside world. But no government in the twentieth century reached a level of control as absolute as that of North Korea. For the regime to have advertised its distress to the outside world would have been out of character, even unimaginable.

Yet, as the North Korean famine relief effort blossomed, it became apparent to me that some relief workers actually admired the egalitarian public distribution system that was theoretically sharing the misery equally among the general population. While these relief workers and scholars were troubled by the regime's repression of civil liberties, they would always add that no one was starving, which counted for a great deal. If only they had been correct. Some were simply naïve and, having developed personal friendships with some North Koreans, may not have realized that they were being systematically deceived. More skeptical relief workers believed that the North Korean regime had exaggerated or wholly fabricated the crisis to collect more international assistance and further its political objectives.

The purity or baseness of the motives of those of us managing any crisis relief operation does not absolve us of responsibility for determining what is happening to the people we are supposed to be serving. In North Korea, however, ominous reports were coming from the border region, gathered by other NGOs and responsible journalists, yet many groups working within North Korea steadfastly refused to take any account of these reports. Some agencies did not want to admit that their work to stop the famine might have been ineffective or, worse still, manipulated by the central government to serve their political objectives.

When I raised these issues with Catherine Bertini, a respected humanitarian relief official and director of the WFP, her response was instructive: "What should we be doing differently if the revisionist interpretation proves correct and a terrible famine is occurring in front of us?" This question will be addressed in later chapters.

4

SURVIVING THE FAMINE: ALONG THE CHINESE FRONTIER

EVIDENCE SEEMED TO BE MOUNTING that a great famine was sweeping across North Korea, but I felt uncomfortable with my understanding of its dynamic, with the estimates of deaths, and with the contradictory data coming from NGOs inside the country. My suspicions rested on refugee interviews conducted by people I had never met, media accounts of defectors' stories written by journalists who—the British journalist Jasper Becker excepted—generally knew little about famines, and UN and NGO field reporting that contained ambiguous and often contradictory information. Perhaps I had misinterpreted what was happening or mistakenly read into the North Korean famine the record of famines elsewhere. Perhaps the more cynical NGO and UN relief workers on the ground in North Korea were correct: the famine never happened, and the regime had manufactured evidence to increase food aid donations for an otherwise manageable food shortage. The possibility, however remote, gave me pause more often than I publicly admitted.

The first in-depth reporting from the Chinese–North Korean border came from Jasper Becker, the Beijing-based journalist for Hong Kong's *South China Morning Post.* His twenty dispatches written between 1996 and 2000 are a rich source of anecdote and insight into conditions inside North Korea. Becker's authoritative reports drew from his previous research into famines; his January 1997 book *Hungry Ghosts,* on the 1958–62 Chinese famine caused by Mao Zedong's Great Leap Forward, was one of the best accounts of the disaster. Becker understood totalitarian famines better than most of the humanitarian relief workers managing the relief effort and in the second edition of his book included a post-script on the North Korean famine.

The first systematic evidence of the unfolding tragedy in North Korea was provided by the refugee interviews conducted by a South Korean Buddhist monk, the Venerable Pomnyun. Since 1993, Pomnyun had been doing humanitarian work through the NGO he founded, the Korean Buddhist Sharing Movement, in the ethnic Korean region of China along the North Korean border. Through this work he had developed an extensive network of friends who provided information on what was happening inside North Korea, though he himself was never allowed inside the country. In June 1997, one of his Korean Chinese friends described the famine, but Pomnyun initially doubted the story until his friend took him to the Tumen River, which divides China from North Korea in the east. There Pomnyun could see children on the opposite shore who appeared acutely malnourished. Troubled by the image of these emaciated children, he began interviewing refugees crossing over into China. Any doubts he had about the severity of the crisis disappeared during these interviews.

When Pomnyun returned to South Korea, where North Korea had been the central public policy issue for a half century, his first attempts to publicize the suffering were distorted by the political whirlwind surrounding anyone remotely sympathetic to Pyongyang. Political figures and the media suspected his motives, dismissed his reporting, or reinterpreted it to support their biases. The anemic political left in South Korea criticized him for embarrassing the North Korean government with exaggerated reports of mass starvation, while members of the dominant political right—particularly the security and military apparatus—harassed him, refused him permission to travel to North Korea, and confiscated his photographs and documents. They did not want anyone creating sympathy for the victims; doing so would only increase pressure on donor governments to provide aid to the famine relief effort, which in their view would forestall the collapse of the hated Northern government. Pomnyun had thus succeeded in annoying everyone simultaneously. To me this only increased his credibility; he was willing to annoy everyone to expose a painful truth no one wished to acknowledge.

At the same time that Pomnyun and Becker were collecting their anecdotes at the border, through World Vision, I asked leaders of the

Korean American community who had relatives in China if they would have their relatives interview refugees about the famine. I wrote nine questions asking refugees about mortality rates in their village between January 1 and June 30, 1997, and the Korean Americans translated them into Korean. Nearly four hundred interviews were conducted in July and August 1997, but only thirty-three were complete, as most refugees were too frightened of arrest and deportation to answer more than a few questions. Data from large cities was excluded, as refugees would not likely know death rates for the general population; in rural areas, however, an apparent 15 percent of the population had died. While hardly a scientific survey, it succeeded in aggregating anecdotes to render some judgments about the existence and severity of the famine. The survey caused a firestorm within World Vision, pitting the Western-run offices in Australia, Canada, and the United States against the Asian-run offices in South Korea, China, and Thailand; the latter argued that the publication of the survey would enrage the North Korean government, which indeed it did. UN agencies and NGO offices in Pyongyang complained that the survey endangered aid agency presence in North Korea.

Médecins Sans Frontières, the respected European NGO focused exclusively on humanitarian relief work, had been having the same internal debate as World Vision concerning the nature of the North Korean crisis. MSF staff from the China office who had traveled to the North Korean border to interview refugees heard the same stories about the devastation of the famine as those provided to World Vision and the KBSM. They released their initial results to the international media in the spring of 1998. This action angered the MSF staff working inside North Korea, as they said they saw no evidence to support the claims of the refugees. An acrimonious dispute ensued within the worldwide organization, during which time the staff who had conducted the refugee interviews were fired, rehired, and then dispatched back to the border to conduct much more extensive interviews over the summer of 1998. That August, MSF published twelve pages of transcribed refugee interviews conducted on the Sino-Korean border. On September 30, MSF's international director general, Eric Goemaere, announced that, despite having worked in North Korea for sixteen months, MSF was leaving the country because of the abuses of humanitarian aid that the refugee interviews had revealed. The transcribed interviews described "corpses in the

streets," large-scale movements of famine refugees into China, and farmers markets that had become the major source of food for urban areas,
though at highly inflated prices. They also told of abandoned children who
roamed city streets begging for food, masses of people harvesting wild
famine foods to survive, and families selling all they owned—including
their homes—to buy food. Several refugees who had deserted from the
army reported unrest in their units because of inadequate rations; they
said their commanding officers had ordered them to raid food stocks on
the collective farms. The refugees described harrowing trips in train cars
packed with displaced people escaping the famine; when people died
along the way, "bodies were simply thrown out of the door." The MSF
interviews also revealed one piece of information absent from the KBSM
and World Vision surveys: the party cadres and military were apparently enriching themselves by selling food aid they had diverted from
aid agencies.[1]

The *Washington Post* had shown only sporadic interest in the famine
during 1997 and 1998, with stories appearing occasionally each year,
none providing particular insight or depth. In early February 1999, however, John Pomfret, who had written before on the crisis, traveled to the
border and conducted in-depth interviews with twenty refugees and
border officials. His lengthy report on conditions in North Korea described "a grotesque landscape of crumbling families, homes without
electricity or heat, and towns and villages where promised foreign food aid
did not arrive, or was reserved for ruling party elites whose neighbors
survived on twigs, leaves, corn stalks, and frogs."[2]

Pomfret quoted Western diplomats describing the border region.
"This is a wild zone. Everybody has three identities and four ID cards.
It's one of the ends of the earth." Chinese officials told Pomfret that
"intelligence operatives from several countries—Japan, the United States,
South Korea, and Russia—frequent the region in efforts to monitor
events across the border. The area is also thick with agents from China's
State Security Ministry." The Chinese were particularly troubled by the
constant stream of famine refugees illegally crossing the border, as many
as three hundred thousand. The Chinese police, Pomfret reported, were
searching homes, rounding up refugees in sweeps, and forcibly repatri-
ating them to North Korea, where they faced prison and likely starvation. In the summer of 1998, North Korean border guards were given

orders to shoot to kill if they saw refugees crossing the border; Pomfret reported that five bodies with gunshot wounds were found around Tumen, China, though shooting incidents seem to have diminished by February 1999.

EVENTS ALONG THE BORDER

The border between China and North Korea runs in a northeastward direction for 880 miles from the Bay of Korea to the Sea of Japan and has three geographic divisions. The first part runs northeast from the Bay of Korea along the Yalu River until the river takes a sharp bend southward. Along this portion of the border, the Yalu—known in Korean as the Ab-Rok Gang—is deep and wide, making refugee crossings dangerous and unlikely. Even more discouraging for refugees was the fact that the Chinese frontier along this part of the border is populated by Han Chinese who speak no Korean.

The next stretch of border appears on the map as a semicircular southward diversion that marks the confluence of the Yalu and the Tumen River, known in Korea as the Dooman River. The Chinese side of this part of the border is covered with a thickly wooded and thinly populated forest area up the sides of Mt. Paekdu. Although some particularly enterprising refugees attempted to traverse this discouraging landscape, few made it past the forest, as they were already weakened by the famine. This mountainous journey is even more forbidding in the winter, when temperatures can drop to between −30°F and −40°F. Nevertheless, the Tumen, narrower and shallower than the Yalu, provided a much more tempting means of escape, and many refugee flows tended to concentrate on this end of the border.

The third section of the border extends toward the north and east until it meets the Sea of Japan. For would-be refugees, this area presented one advantage the other two did not: residents on the Chinese side are ethnic Koreans. The Korean Chinese population, estimated at one to two million people, immigrated in several successive waves from the end of the nineteenth century. They are loyal to the Chinese Communist Party and the central government, display little Korean nationalism, and cause no trouble. They are also hard working and industrious, and their low birth rates do not threaten the ethnic Han Chinese. These characteristics explain why Chinese authorities traditionally left them alone to help their relatives coming across the border.

What began happening along the border beginning in 1997 was not traditional. The dramatic increase in the flow of refugees into China so alarmed the central and provincial authorities that they imposed severe penalties on anyone helping the famine victims. One evening in June 1998, between 10 p.m. and 2 a.m., Chinese authorities conducted a door-to-door census in the ethnic Korean region to locate and repatriate food refugees. Upon their return to North Korea, the refugees were beaten by the border police, imprisoned for a month or more in displaced persons camps, known as 927 camps, and then returned to their home cities and towns. Many Korean Chinese were being called into police headquarters under suspicion of helping their North Korean relatives, interrogated, and then released. By 1999, reports of such interrogations no longer included any mention of torture or mistreatment, but tensions along the border grew as population movements increased.[3] To discourage further immigration, the Chinese authorities imposed fines equal to a year's wages on anyone caught hiding or assisting North Korean refugees.

Pomnyun had regularly invited me to accompany him to this frontier region to interview refugees myself. But the North Koreans believed anyone who journeyed to the border region was a South Korean or American spy, and I did not want to endanger World Vision's program in the country. By June 1998, however, I had resigned from World Vision and taken a fellowship with the United States Institute of Peace to complete this book: I was free to travel and write, unencumbered by operational NGO constraints. In September 1998 I accepted Pomnyun's invitation. I had conducted field assessments and run relief efforts in eight other wars and famines over the past decade; perhaps I could see comparable coping patterns along this border region.

Pomnyun, his English-speaking assistant Jihyun Park, and I arrived in Yanji, China, in mid-September for a ten-day field trip. Yanji, a city that had been built over the past several decades, has three hundred thousand residents, is the capital of the Yanbian autonomous region in Jilin province, and lies fifteen hours by car from the North Korean border. While ethnic Koreans had once been the majority, inexorable population pressures had led to Han Chinese migration into the region. By the time of my visit, ethnic Koreans constituted only 40 percent of the population of Yanji, but Yanbian's small towns and rural areas were still heavily Korean, which is why many North Koreans sought refuge there.

The airport, funded and built by South Koreans, was modern and efficient for what the Chinese call a frontier outpost in a remote border region. The modernity of the airport and the prosperity of the city were a function of South Korean business investments in a region full of Korean-speaking workers. South Korean tourists were also drawn to Yanbian because of Mt. Paekdu, known in Korea as Paik-doo San, the legendary birthplace of the Korean people and their culture. The 1997 economic crisis in South Korea had begun to take its toll on tourism from the South, but, crisis or not, most South Koreans yearn to visit the mountain before they die and—judging by the number of hotels and restaurants in the city—many do. Even after the June census and repatriation, the presence of North Korean refugees in Yanji, while not apparent to a newcomer, did not require much effort to discover. They were hiding everywhere: in parks and alleys, near and around the marketplaces, and in the garbage containers behind the city's countless restaurants. I succeeded in interviewing twenty-four North Koreans. Of these, nineteen were working-class people from small towns and the large industrial cities strung along the other side of the Tumen River, one was from Pyongyang, several were from South Hamgyong Province, and one was from a city in the southwest.

I also spoke with several Korean Chinese, many of whom asked me how long the famine would continue and how long they would have to support their relatives. Some families had begun to turn away even their relatives. In the earlier phases of the population movement into China, refugees begged for food or sought work at ginseng plantations spread out in the rural areas of the province. But by mid-1998, the severity of the crisis, the saturation of the job market, and the inadequacy of begging had driven some to theft and murder to obtain food. Even China's ethnic Korean population no longer welcomed them. One retired truck driver in a Chinese border city told me that the communist founders of China and North Korea had lied to their people for decades about capitalism, which they claimed benefited only the rich and impoverished everyone else. He continued,

> That was a lie. It is communism that impoverished everyone except for the cadres in both countries and is causing the famine in North

Korea. Under Deng Xiaoping and Jiang Zemin, China has adopted beginning capitalism, even though we do not call it that, and the common people have never been so well fed and prosperous. I tell all my North Korean relatives who ask me for help that they must take the Chinese example and adopt our system or the famine will never end.

He was not alone in these sentiments.

A long cement bridge across the Tumen River connects Tumen, China, with Namyang, North Korea. A Korean Chinese merchant's wife said the bridge was once well traveled. North Koreans would send letters to their Chinese relatives, pleading for help; later they would meet at this bridge, where the relatives would provide food or money. As the famine grew in intensity, however, fewer and fewer people met at the bridge. The merchant's wife told me,

> In 1996, one hundred to two hundred Korean Chinese would cross each day; by 1997 the visits dropped to fifty a day. This year [1998] three to four people cross over [daily]. It is not because the North Koreans stopped coming—they are still there. The decline in exchanges has taken place because the Korean Chinese are tired of the constant requests and aren't coming anymore. If you look across the river you can see people in the apartment porches, sitting; they [were] sent there by the [North Korean] security police last year. It used to be that three hundred to four hundred poor North Koreans would crowd together on the streets waiting for their relatives from China. It became embarrassing to the authorities for so many beggars to be seen by us, so they forced them to disperse into the apartments. Some people will wait months for their relatives who never come. Some die waiting.[4]

Several elderly ethnic Koreans who had been supporting their relatives in North Korea for years told me they had stopped because they were unable to support themselves on their modest income; they said they felt terribly guilty about their decision.

These Korean Chinese and their North Korean relatives had maintained their ties of blood and kinship for a century, ties that had served as one of the most effective famine-coping strategies for people living in the northern provinces. When crises threaten, people instinctively turn to their extended family for help. During the famine of the Great Leap

Forward, Korean Chinese had turned to their more prosperous North Korean relatives for help. The success of Deng Xiaoping's economic and agricultural reforms in the 1980s and the collapse of the North Korean economy in the 1990s reversed the economic circumstances of the two societies: the famine had moved south from China into North Korea, and prosperity had migrated north.

SURVIVAL STRATEGIES

The mechanisms people use to survive famine are no mystery, though in each famine new twists and turns sometime appear.[5] The authors of the annual FAO/WFP crop reports from 1995 to 1999 observed some of these coping mechanisms. By June 1997, their interim reports were full of these indicators, which would normally be sufficient proof that a famine was under way. In the case of North Korea, however, expatriate relief workers had no access to mortality rates and saw no mass burials or emaciated people, so they kept reporting that famine was merely looming when in fact it had arrived.[6]

North Koreans used coping mechanisms that fell into three broad categories: reduce the number of mouths to feed in the family, move to another region that has more food, or find alternative sources of food outside the traditional public distribution system.

Reduce the Number of Mouths to Feed

If the decline in the amount of food available to a family cannot be slowed, then reducing the number of mouths to feed means the remaining family members will eat a little better, improving their survival chances. A team of researchers from The Johns Hopkins University School of Public Health conducted the most comprehensive and scientifically rigorous analysis of refugee data and found evidence of a substantial increase in family breakup and a decline in family size.[7] Refugees I interviewed gave graphic accounts of how they were separated from their family members. Some refugee families remained intact despite the harrowing trek to the border, but upon encountering police or soldiers on either side of the Tumen River they ran for cover, losing track of their relatives in the process.

Population Control and Family Planning. At a minimum, having no
more children reduced the potential burden and protected the declining
food supply. In refugee interviews conducted by KBSM, women spoke
of taking measures to ensure they did not become pregnant, because
they knew that they would not be able to feed a newborn and that pregnancy could threaten their own survival. Other women spoke about post-
poning marriage for this very reason. Some women sought abortions if
they did get pregnant. Even if they had not deliberately tried to avoid
pregnancy, however, malnourishment and subsequent infertility would
have acted as an effective birth control measure.[8] Both the KBSM and
Johns Hopkins surveys showed sharply declining birth rates among
North Korean women as the famine progressed: the Johns Hopkins survey
showed a reduction of 50 percent in birth rates from 21.8 per thousand
in the early 1990s—before the famine—to 11 per thousand by 1997.[9]
But in the 1980s, well before the famine began, the regime appeared to
have been pursuing a population control policy.[10] Thus, the reduction in
birth rates may have been a coping mechanism at both the national level
and by individual families as the food supply declined. As the famine
progressed and the population declined even further, however, the authorities appear to have reversed their policy. Refugees interviewed by Becker
and the KBSM consistently reported that the authorities prohibited
birth control devices and abortions.

The Voluntary and Involuntary Starvation of the Elderly. One of the
most chilling strategies North Korean families pursued to reduce their
size was the shedding of family members. Some Southern Sudanese tribes
shed teenage boys to cope with famine. When a boy marries, his parents
face a reverse form of dowry in which they must give cows, the traditional medium of exchange, to the bride's family. Thus girls increase
family wealth, whereas boys decrease it, an economic calculation that
affects survival decisions during crises. North Korea steadfastly remains
a Confucian culture in nearly every respect, though its rhetoric may
translate Confucian values into more modern totalitarian form using the
language of *juche* and Marxism-Leninism. In the Confucian worldview
the elderly are held in the highest esteem because they are the transmit-
ters of traditional values and keepers of family memory. Confucianism
has transformed reverence for the elderly into a religious ritual where

ancestors are worshipped.[11] Nevertheless, many sources confirm that some families cast out their elders so the young would have a greater chance of survival. Some anecdotal reports told an even more powerful story of grandparents choosing not to eat so the rations available to their grandchildren would be larger. In the conflict between reverence for the elderly and the continuity of the family line, the latter instinct often won, sometimes with the encouragement of the victims, sometimes despite their opposition.

The Phenomenon of Abandoned Children. The elderly were not the only individuals put adrift as a means of extending a family's meager food supply. During desperate and chaotic migrations, children were sometimes inadvertently separated from their families or were purposely abandoned. In other cases, parents fed their children before they themselves ate, and by dying first left their orphaned children to fend for themselves. Officials told us that in some cases children were not actually orphaned but merely abandoned, as the families had no food to feed them. The abandoned child phenomenon reached even the prosperous capital. One North Korean official who had defected told me of being recruited into a posse that searched for abandoned children in Pyongyang; his cadre team scoured the city streets for these children and turned them over to the authorities for warehousing.

In the spring of 1997 and again in the summer of 1998, three different NGOs independently observed gangs of abandoned children stealing food to survive. One aid worker visiting the Najin–Sonbong trade zone in the Northeast in 1998 watched a gang of starving children run alongside a slow-moving truck carrying bags of grain. As they ran, they poked sharp sticks into the bags, and children behind them carefully collected the corn pouring out of the bags. One NGO working in a remote province investigated rumors of a building being used to house several thousand abandoned children; indeed, the workers discovered 3,800 dirty, ill-clad, and unsupervised children locked in an old warehouse. Although the children were suffering from moderate malnutrition, they were not dying; they had been there for only a few days, after having been swept up off the streets of a neighboring city. The very existence of these abandoned children was a sign of the advanced breakdown in the social order.

One merchant who had kept his family alive as a trader until he migrated to China told me of an incident one day in his city's farmers market:

> A three-year-old boy and his four-year-old sister . . . were in poor health. The boy lay motionless on the ground, with his sister sitting next to him listless. The parents had hung papers around the neck of each child with their names and ages and then deserted them in the market hoping some merchant would pick them up and adopt them. The group of us took pity on them and bought two boiled eggs and placed them next to each child with the instruction to eat them quickly before another abandoned child came by and stole them.[12]

Early one morning Pomnyun took me up into the thickly forested hills behind Changbai, a prosperous if remote frontier city that rests on the Tumen River across from the North Korean city of Hyesan. There I interviewed a thirty-eight-year-old widow from Unhung, Yanggang province, whose husband had been beaten to death and robbed while carrying home a small bag of corn on June 20, 1997. Both of her parents had starved during the famine. She had crossed over into China for the third time on August 25, 1998, after her uncle in Hyesan, North Korea, from whom she had sought help, told her he had no food either. On their first crossing into China, she, her four-year-old son, and her eight-year-old daughter had been caught and sent to the Hyesan 927 camp for internally displaced persons. The camp held more than five hundred people, and two to three people died each day. Forty people were crammed into her small room; it was impossible to lie down to sleep at night, so people slept crouching. After they were released, she kept her two children alive by denying herself food, and she expected to die before they did; this caused her great anguish, because she knew they would be abandoned on the streets. She told me she and her children had survived after one of their border crossings because a poor, elderly Chinese couple had taken in and fed them. They could not let her stay any longer, though, because they had gone through all their food reserves. She and her children were again deported, but they managed to return. When I spoke with her, her plan was to try to give away her two children to any Chinese family who would take them, so she could then try to move into the interior of China and marry a Chinese farmer. She told me 40 percent of the houses in her *ban* were abandoned, because the people either had starved or were on the move.[13]

Human Trafficking. A common way North Korean families reduced the number of mouths to feed was by selling daughters and wives to "human traffickers." This practice was also common in the European famines of the eighteenth and nineteenth centuries and in the African and South Asian famines of the twentieth century.[14] As we drove through one village famous for human trafficking, Pomnyun told me the bordello trade in young girls was on the increase. Yet some North Korean girls were destined not for service in Asian bordellos, but for marriage to young Han and Korean Chinese farmers who could not otherwise find brides. Before the easing of Chinese population control policies that prohibited more than one child per couple, families often killed their infant daughters out of a desire to have male heirs.[15] This terrible practice disturbed the gender equilibrium for people born during this period, and by the late 1990s there were not enough young brides for the young men. The shortage was particularly acute in the rural areas of China, and North Korean girls accepted marriage "offers" out of desperation, not choice; at times they were treated little better than chattel slaves.

In July 1999 the KBSM released the first comprehensive study of the size of the population movements into China, the coping mechanisms food refugees used once they arrived, and the hardships they endured in China.[16] KBSM staff surveyed refugees in 2,479 villages in three Chinese provinces north of the Tumen River. These provinces together have a population of more than 100 million people, and they have the largest concentration of ethnic Koreans in China. The KBSM estimated that there were between 140,000 and 195,000 refugees in China at the time of the study, mostly concentrated in the villages with the highest proportion of ethnic Korean Chinese. The KBSM did not count refugees on the run or in hiding, nor did the number include gangs of children abandoned onto the streets. Chinese police searches forced the KBSM teams away from the larger cities that tended to have a heavy presence of refugees, so the study overrepresented rural areas. Of those refugees interviewed, about three-quarters were women. Half of the women had been sold for marriage by human traffickers, but some were in marriages arranged through relatives. Sixty percent were between twenty and thirty years old.[17]

Some women sold into marriage reported being treated like chattel, imprisoned in their new homes for months at a time. A twenty-one-year-old female refugee from Taedong-gang, South Pyongan province, reported,

> A human trafficker sold me to an anonymous man living deep in the mountains of China. He had a dark complexion and was around forty [years old] and below 160 cm [5 feet] tall. He spoke incomprehensible Chinese and confined me in a room, locking the door. When night fell, he appeared, reeking of alcohol, and ruthlessly abused me. I was unable to move due to hunger. I cried and cried because of pain and grief until dawn. He shackled me like a dog so I could not get away. I suffered such a miserable life for half a year.[18]

Some women were sold and resold four or five times and abused by each of their owners, but others reported that they had married well and were happy. Most spoke with great pain of their abuse but said it was better than starving to death in North Korea. The marriages are illegal, however, and many husbands abandon their North Korean wives before the police discover them, to avoid heavy fines.

As Pomnyun reported, not all women were sold into marriage; some were sold to bars as prostitutes. A twenty-seven-year-old female from Onsong-gun, North Hamgyong province, explained:

> I worked at a karaoke bar as a serving staff. . . . I had to sleep with customers; otherwise, the owner threatened to report me. As a result, I got venereal disease. I gave my money to the owner, but he didn't give me all my money back. He only gave me half of my money and dismissed me. Since I had no other way, I relied on an old man over fifty . . . . Since we couldn't communicate at all, he also was infected through me. He cursed and battered me. Then he took me to a hospital several times. Sometimes, I wished to die, but at other times, I think it is much better to be here than go back to North Korea and die from hunger.[19]

The otherwise unremarkable Chinese farming village of Nampong, which sits on the banks of the Tumen River, was home to one of three gangs of human traffickers along the river who trade in these young women. When I asked who made up the gang, Pomnyun replied, "Everyone who lives in the village." His comment, although an exaggeration, indicates how widespread the trade had become. Demand was high, and so too were the profits; the supply of young girls was plentiful, and their prices attractive. Parents would sell their daughters for $25, and the traffickers then resold them to Chinese farmers for $250. The price increased if a girl was moved further into the interior of China, or if she was particularly beautiful. Refugees explained with considerable amusement that beauty was unnecessary, because Chinese farmers were so desperate for children and companionship that they would take any woman, no matter how homely. Increasingly, brazen traders resorted to kidnapping to avoid the initial investment. Female refugees who arrived in China unaccompanied by male family members were at great risk.

The competitiveness of human trading was so fierce that it even caused problems for some of the NGOs. Three KBSM staff—one young man and two young women—were in one river village trying to help refugees and were mistaken by one of the human trafficker gangs as competitors. The male staffer barely escaped a beating and the two young women were nearly kidnapped because they were thought to be North Korean refugees. The three NGO staff departed with great haste.[20]

Pomnyun and I had dinner in Changbai with a fifteen-year-old girl named Moon who, because of stunting, appeared to be ten; her story was probably illustrative of so many others. She, her mother, and her brother had left Hamhung, the second largest city in North Korea, after they ran out of money. Her malnourished father had died of disease in February 1996. They had sold their family home after her father's death, and her mother had used the money to run a small business in the markets, but it was never successful enough to feed the family.

Moon attended school, but as the famine grew worse the teachers began demanding food from the students; if they refused they would be given poor grades and marked down as discipline problems. "All the kind teachers who made no demands died of starvation. The cruel teachers who threatened the children survived," she said. She had escaped into China four times; each time she was caught and sent to the Hyesan 927 camp, where she was beaten for her independence. She managed to escape out the window of her room using rags tied together, but on the way down a guard frightened her, and she fell five stories to the ground. She hurt her legs so badly she could not walk for nearly two months. After her next escape her mother sold her for $25 to a Chinese peasant family far inland from the river who claimed they wanted to adopt her.

Moon spent one night at the family's farmhouse before she fled. The people were very nice, she said, but they spoke only Chinese and she suspected they intended her to marry their son, a border guard who was to arrive the next day. She stole away to the village train station, crept into a tool chest in one of the cars, and arrived the next morning back in Changbai, where she later met us. Unlike many of the other refugee children we saw, whose clothing had turned to dirty rags and who had skin infections, she had kept herself relatively clean and her clothing in good repair, so she was not readily identifiable as a refugee.[21]

Chinese provincial officials tried to stem the flood of purchased brides, but they were only occasionally successful. At the end of 1998, two men were arrested for trading two cases of cigarettes for three women. One woman was sold for $362 and the other was about to be sold when the trader was arrested.[22]

Most of the population movements across the river took place at night because border security had increased so dramatically during 1998: soldiers were posted every fifty meters on both sides of the river, and one could see their foxhole-like hiding places strung along the riverbanks. The support of the border soldiers, however, could easily be purchased. Many refugees told of bribing the soldiers with nothing more than promises that, on their way back from China to North Korea, they would pay the soldiers what they demanded. The soldiers often accepted the return offer of payment, perhaps because enough of the refugees actually met their end of the bargain. The porosity of the border encouraged smuggling of other products that, when imported legally into China, incurred steep duties. The higher the duty, the greater was the incentive for smuggling. A smuggling ring trafficking in used Japanese automobiles, for example, operated along the Tumen River. Its operation was evident in all the narrower and shallower fords in the riverbed, and Chinese border authorities erected cement barriers where smugglers most frequently drove the cars across the river at night. One UN relief worker told me that the North Korean economy seemed to be improving in the summer of 1998, as a large number of ships carrying Japanese cars had arrived in Nampo. I suspected most were imported to be smuggled to China.

Not only were young women purchased, but able-bodied North Korean males were also in demand as farm laborers on ginseng plantations; they had a reputation of being hard and tireless workers. But the number of refugees was so high that it may have depressed the labor market. North Koreans' tenuous status as illegal migrants was even more damaging to their negotiating position: if turned over to the authorities by a dissatisfied employer, they were stripped of their earnings and belongings and returned to North Korea to the camps for internally displaced persons (on which, more below).

Mass Suicide as a Final Resort. The most gruesome of all coping strategies was mass suicide. I suppose this is not truly a coping strategy, but their final failure: an utter loss of hope. I had never heard of such a phenomenon in ten years of famine relief work. Robert Conquest had recorded instances of individual suicides during the Ukrainian famine of 1930–33.[23] And in refugee camps in Bosnia and Congo I heard of older men, particularly those from the upper class, who took their lives because of the humiliation of utter dependence and absolute deprivation. But when I first heard of a mass suicide, I thought the translators had misunderstood the refugee, or that the practice was an isolated incident. But the number of unsolicited stories in the KBSM surveys and among the refugees I interviewed were too numerous to ignore.

Mark Kirk, then a congressional staffer and now a member of Congress from Illinois, visited the North Korean border and videotaped several refugee interviews. One woman told of two cases of family suicides in her hometown in North Hamgyong province; she wept as she spoke because they had been neighbors. In most cases the suicides were committed by younger couples with smaller children; the couples had been denying themselves food for so long they feared they would die before their children did and that their children would be left to fend for themselves on the streets. Rather than have the children die alone, parents would collect their remaining assets and purchase a bowl of rice for a last meal, mix it with rat poison, and die together. One refugee reported that people in her village had found an entire family hanging from trees in the forest. Another reported to the KBSM, "The number of suicides is increasing. In the beginning they were the workers and the farmers. Now the officials are killing themselves. The situation has become so extreme that some people are eating their own children."[24] I later learned that, during the Chinese famine of 1942, whole families committed mass suicide in much the same way that Korean refugees described to me.[25]

In traditional Korean culture, families that had been wrongfully accused and publicly humiliated by a royal official would commit suicide, believing that they would return as spirits to haunt the offending official. Some famine refugees expressed unbridled rage at party officials for allowing the famine, accused them of stealing food while they starved, and insisted they be brought to justice for their crimes. While no evidence connects popular rage over the famine with the suicides, like much of what we saw in North Korea, its connection to the historic culture of the country could not be discounted easily.

Move to Another Region to Find Food

People move during famines for a variety of reasons. Men tend to move before their families do to seek day labor in cities, to send some of their earnings back to their families, and to increase their own chances for survival.[26] Many of the internally displaced people I interviewed during the Somalia famine in August and September of 1992 were moving toward the camps run by humanitarian organizations rumored to have food, or to escape clan fighting. The population of Somalia's capital, Mogadishu, increased by as much as 25 percent after the arrival of the U.S.-led military forces, as people left their villages for the city because they believed the international force would guarantee both food and safety from the clan wars.[27]

Escaping to China became one of the primary means for surviving the North Korean famine. One refugee from a province just north of Pyongyang observed that, in his village, "most of the people who have passed away are those who have never been to China. I only [came] here in [the] hope [that I might] get some food, but the security was extremely tight.... Over half of the people in our village left the village for food and the majority of those have crossed the border to China."[28]

The regime's population control system had broken down, not because the regime was liberalizing, but because it was unable to provide food to people with ration cards. Under the old system, people needed a permit from the local public security office to travel outside their village. Every person in the country was also registered by household. This central government policy had been instituted to avoid overcrowding in urban areas and to make migration from rural areas to the cities exceptionally difficult.

The prefamine population control system constrained movements enough so they were not as extensive as in some African famines. By North Korean standards, however, the population movements were massive. Some national statistics exist on nonfamine population migration, though the North Korean definition of migration would not be regarded as such in most societies. In North Korea, for example, leaving one's *ri* (precinct of 1,900 people) or *dong* (village of 7,600 people) to move to a neighboring one to get married is defined as migration. During the 1980s, between eight hundred thousand and one million people a year left their villages, but it is unclear what proportion consisted of precinct or village moves.[29]

The MSF interviews provide some insights into the breakdown of the traditional permit system that controlled population movements:

> Travel nowadays is possible, providing you are discreet and do not shout about where you are going nor where you come from, because the tight restrictions on traveling which used to make it very difficult to move about are not so rigidly enforced. However, there is a 50 won fine for unauthorized traveling if you are caught.[30]

Large-scale, famine-induced population movements into China took place on an accelerated scale by the autumn of 1996. Given the difficulty the refugees faced in traversing the mountain ranges to get to the border, the size of the migration is impressive evidence of the famine's severity. The Chinese and North Korean authorities in 1998 had begun constructing guard stations along the Tumen River to catch attempted migrants. Yet, in some ways the North Korean regime's attitude toward emigration had relaxed. Prior to the famine, the authorities executed anyone caught escaping. During the famine the penalty was a beating, the confiscation of personal belongings and any money earned in China, and confinement in a 927 camp for a period of months before the refugee was imprisoned permanently in his or her home village.

The 927 Camps for the Internally Displaced. On September 27, 1997, Kim Jong Il ordered his 210 county administrators to set up facilities—named 927 camps after the date they were ordered—to imprison internally displaced people.[31] These camps testified to the central government's alarm over bands of desperate, dying people wandering around the country. These people were called by one NGO manager "the goners," because of their low survival chances. In a December 1996 speech, Kim Jong Il complained of chaos and anarchy in the countryside, perhaps a reference to these population movements. The internal permit system was designed to control population movements, but another regulation ensured its enforcement: people could receive their food ration only in their home village. If they left their village without an official permit, they would starve unless they had relatives willing to share their rations. When the public distribution system collapsed and people no longer relied on the state for their food, the controlling power of this regulation ended.

Hwang Jang Yop, the highest-ranking North Korean to have defected to South Korea, gave a press conference after his defection in which he confirmed the use of food distribution to control the population, the paralysis of that system, and the consequent movement of people:

> North Korea controls people with food. If food [were] not distributed, people would end up dying. North Korea controls the entire country and people with the food distribution. In other words, the food distribution is a means of control. However, at the moment, the food rationing is not being carried out well in Pyongyang. With the exception of Pyongyang, all other regions are in a state of paralysis, and thus it is difficult to control the people. People are roving back and forth from the east coast to the west coast. If you consider this, you can understand how serious the food situation is.[32]

Many refugees in China had been captured by police on a previous attempt to cross the border, been sent back to North Korea, and spent time in these notorious 927 camps, which were usually located in the county hotel. The camps had no heat despite the arctic winters, the sanitation was terrible, food was scarce, and contagious disease and death rates were high. The refugees reported that each camp held between three hundred and fifteen hundred people, forty to fifty people to a room. Countrywide, these camps housed between 60,000 and 315,000 displaced persons at any one time before the people were forcibly returned to their home villages. Although there have been no comprehensive studies on turnover rates in the camps, stays were intentionally temporary and ranged from several weeks to two months. Conservatively extrapolating the population figures at a turnover rate of six times a year would mean that a minimum of 378,000 and a maximum of 1.9 million people per year passed through them. Yet, the population figures in these camps by no means reflected all internal population movements from the famine. Many internally displaced people avoided capture, others died as they moved in search of food, and still others successfully escaped to China. By the summer of 1999, the central authorities had shut down the 927 camps and transferred the remaining inmates to remote prison camps far from public view.[33]

Deaths along the Journey and Proof of Mass Graves. Historically, a large percentage of people fleeing from famine have died during their journeys. When people leave their home villages and towns they lose their most effective coping mechanism: their extended family and friends. Sanitary conditions, water, and food availability all rapidly deteriorate. The proximity of displaced people to one another in temporary shelters increases the risk of epidemics. Unlike refugees or internally displaced people in other emergencies, who find help and protection in refugee camps run by international organizations, North Korean refugees had no place to get help. It is likely that for every refugee who reached China, one died along the way. Refugees provided many anecdotes of deaths they encountered during their journey. One American researcher interviewed two boys who left their home village; they reported that four others had left the village with them but died en route.[34] Many refugees deliberately planned their escape to China across the Tumen River during the coldest months of the winter, when it was covered with ice. But these months are the most inhospitable for travel, as there are no wild foods available in the countryside and the temperatures drop well below zero Fahrenheit in the mountain ranges that the refugees must cross before arriving at the Tumen River. These temperatures are particularly deadly for malnourished people, as they are much more vulnerable to hypothermia. Most of the refugees did not own warm clothing, making the cold even more dangerous. During the frigid winter months in early 1998, KBSM staff counted several dozen bodies along the Tumen River in one limited area.

Another bit of evidence suggests high mortality rates among the internally displaced: the presence of mass graves in North Korean cities along the Chinese border. While Pomnyun and I were wending our way along a dirt road that hugged the banks of the Tumen River, we passed by the city of Musan on the opposite side. On the outskirts of the city on the side of a high mountain was a graveyard full of new mounds and tombstones. Two trucks were parked there, and about thirty men were carrying from the truck what appeared to be bodies wrapped in white vinyl sheets; the men were dumping the wrapped bodies into a large pit. When they finished, they all stood around the pit, heads hung and arms folded, apparently in silent meditation. Then they began shoveling dirt into the pit, after which they collected their things and left on the trucks. Pomnyun later gave me two videotapes of similar mass burial ceremonies along the Tumen River, one that he had recorded and the other that a South Korean television station had videotaped. They both showed the same unmistakable evidence of the existence of mass graves of perhaps scores of bodies.

Despite a half century of marxism, North Korea is still a thoroughly Confucian society, and traditional practices include the worship of ancestors, the continuation of the bloodline, and the proper burial of the matriarchs and patriarchs of the family. Steve Linton, a scholar of North Korea, writes:

> Moving an ancestor's grave is one of the most important decisions one can possibly make in Korean tradition. Because the final resting place of the dead is believed to influence the fate of future descendents, ancestral remains are sometimes moved to a more propitious location several years after interment. This is especially true if a lack of preparation (or lack of financial resources) mandated a less than suitable arrangement at the time of death.[35]

Korean culture would thus suggest an abhorrence of mass graves except under the most extraordinary circumstances. Graves along the Chinese border therefore were likely to hold the remains of people who died apart from their families and away from their villages and neighborhoods: people on the move who failed to make it to the Chinese border.

A Refugee Boy's Story. Pomnyun and I found Kim feeding on a crust of bread in a garbage dump in Changbai. He told us he was sixteen years old; because of stunting, a common characteristic of refugee children, he appeared to be ten to twelve. His body was covered with scabies, a skin disease spread by poor sanitation and frequent among children in refugee camps, and his hair was filled with lice. Only Pomnyun's serene manner and kind words convinced him to speak with us; he was terrified we were secret police who would beat him and send him back to the 927 camps in North Korea. Pomnyun told the boy we were merchants interested in doing business on the border, but that we wanted to find out what was happening in North Korea before we arranged any transactions. Some critics had suggested that the refugees giving testimony on the border were South Korean agents trying to embarrass the Northern government. If Kim was a recruit to the South Korean intelligence service, he succeeded in fooling Pomnyun and me. He said he had no relatives in China; in fact, he had few relatives alive anywhere as far as he knew. His physical condition and presence in the dump lent some credibility to his claim. This was his second trip to China to search for food. He had eaten three meals in the previous five days, so we fed him as he talked.

His parents had sold the family home for 2,000 won ($15) two years earlier to create some capital to start a barter business that they carried on for two years before it could no longer feed them. The family had broken up after his parents sold their home, though they remained in the same village: he and his father went to live with his father's brother, and his sister and mother went to live with her brother. While at his uncle's, he and his father survived on the roots of corn and rice stalks and on wild greens harvested in the mountains; such meals gave him severe and painful constipation. He said cows had died on the collective during the 1997–98 winter from lack of fodder, but party cadres in a more prosperous neighboring village came and took the carcasses. He explained that, had villagers eaten the cow in their village, they would have been executed. Both his parents eventually died in the famine. His malnourished mother succumbed to a paratyphoid epidemic that swept through his village the previous summer, and his father died of starvation in August 1998 while Kim was attempting to bring food from China back to his family. According to his neighbors, his ten-year-old sister was on the streets of his home city begging for food, but none of the neighbors would take her in because they could not feed even their own families.

After the Chinese police captured Kim on his first crossing, he was beaten with a metal bat and returned to North Korea. There he was beaten again and imprisoned in the Hyesan 927 camp. Of the three hundred people in Kim's camp, he said forty were sick with paratyphoid, as sanitation in the camps was squalid and food rare. On average, he said, two or three people would die each day, and their bodies were combined with those collected at the railroad station and marketplace in the city and dumped in pits that held twenty to thirty bodies. Kim knew this because the camp prisoners served as the laborers who buried the bodies each day. On his way back to China he clung underneath a slow-moving train, and when one of the trainmen saw him there he attempted to dislodge him by kicking him, landing a blow that, as he showed us, broke one or two of his ribs.[36]

The Famine Trains. Many people tried to escape the famine using the dilapidated train system on which Kim traveled. Kim Jong Il also mentioned the trains twice in his famine speech of December 1996:

> On my way to the Chollima Steel Complex, I saw people lined up along the street trying to get grain. I heard that other places are also brimming with people trying to get grain, and that train stations and trains are crowded with people. Heart-aching occurrences are happening everywhere. However, the responsible provincial, city and county party secretaries and other functionaries merely get together in offices or conference rooms and hold study sessions or lectures, instead of making any practical efforts. . . . The state of the railway system in the country is beyond description and trains are overcrowded.[37]

Refugee descriptions of the train system bring to mind images of trains taking Jews to their death during the Holocaust. The only difference was that the Jews were forced onto these freight trains, whereas North Koreans desperately wanted to get onto the trains to escape the famine. North Korean authorities made faint efforts to prevent them. I asked one displaced twenty-seven-year-old former factory worker from Hamhung City who had taken four trips to the Chinese border to describe his journeys:

> *Kochibis* [wandering swallows—the Korean term for internally displaced people] could always get onto the trains without tickets. The trains have specially reserved cars for soldiers, internal security police, and party cadres; other cars are reserved for mail and luggage, though some *kochibis* sneak onto these cars if they can. There are five passenger cars for the common people. The windows in these train cars have all been broken either by people trying to get on these packed trains or they are broken by overcrowding on the trains.

When train cars were outrageously packed and crowded with people, including riders hanging in the entrance, [lying on the] roof top, or [hanging] underneath the train, about 700 people boarded per train car. The ordinary occupancy limit is 180 people, including 120 seats, per train car. Because of overcrowding some people were suffocated, weakened, or starved to death in the cars. When the train would stop [because of electrical failure], people used to get out for a rest and immediately return before departure. Toilets also were packed with passengers. As a result, women would urinate inside the trains. Men manage it inside as well, or between the car connections. Dead bodies were taken off at train stations. I hadn't seen many bodies along railroad tracks. Some riding [on the] roof top accidentally died when they stood up and touched the electrical lines above the train.

When I went to Kangwon province, I saw seven dead bodies. I had seen about three bodies in a month in my trip to other regions. Altogether, I saw twenty dead bodies during my trip from North Korea. Some people riding over train car connections were trapped [and squeezed] to death because of a sudden train stop. Some hanging over the train car entrance fell to their death.

Railroad station waiting rooms were overrun by lice and stench [from *kochibi* sewage]. In Heungnam station, dead bodies were left without getting anyone's attention. . . . *Kochibis* appeared in 1995 for the first time and their number grew rapidly over 1996 until now.[38]

I interviewed one older Japanese woman who had immigrated to North Korea to take a husband in 1963 and was now leaving. The elderly lady hung her head and wept when I asked her to describe what had happened on her journey to China.[39] Her husband had starved to death along with two of her six children, and she told me the cold on the train ride was deadly because the windows had no glass in them. Refugees would try to use their clothing to block the mountain winds that swept through the dismal cars.

Similar accounts were repeated by other refugees, not only in the interviews I conducted, but in hundreds of narrative accounts collected by KBSM. Many accounts mention the same grim stories, the same squalor on the trains, the same accidents that kill people during the trip, the crushing and suffocation of people on the train cars, and the same apocalyptic scenes in the railroad stations. Jasper Becker's border reports also carry similar accounts:

At Hamhung's city railway station Ms. Kim and many others waited for days for a train. Each morning, railway staff dragged away twenty corpses, so many in fact that they no longer bother to register the identity of the victims. Indeed, many had swapped their documents for food long ago. When finally a train left, it was crammed full and took three days to travel the 480 kilometers to Hyesan, the border town, due to frequent power blackouts. On the train railway guards seized her food and beat her because she had no ticket or documents. When the train arrived, eight people in her carriage had starved to death.[40]

One person from the southwestern rice-growing area, who had traveled to China on a train in the summer of 1998, told me,

There are no train schedules. You go to the train stations and wait until a train appears, sometimes for hours or even days. The trains are not maintained nor are the tracks, and as a result the train ride is very rough. Many of the ties have rotted and not been replaced and so the train moves on the tracks up and down like a ship in a stormy sea. They must travel very slowly or they will slip off the tracks. I saw a wrecked train on the side of the track we were traveling on and I heard many other reports of train wrecks.[41]

*Find Alternative Sources of Income and Food*_____

Individuals who are able to escape a famine and get help from relatives, or those who have relatives abroad who send them remittances, are more likely to survive famines than those without such resources. During the Ethiopian civil war, the Eritrean rebel movement surrounded the capital city of Asmara, shutting off all but UN food airlifted into the city. Yet a huge gap existed between the tonnage being brought in by the UN airlift and the amount people needed. But virtually every family had relatives in Europe, the United States, or Canada who were sending remittances to their families in the city, and food was being purchased outside the city and smuggled in by bribing the soldiers on either side of the combat lines. These remittances, along with the UN airlift, prevented large-scale starvation.

In the case of North Korea, the effect of this cross-border movement and of cash remittances from the ethnic Korean diaspora in Japan, Australia, the United States, and Canada cannot be ignored, but it is not easily calculated. Although the level of cash remittances sent to family members inside North Korea can be estimated, it is nearly impossible to tell how many families inside North Korea received them. The greatest limitation on remittances as a coping mechanism is that much of the emigration that produced this Korean diaspora took place after the Korean War and thus came nearly entirely from South Korea. The South Korean government has tried to discourage remittances from Korean Americans, arguing that the North Korean government would divert the money before their relatives would receive it. Refugees told the KBSM that the central authorities often held remittances in special reserve accounts that the recipient could access only after waiting for months and sometimes years, and that the central government would sometimes confiscate some or all of the funds arbitrarily.

The large Korean diaspora in Japan, cultivated for years by Kim Il Sung, historically provided large remittances to North Korean relatives and to the North Korean government. Direct subsidies to the North Korean government went through Chosun Soren, a pro–North Korean organization within the Korean Japanese community and funded with the proceeds from *pachenko* (gambling) parlors they run. The Japanese government lacks a rigorous method for tracking how much in family remittances and gambling revenues the diaspora sends to North Korea each year, but four changes beginning in the mid-1990s led this source of financial subsidy to diminish. The first was the economic slump in the Japanese economy, which affected the prosperity of the Korean community. The second was the death of Kim Il Sung and the failure of Kim Jong Il to cultivate this diaspora. Third was a generational turnover, as the younger generation feels little loyalty to North Korea and its regime. And fourth was the mishandling of the elderly Korean Japanese who had gone home to visit relatives. Remittances have declined to a trickle.[42]

Wild Famine Foods. Many refugees tell stories of foraging in the mountains for wild famine foods. The general rule repeated to me by refugee after refugee was that if it was not poisonous, they would eat it. One refugee from Hamhung City said his sister had died from eating wild foods she did not realize were poisonous.

Pyongyang aggressively encouraged foraging for wild foods, a practice that had been occurring spontaneously for years. By the summer of 1996, wild foods amounted to 30 percent of the North Korean diet.[43]

I had seen evidence of this during my trip in June 1997, but by 1998 this effort had reached massive, darkly comic, proportions. Pyongyang produced an instructional videotape, obtained by Mark Kirk of the House International Relations Committee in 1998, on the harvesting and processing of "substitute food." In my decade of involvement in famine relief efforts, I had never seen such a bizarre manifestation of a hunger coping mechanism than this videotape. It showed, for example, how to harvest pond weed, dry it out, and make it into flour to be mixed with wheat or corn flour as an extender. In one part of the tape, corn husks, oak leaves, and grass are ground up into powder and passed through a noodle machine. The resulting noodles have little nutritional value, cannot be digested by the human system, and in fact cause severe gastrointestinal problems for those hungry enough to eat them. The exact nutritional value of the substitutes is unclear, as their testing by the WFP was inconclusive: the substitutes were mixed with corn and wheat flour in unknown proportions, so scientists analyzing them could not determine what calories were attributable to which part of the food.[44] Some alternative foods do have nutritional value and are traditional in the Korean diet. These include mushrooms, pine nuts, acorns, grasshoppers, some shoots, and seaweed. They cannot take the place of stable grains such as rice and corn, however, both because urban families do not have access to them and because these foods have limited caloric values.[45] A senior North Korean official told me that it was official policy for the party cadres to eat one to two meals a day of the substitute foods. If this had been enforced, which I doubt it was, it might have brought the country closer to an elite-led revolution than any other action of Kim Jong Il.

While I was in Pyongyang, Ambassador Kim Soo Man, my host, gave me a volume of Kim Il Sung's autobiography as a gift; only later did I learn that it was one of seven volumes so far translated into English. I suspect the choice of this particular volume was no accident, as it contained the wartime exploits of Kim Il Sung against the Japanese in the 1930s. The following account of the suffering in Kim's unit strongly calls to mind the suffering engendered by the famine:

> At the beginning of the march we had two meals of gruel a day. As the food ran short, we had just one meal a day. Finally we went without food altogether, only eating snow. Our vision became

blurry and when we got up to continue the march, we felt dizzy and could hardly walk. This is why, whenever I talked to cadres after liberation, I used to say people who have experienced starvation know how valuable rice and peasants are and that no one without his experience can claim to know all about revolution. . . . There are many short men among the anti-Japanese veterans because they did not get proper nutrition in their youth and because they had to go through all kinds of hardships. These factors stunted their growth. When we were fighting in the mountains, we often had to do without proper food, eating such things as wild herbs, grass roots, tree bark, malted wheat, rice bran, the residue left over from brewing, and so on. We ate mainly coarse food at irregular times, so we suffered from all sorts of troubles of the digestive canal.[46]

I later discovered that, as the crisis intensified, the North Korean electronic media had been quoting these passages extensively, comparing the most difficult periods of 1997 to the period of the Great Leader's heroic efforts against the Japanese nearly six decades earlier. All this was intended to build patriotic fervor and direct an exhausted population's anger away from the regime's failure.

During famines, people often engage in begging and in gleaning, a traditional technique of hand-picking grain left in the fields after the harvest or accidentally spilled on the ground in the markets. Two North Korean refugees told the KBSM that they had gone into the fields just after the corn crop had been planted and dug up all the planted seed; in one case they had dug up potato cuttings to provide a couple of meals. During famines, frequently farmers eat their seed if they calculate that they will not survive until the next harvest, so relief workers as a standard practice do not distribute seed for planting unless they also provide a good ration with it to reduce the farmers' incentive to eat the seed. In a marxist system where the seed is owned, controlled, and planted by the collective, farmers simply wait until the crop is planted and then dig up the seed. I could find no reports of this practice occurring in the rice-growing areas, probably because rice is first grown in small, sheltered, water-flooded seed beds and would be difficult to collect.[47]

Some refugees from coastal areas spoke of harvesting seafood such as shrimp and squid from the ocean and then transporting it to China for sale or barter for corn.[48] While some nutritionists criticized the practice for reducing the meager levels of protein in the North Korean diet, it made great sense as a coping mechanism.[49] Survival depends on caloric intake, and the least expensive calories in the region come from corn; a kilogram of seafood would purchase twice as many kilograms of corn, if not more. Thus, the refugees sold higher-value protein to purchase lower-priced corn. Refugees provided a number of reports of rice being bartered or sold for corn, as rice is 50 percent to 60 percent higher in price per kilogram. Hilary Mackenzie, the Canadian journalist, reports that in Hamju, outside Hamhung City, clams were collected and bartered in China for rice and flour: "one ton of black clams fetches 2.5 metric tons of wheat flour."[50]

As the famine progressed, desperate county and provincial officials converted grain mills into factories manufacturing substitute foods. Seaweed, pond weed, pine tree bark, rice plant roots, and corn stalks and cobs were ground into powder and mixed with corn meal or rice flour to extend the food staple. One senior minister in Pyongyang admitted to WFP director Catherine Bertini that the widespread consumption of substitute foods was causing terrible digestive disorders. The human system wastes needed calories in trying to digest these foods, so they cause a net nutritional deficit in addition to incurring digestive side effects. North Korean officials ignored humanitarian agency warnings to stop the practice.

Traditionally, farmers facing famine will slaughter their domesticated herds before the animals die from lack of forage. Alternatively, they will try to sell the animals before the price drops from the glut of animals everyone else is selling; these price drops are a common prefamine indicator. Although no information exists on the sale of meat in the farmers markets, there is substantial information on the consumption of the animal herds. The North Korean minister of agriculture told senior WFP officials that he had instructed the collectives to eat the grain-consuming animals during the winter of 1996–97 before they starved from lack of feed. The central authorities had made a strategic decision to replace the grain-eating animal population with goats, which could survive entirely on grass and forage. The only animals protected by central edict were the oxen herds, as they were essential, not for meat or milk, but as draft animals to replace motorized equipment for which the farmers lacked either spare parts or fuel. Without the edict, farm families would only have consumed domesticated animals beyond their reproduction capacity if they believed they would be unable to survive until the next crop.

Hilary Mackenzie reported similar behavior:

> I witnessed the consumption of domestic animals throughout the country. Chickens, rabbits, and dogs all were consumed. I saw no goats or domesticated animals as I toured the country. Duck farms were pointed out to me but I did not go in one. The only animals were a few oxen in the fields. In Onsong, puppies were turned into dog meat soup. The family said it was wolf. The same family had pig sties but could not feed the pigs, so they ate them.[51]

The UN Development Program agricultural roundtable document of 1998 claimed, "Data gathered for the purpose of this study indicate a reduction of 37 percent for cattle, 36 percent for sheep and goats. More importantly, grain eating pig and poultry populations declined by 57 percent and 90 percent respectively."[52] The study connects the floods and the reduction in animal population, reflecting the regime's explanation for the disaster, but avoids the uncomfortable conclusion that famine had led to the destruction of the animal herds.

The most direct and simple means by which vulnerable families survive any famine is by increasing their food supply through informal, nontraditional, and even illegal means. The measures North Korean families took to obtain food suggested coping mechanisms had been developed over years of sustained deprivation. The most commonly mentioned one-time method for getting cash was to sell family effects: clothing, furniture, pots and pans, ceramics, and finally the house itself.[53] Families descended from landlord or business wealth that were able to keep some of their family heirlooms during the communist period often sold these to buy food. One American diplomat in Seoul told me North Korean antiques and family heirlooms began appearing in South Korean antique shops in 1996, as traders had purchased them from North Koreans along the border with China.

A seventy-two-year-old former South Korean prisoner of war, Chang Mu-hwan, who escaped from North Korea in October 1998, even told of an illegal cross-border trade in human blood. Smugglers were seeking to purchase blood from families in need of cash.[54]

CRITICISM OF THE BORDER SURVEYS

Criticism of the border reports came from several sources, each with a different objection. Eric Weingartner was hired by a group of NGOs (World Vision among them) to coordinate private relief shipments into North Korea and had been attached to the WFP staff for administrative purposes; his periodic reports dismissed evidence of high mortality rates, particularly if they came from the border. Weingartner worked in the WFP headquarters in Pyongyang and his views were indistinguishable from those of the WFP staff. He held the border reports suspect for two reasons: First, he believed they were conducted for fund-raising purposes—a common attack by critics of NGO operations—and second, he argued that the refugees had invented the famine to avoid deportation back to North Korea.[55] In fact, fund-raising had nothing to do with the motivation behind the surveys, and in any case the *Washington Post*, the *South China Morning Post*, and Johns Hopkins University were not NGOs. Weingartner's second and more substantive criticism is directly contradicted by the behavior of the refugees, all of whom indicated that the overwhelming majority had come to China to get food for their families, not to stay; in fact, many voluntarily returned to North Korea.[56]

A common criticism of the refugees was that they invented a famine where there was only a food shortage, so their Korean Chinese friends and relatives would give them food for their families. Although it is true that the refugees may have exaggerated the severity of the crisis to make a compelling case for charity, one doubts they would make the long and dangerous journey to China if they did not face a genuine, life-threatening crisis. Migration is a coping mechanism of last resort when the suffering is intolerable, not something people do when they are somewhat hungry. The very existence of mass population movements in itself should have been sufficient proof of the later stages of famine. Had only a few interviews been conducted, Weingartner's arguments might have had more weight; perhaps a few dozen refugees might have contrived stories for deceptive purposes, but orchestrating such a deception over the course of 2,300 individual interviews is implausible to say the least.

Perhaps the most striking characteristic of the refugee stories was how closely they reflected the general experience of other famines. The KBSM survey asked people how they stayed alive during the famine—

a simple way of asking about their coping mechanisms. The refugees certainly had not read the literature on famines to better inform fabricated stories. Yet they all graphically described their experiences in ways that precisely paralleled other famines and told similar stories of famine deaths.

One last school of criticism of border information has suggested that the area is full of secret agents of the regional powers—China, Japan, North Korea, the United States, and South Korea. These agents have allegedly been spreading misinformation about the severity of the crisis to advance their governments' political agendas. If this was the case, the secret campaign was extraordinarily well organized, given that more than 2,300 sick or malnourished refugees testified to the effects of the famine on their immediate families and their neighborhoods. The notion that more than 2,300 South Korean intelligence agents scheduled their own starvation to coincide with their arrival at the border, so that they might be more believable as refugees, is simply implausible.

The secret agent theory fails on an even more telling point. Namely, which government's interest would been served by the invention of a fictitious famine? Until the summer of 1996, U.S. intelligence reports denied the existence of the famine. China would certainly not want reports of a famine in the news media, as it might attract international relief efforts along the border that would act as a magnet for more refugees to cross into China, a population movement that the Chinese authorities assiduously attempted to avoid. According to Jasper Becker, official Chinese media coverage until March 1998 discouraged alarmist views of the North Korea crisis. The South Korean Central Intelligence Agency and other South Korean government sources also publicly downplayed the crisis until mid-1998, in their case because they did not want private or international donors to subsidize a government they wanted to collapse; media accounts would only encourage more aid. The Japanese government would have no motive to falsify data collection along the border, since it refused to give any aid and regularly denied the existence of the famine publicly even while its internal intelligence reports showed a famine was under way.

This leaves only the North Korean government as the potential manufacturer of exaggerated reports of famine. Yet the regime believed such reports would have undermined national security by showing the system to be failing and its people starving, information that might encourage an attack by South Korea and the United States. The North Korean government was getting food aid in any case, so it had no need to create a famine that it did not want to admit existed in the first place. If it had wanted to admit to its failures, it could simply have invited the international media into the country to take contrived pictures of starvation so it could get more food aid.

THE EROSION OF KIM JONG IL'S BASE OF SUPPORT

The notable aspect of the coping mechanisms practiced in this particular totalitarian famine is that most were illegal under North Korean law. The people who did survive without deaths in their family or a reduction in their meager family resources were those who violated the law and trashed the system. Some of the senior military leaders and the party cadres not unexpectedly used their political power to protect their families, while others enriched themselves at the expense of the system and embraced crony capitalism in the process. All had bid the old communist economic order good-bye and by their behavior renounced Kim Jong Il's failed leadership. The urban poor who trusted that the Dear Leader would feed them through the public distribution system either died or survived on the edge of starvation, more impoverished and destitute than when the famine began. The abject failure of the regime's measures to stem the catastrophe effectively killed off its own base of support, though the leadership certainly did not intend this outcome. This was not a prescription, even in a dictatorship, for the political survival of those administering the system.

As Pomnyun, Jihun Park, and I boarded the plane at Jilin on our way to Seoul to interview defectors from North Korea, I looked back at what I had just witnessed along the frontier. For two years I had been searching for unimpeachable evidence for the North Korean famine. I had found it. These interviews provided the raw data needed to construct a microeconomic theory to explain what caused the famine, who had died, and why.

5

THE ECONOMICS
OF THE FAMINE

WHAT I SAW ALONG THE NORTH KOREAN–CHINESE BORDER in September 1998 bore striking economic similarity to other famines I had witnessed. Reports from NGOs and the United Nations lacked any economic analysis of what was happening to the collapsing food security structure that had traditionally fed the country. Aid workers argued that North Korea lacked market mechanisms by which they could quantify the famine, but this observation was greatly mistaken. Economic forces were at work, some underground on the black market and some openly in farmers markets, but they were not easily observable because the state ideology resolutely denied their existence and thus required the police to disguise them from foreigners.

Most analyses of the North Korean famine have been conducted using the disciplines of public health, nutrition, national agricultural production, and food aid distribution. But famines at their core are principally economic and political phenomena with public health and nutritional consequences, not vice versa. For decades there has been a debate between two competing economic theories of famine: the food availability decline theory of Thomas Malthus and the entitlement theory of Amartya Sen, the Nobel Prize–winning economist. Malthus, an eighteenth-century Methodist minister from Great Britain, argued that population growth rates will eventually exceed the growth in food supply, given the temporal limit of available land. As the gap widens between the food needs of the population and the capacity of the agricultural system to produce enough food, famine will reduce the population to a more sustainable level. Malthus believed the gap between food requirements and total food supply is what causes famine deaths. But this theory fails to explain why some people prosper during famines and others starve. Starvation is seldom experienced equally in a famine, even in a totalitarian system, because food distribution becomes linked with the political objectives of the state. Anecdotal reports of people who lived through the Chinese famine of 1958–62 have shown that former landlords and businesspeople whose wealth was confiscated after the Communist Revolution suffered more deprivation than other groups because they were seen as class enemies.[1]

Under Sen's theory, in contrast to Malthus's, a family's access to food—whether through purchase or barter on the market, production on the farm, or availability of food rations in a socialist system such as North Korea—determines who lives and who dies.[2] If food prices increase rapidly at the same time that wages are static or dropping, families will starve unless their coping mechanisms save them. When the state controls food production and distribution, as it does in a totalitarian system, it inevitably uses this system to tighten its control over every aspect of life. This control frequently involves rewarding those with power and neglecting those without it. Thus, in totalitarian famines, the political objectives of the state have a profound influence over who lives and who dies, as Sue Lautze has pointed out.

The previous chapters established the existence of a great famine in North Korea in the 1990s, but its political economy must be examined to fully understand its causes and unique dynamic. To do this one must consider several elements of the public distribution system (PDS): how it was supposed to operate, how it slid into paralysis as the national economy unraveled, what central government decisions were made as the crisis grew more severe, and how these decisions contributed to the deadly progress of the famine. The perverse interaction between the PDS and the newly burgeoning farmers markets, the market price of grain, and its widespread hoarding drove the country's food system into chaos.

The North Korean famine was caused by a collapse of the PDS as the principal means by which the North Korean people obtained their food supply. This collapse was driven by four separate forces, two of which arose from central government decisions. The first force was steadily declining agricultural production caused by poor agricultural practices, perverse economic incentives, a declining volume of inputs such as fertilizer and pesticides, and several years of natural disasters, beginning in

1995. The second related force was the precipitous decline in food subsidies from the Soviet Union and China. Most analysts of the crisis understood these first two forces well.

What they overlooked were the third and fourth forces, which transformed a small, regionalized famine into a national catastrophe resulting
in the massive death tolls of 1996 and 1997. Pyongyang's decision to
triage the northeast region of the country by cutting off food subsidies to
the eastern coastal plain in 1994 and 1995—the third force—killed more
than a million people. The fourth force was the central government's
decision to reduce farmers' per capita rations from 167 kilograms per
year to 107 kilograms after the disastrous harvest of 1995. This decision
ended the voluntary cooperation of the peasants in supplying their surplus to the urban and mining areas. Peasants realized their own survival
required them to take other measures, including widespread hoarding of
the 1996 harvest, particularly in the corn-growing areas. Thus they reduced the amount of time they devoted to cooperative farms and spent it
instead on private and secret plots. This fourth force precipitously reduced
the total amount of food in the PDS—a system already reeling from the
double blows of reduced subsidies and declining local production. In the
place of the PDS a new, privatized system of food distribution arose that
supplied the population in urban and mining areas with their food.

THE PUBLIC DISTRIBUTION SYSTEM

During the period of the Soviet collapse in late 1991 and early 1992, I
was working as the chief humanitarian relief official of the U.S. government. In that capacity, I sent Fred Cuny and a technical team to the former
Soviet states to determine whether a crop failure in the summer of 1992
and the economic turbulence issuing from the political chaos would lead
to a famine. Cuny was one of the most able field officers in the humanitarian aid community and an internationally recognized expert on famine.[3]
Lawrence Eagleburger, then deputy secretary of state, feared that food
riots in the larger cities could undermine or even collapse the fragile new
reform government of Boris Yeltsin. Cuny spent six months studying the
traditional Soviet food distribution system to understand how it functioned and whether the country was at risk of widespread starvation. He
concluded, in what may be the only extant study of the Soviet public

distribution system, that the inefficient system was in fact still in working order, despite political turmoil and economic collapse. It persisted mainly because collective farms were still dumping much of their grain surplus into the system, and because the United States had sold the Soviet Union a massive amount of grain at highly subsidized rates to make up for the 10 percent reduction in food production the previous summer.[4]

The North Korean and the Soviet public distribution systems were remarkably similar. The North Korean agricultural system was modeled after its Soviet counterpart, so it is not surprising that the Soviet PDS served as the model for that of North Korea. When it operated at peak efficiency, the North Korean system—like its Soviet counterpart— theoretically provided the basic necessities to the population at heavily subsidized rates as payment for work. The more important the work was to the state, the higher the ration the worker received. The internal security apparatus and party militia, for example, reportedly received three times the rice ration that military officers of equal rank received—a source of considerable friction inside the North Korean system.[5] Stalin himself wrote that the pure marxist doctrine of paying everyone according to their needs was impractical and declared that some gradations of salary were permissible to reward work that was more important to the state.[6] In the North Korean industrial sector, miners received the highest rations, if the mines were functioning, because they produced a commodity tradable for crucial foreign exchange.[7] But when the mines shut down for whatever reason, it appears that miners' salaries and rations were also shut off. The North Korean military and collective farmers were provisioned separately: the farmers received an annual ration after the harvest, while soldiers were fed through their own mess system, which received the first call on the harvest each year.

The North Korean central government created sixty-four subcategories into which the population was divided and ranked from the most to the least favored. Each person was required to wear a pin with Kim Il Sung's image on it (they now receive a pin with Kim Jong Il's), and its design indicated their rank.[8] This classification system was even used to proscribe social interaction: a person of higher rank marrying a person of a lower rank was demoted to the lower rank.[9] Food ration levels were traditionally determined by a combination of social rank, the importance of one's profession to the state, and political status.[10] As the famine intensified, class mobility suffered: no one could move up through the ranks, but one could move down to a lower rank.[11] This decision was made presumably to preserve the remaining benefits for the existing core class, rather than have it diluted with new recruits.

Most important for the purposes of this study, it has been noted that social rank within the hierarchy "may affect one's treatment under the legal system, one's allocation of rations, one's ability to receive permission to travel, and a multitude of other factors affecting one's livelihood."[12] One study suggests these categories were relaxed somewhat in the 1980s, a move that probably reflected Kim Il Sung's complete control and unchallengeable power, as any opposition to him had long ago been eliminated.

The traditional food allocation system, a subset of this social structure, was based on twelve hierarchical ranks, with Kim Il Sung and his family at the top. Prisoners in the North Korean gulag, at the bottom, were assigned a ration of 200 grams of grain a day, substantially less than needed for survival. One North Korean who escaped to Japan before the famine told human rights investigators that most prisoners starved to death within two years.[13] These conditions could not have improved during the famine. Below the five top ranks, which consisted of the Kim family and the party hierarchy, were seven other ration categories. Miners, defense workers, industrial workers, and fishermen received 900 grams. Military personnel serving along the demilitarized zone with South Korea, as well as high-ranking officers, received 850 grams. All other military officers, light industrial workers, teachers, engineers, college students, and most residents of Pyongyang received 700 grams. Residents outside Pyongyang received fewer than 700 grams. High school students, disabled persons, females over age fifty-five, and males over age sixty-one received 400 grams. Preschool children received 200–300 grams. And, as stated above, prisoners received a mere 200 grams.[14] Trevor Page, the first WFP director in North Korea, told Jasper Becker that by February 1996 the famine had driven the central authorities to reduce these categories to three.[15]

Marxist systems affect famine victims in very different ways than do traditional, free market economies, because wealth is more difficult to accumulate. Instead, politically powerful people try to gain access to the resources of the state. Access to these goods and services is the equivalent of the ownership of wealth, and it protects party elites and their families from vulnerability during crises.

In the North Korean famine, farmers also ate while others starved, not because the state fed them, but because they too had access. Their access, however, involved land on which to grow food; they could divert the crop before it was harvested, some had secret plots in the mountains, and most maintained sanctioned private plots on the collective farms. One human rights study written well before the famine reported that non-privileged families preferred living in farming areas for this very reason.[16] The survey of famine refugees conducted by the Korean Buddhist Sharing Movement (KBSM) showed that few farmers were crossing the border: farmers constituted only 4 percent of the refugees but 25 percent of the population as a whole. Another 15 percent of the overall population worked in rural areas in nonagricultural employment.[17] After this anomaly was discovered, the KBSM began asking refugees directly where the famine was most severe: 70.4 percent said the city, 1.9 percent said rural areas, and the remainder either did not know (24.3 percent) or suggested the two areas were equally deprived (3.4 percent).[18]

At the end of each harvest, government officials would provide collective farmers with a year's ration for themselves and their families, whereas the rest of the population received rations twice a month from the PDS. After the farmers' basic rations were distributed, the harvest was divided among several other pools, the first being seed for the next crop. Then the central authorities set a prohibitively high grain quota for the PDS that had to be met. This quota was "purchased" from the farmers at a predetermined, fixed price: 0.46 won per kilogram for rice and 0.15 won per kilogram for corn. The state then sold the grains to the population, through the PDS, at the heavily subsidized price of 0.15 won per kilogram of rice and 0.08 for corn.[19] The price per kilogram on the farmers markets, however, was 8 won for rice and 4 won for corn.

This system worked reasonably well as long as the collective farms received their inputs in the form of farm machinery, spare parts, tractor fuel, fertilizer, pesticides, herbicides, and some consumer goods. Beginning in the early 1990s, however, these inputs disappeared over the course of several years, causing steeply declining grain harvests (see figure 2). As production declined because of the input failure, farmers markets arose to meet the needs of the people. The PDS was unable to meet those

Figure 2. Cereal Production in North Korea, 1989–98

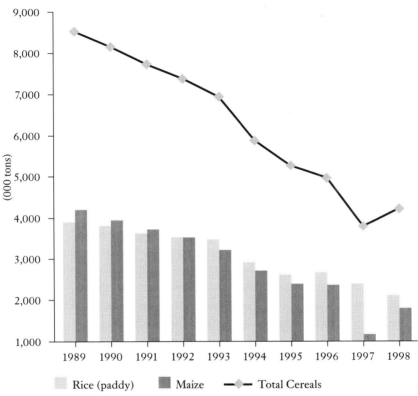

Source: FAO, Global Information and Early Warning System.

needs because of declining production, preharvesting, and diversions by farmers, and because food subsidies from China and Russia were in decline. The price of rice and corn in the farmers markets (and on the black markets) was seventeen and twenty-six times higher, respectively, than the price at which the state purchased the two grains from the collectives— or fifty times higher than the subsidized cost of the grain through the PDS. This created an irresistible incentive for farmers to hide food from the state and sell it on the markets. Party cadres and military officers with political power also diverted PDS food, commercially imported Chinese food, and even donor food aid so they could profit by selling it in the farmers markets. The more the PDS slipped into chaos, the more robust and pervasive the farmers markets became, which in turn meant that even more food was withdrawn from the PDS and into the farmers markets, creating a vicious cycle.

The cash salary received by a farmer, miner, or factory worker was supposed to pay for all necessities, but at heavily subsidized rates. The average factory worker earned between 60 and 90 won per month, which would buy enough corn or rice from the PDS to feed a family, though grain purchases were limited depending on social status. But as food shortages grew more severe, the ration that families were allowed to purchase from the PDS declined and finally ended entirely, which drove people to search for other means to feed themselves.[20] Given that the PDS was the sole food source for miners and urban workers, its precipitous collapse would have meant mass starvation, absent some other system to take its place. Farmers markets took the place of the PDS as the new food delivery system for these areas, though at highly inflated prices.

Evidence that the PDS between 1994 and 1998 ceased to function as the primary food source for much of the nonagricultural population comes primarily from refugee interviews. Information from within the country was understandably unreliable; after all, the PDS was the recipient until 1997 of substantial amounts of UN, Red Cross, and other NGO food aid. If the system had collapsed, the regime would not have wanted to advertise it.

Even the WFP acknowledged in its 1999 post-harvest assessment that the PDS had ceased to function in North Hamgyong province, though its acknowledgment was four years too late; moreover, while the PDS had stopped functioning there in 1995, no WFP or bilateral food aid was distributed there until mid-1997. Although the Johns Hopkins and KBSM researchers conducting refugee interviews did survey a disproportionate amount (60 percent) of people from North Hamgyong, which one might think would skew the results, 20 percent of the 1,679 KBSM interviews came from South Hamgyong province and 20 percent were from the rest of the provinces, and they all show a similarly steep decline in the population's reliance on the PDS. Before Kim Il Sung's death, according to the surveys, 60 percent of the population relied on PDS food, while 40 percent lived in rural areas and were outside the PDS. In

1996, the percentage of rural inhabitants remained the same, but by then only 6 percent of the population relied solely on the PDS for food.[21] When I visited the Chinese border I interviewed refugees from other regions of North Korea, and their descriptions of the PDS collapse were remarkably consistent: all reported that food distributions were made only on a half-dozen national holidays, rather than twice a month.

THE HISTORY AND OPERATION OF FARMERS MARKETS

Few UN and NGO field reports conclude without some mention of the phenomenal increase in the frequency of, selection of products in, and size of officially sanctioned farmers markets as the famine unfolded. Every one of the refugees I interviewed along the North Korean border, regardless of his or her home region, explained how crucial these markets had become to their own survival, provided that they had currency to buy food or items to barter for it. Without these markets the urban areas would be even more depopulated than they had become. But the rise of farmers markets amounted to a de facto privatization of an important part of the North Korean economy, and the regime's ideological embarrassment may have been one reason officials prevented any expatriate visits to observe these markets or to study food prices in them. Another reason may have been that the amount of stolen contraband and diverted food aid sold in the markets may have been too large to disguise.

The South Korean Unification Ministry released a study in January 1999 reporting that between 300 and 350 farmers markets were operating in North Korea, a sharp increase from the mid-1990s. The report claimed that 60 percent of people's grain needs and 70 percent of their other daily necessities came from the markets, three to five of which operated in every city and one or two in each county.[22]

Most NGO and the UN agency reports noting the phenomenon of farmers markets imply that they are new. In truth, their history during the communist period dates back to the end of World War II. Farmers markets were a vibrant and important part of the peasant economy from 1945 to the beginning of the Korean War in 1950, which disrupted their operation, and then from the end of the war in 1953 until 1958, when the forced collectivization of agriculture was completed. From 1958 to 1980 the markets functioned on a modest scale with heavy restrictions. In a 1969 speech, Kim Il Sung first officially sanctioned the farmers markets:

> The peasant market represents a form of trade whereby, at definite places, the peasants sell directly to people, part of the agricultural produce, both of the collective economy of the co-operative farms and of the sideline work of individual co-operative members. . . . In the peasant market, prices are determined spontaneously according to supply and demand and, therefore, the law of value operates somewhat blindly. The state does not plan supply and demand or prices for peasant markets. . . .
>
> Since the co-operative economy and individual sideline production are in existence under socialism, it is inevitable that the peasant market exist, and this is not such a bad thing. . . . There is more good than bad in the continued existence of sideline production and the peasant market in socialist society. We are not yet in a position to supply everything necessary for the people's life in sufficient quantities, through state channels. . . . Under the circumstances, what is wrong with the individuals producing things on the side and selling them in the market? Even though it is a backward way, it should still be made use of when the advanced ways are not sufficient to cover everything. . . . As long as the state cannot produce and supply enough of all of the goods necessary for the people's life, we must strictly guard against the "Left" tendency to abolish the peasant market so hastily. . . .
>
> As for other methods of control, we can only take some technical measures such as regulating the volume of sale per buyer . . . to limit somewhat the tendency towards concentration of goods in the hand of a few people.[23]

Beginning in 1980, as national economic expansion slowed and began to decline, the markets' health consequently improved.[24] The vitality of the farmers markets appears to be inversely related to periods of major state mobilization of human resources for industrialization and agricultural collectivization. Kim Il Sung's tolerant attitude toward the farmers markets apparently was not shared by his son, however. Upon his father's death, Kim Jong Il attempted to close the markets by central edict. Kim rescinded this decision within three days, after "near uprisings took place in some areas of the country"; the rescission reflected political and economic reality rather than any change of conviction on his part.[25] More than two years later, in a December 1996 speech, Kim attacked the farmers markets as unsocialist:

It is even against the principle of socialism for officials to pass on the responsibility to lower levels, and tell people to solve the food problem on their own. . . . This only makes people wander about in search of rice. In a socialist society, even the food problem should be solved in a socialist way, and officials should not tell people to solve it on their own. Telling people to solve the food problem on their own only increases the number of farmers markets and peddlers. In addition, this creates egoism among people, and the base of the party's class may come to collapse. Then, the party will lose popular support and dissolve. This has been well illustrated by past incidents in Poland and Czechoslovakia.[26]

Kim Jong Il feared that the privatization of the food distribution system and the rise of the farmers markets would make people less dependent on the party cadres for their survival. This in turn would reduce the state's level of control and perhaps lead to the destruction of North Korean communism, as happened in Eastern Europe.

Nevertheless, by 1993 the markets were open daily, so the state gave quasi-official sanction to them and began to tax traders at rates ranging from 30 won per month to between 2 and 15 won per day depending on the size of the individual market space. Chinese merchants were taxed at 50 won per day. In the late 1990s one could find chicken, pig, and dog meat for sale, as well as honey, vegetables, and grain from individual garden plots. These markets would make a capitalist smile, because they were teaching North Koreans the street principles of market capitalism, knowledge that only exacerbated the distortions in North Korea's dysfunctional economic system. As noted by the Korean Institute of Peace and Unification,

Recently one has been able to find grain and household items on the markets that have been stolen from official sources. This incidence results from the double price created between the official [low] price and the unofficial [high] price in the farmers markets, as societal control became loose owing to the economic crisis. The North Koreans have learned the benefit of selling official business products at significantly higher prices [on the farmers markets].[27]

These same sorts of economic forces drew food out of the PDS during the Chinese famine of the Great Leap Forward, as "peasants tried to withhold agricultural products from forced state procurement so that they could get a better price in rural markets."[28] The dual system maintained by the central authorities, whether in China or North Korea, was a disastrous economic policy that caused the collapse of one system even as the other was burgeoning. The state's refusal to embrace capitalism meant that the much higher market prices would not result in increased farm production, because the farmers did not own the land they farmed or the surplus grain they produced. The dysfunctional system created every incentive to steal, rather than to produce, more food. For those who were unable to change their source of food from PDS to market, generally because of income limitations, the dual system meant starvation.

The Korean Institute's report was based on interviews of defectors familiar with the new markets; it claimed that more than five thousand Han Chinese, Korean Chinese, and North Koreans traded in the markets. The North Korean traders—frequently discharged soldiers and the wives of party cadre, internal security police, and retired government officials—had formed a new class of nascent capitalists. The uselessness of the North Korean currency on international markets constrained the expansion of these markets, though. Chinese and Korean Chinese merchants insisted on barter for goods, unless the Korean merchant could provide Chinese yuan or U.S. dollars; one refugee told me dollars were widely used and the preferred currency on the markets. Authorities would impose a 20 percent fee for changing North Korean into Chinese currency, which added another disincentive to making purchases in hard currency. I was able to confirm much of the South Korean report's analysis from refugees I interviewed and from the KBSM's own extensive refugee interviews.

One North Korean merchant from a southwestern provincial city explained to me how the markets functioned. He attributed the rise of the markets, just as the defector I interviewed in Seoul did, to the collapse of the PDS. But what Kim Jong Il was unable to accomplish with his initial order to close the markets in 1994 he has attempted to do more subtly through regulatory harassment. In at least one city, the municipal authorities located the site of the market at the local garbage dump, which sums up what the regime thought of the markets. New internal security units of "economic police" were tasked with ensuring that contraband items were not sold in the marketplace. One refugee explained, "When the economic police raid a market, merchants try to gather their wares before they are confiscated or destroyed. People run in every direction and there is general chaos. The police are allowed to take whatever is not on the approved list."[29] Service in the economic police force must have been a sought-after assignment, as officers (I was told) were allowed to keep the confiscated contraband as a substantial "salary supplement."

The regulations constraining the operation of the farmers markets are posted in the markets, and only five categories of legally tradable items are listed: agricultural products other than grain, used clothes, used furniture, seafood, and wild foods harvested from the countryside, including wild game. Although the sale of grain in the markets is illegal, the practice is widespread and increasing, as the police seem unwilling or unable to control it. This is also true for manufactured goods, nearly all of which come from China. In September 1998, while I was in Changbai, China, on the Tumen River across from Hyesan, North Korea, I watched truckloads of garish living-room–size mirrors being moved across the border into North Korea. One refugee told me that the amount of grain sold in the six large markets in his home city of Hamhung far exceeded the amount of Chinese manufactured goods for sale. The limited market for luxuries or conveniences may reflect the level of deprivation and the limits on family income in Hamhung City.

On June 8, 1998, a bizarre incident in Namyung, North Hamgyong province, provoked an anti-Chinese hysteria. Rumors of the incident were making the rounds in the border area while I was there in September 1998. Apparently, a soldier waiting in the Namyung railroad station extinguished his Chinese cigarette in an ashtray, and it exploded. As a result of this incident, the central government banned the sale of Chinese manufactured goods and state propaganda began attacking Chinese products. The Venerable Pomnyun often went to the Chinese banks of the Tumen River to throw food across to North Korean children on the other side. After the cigarette incident, he said, the children would yell to him that they did not want any Chinese cookies, because their teachers told them they were poisoned. An American field worker in the summer of 1998 reported that Chinese border officials told him that 144 Chinese merchants had been arrested inside North Korea and were being held in exchange for North Koreans, whom the Chinese authorities were being encouraged to arrest. The arrests may have been connected to the campaign against Chinese goods, as they occurred at the same time.[30] The Chinese government was not amused by the ban on the sale of Chinese goods or by the arrest of Chinese merchants, and it angrily protested to the North Korean government. On July 22, Pyongyang lifted the ban and the central authorities announced that the bad Chinese products came from a few unscrupulous merchants and were not the fault of the Chinese people or their government.

The official motivations behind these arrests and the ban on the sale of Chinese goods remain unclear, but one can speculate on their causes. Perhaps Kim Jong Il had had enough of capitalist luxuries being promiscuously displayed in the markets in the middle of a famine that was shaking the foundation of the regime. The presence of these goods on the markets was tangible evidence that some people were prospering as the poor starved, contradicting the egalitarian claims of the regime. Alternatively, Kim may have been angered that the quality of the goods was poor but their price high, because the Chinese were dumping their lowest-quality products on a market with few competitive alternatives. Some North Koreans complained to me of this practice. It could also be that the regime was embarrassed by the continuing appearance in Western media of interviews with Chinese merchants reporting on the severity of the famine. Two years earlier, the *South China Morning Post, Los Angeles Times, New York Times,* and *Washington Post* had begun carrying articles based on these interviews. Pyongyang therefore prevented further "spying" by the merchants by ruining their business or by arresting and harassing them.

Regardless of their motivations, the North Korean authorities were likely becoming uncomfortable with the realities of even such basic levels of market capitalism as these farmers markets. The authorities undoubtedly found obnoxious the open information on which the marketplace thrives, the power of the profit motive to corrupt socialist morals (and officials), the evidence of Chinese capitalist prosperity represented in their manufactured goods, and the unequal distribution of wealth reflected in the transactions of the marketplace. However much the North Korean authorities might have harassed the merchants and their customers and attempted to regulate their exchanges, though, the marketplace resolutely resisted being made to work for the regime's political objectives. Markets have their own dynamic, which states the world over are hard-pressed to control. A marketplace driven by diverted food and by Chinese manufactured goods was the uncontrolled future the regime did not wish to confront, so the authorities attempted to ruin the merchants' business however they could.

Chinese manufactured goods may have made life easier and more comfortable for those who could afford them, but except for Chinese-produced medicine, they were not crucial to family survival. The sale of grain in farmers markets, however, was another matter entirely. For an urban worker or mining family, the collapse of the public distribution system meant slow death by starvation unless some alternate source of food could be found quickly. The rise of the markets was directly related to, and indeed caused by, the PDS collapse. The huge demand for food meant considerable profit for the new merchant class, even before the markets grew more efficient and competitive. A United Nations Development Program (UNDP) report based primarily on official North Korean sources acknowledged the rise of these markets in the border areas, but it denied their existence in the rest of the country.[31] Yet Canadian journalist Hilary Mackenzie said that in the summer of 1997 she flew over a large farmers market in Hamhung City, South Hamgyong province. A food refugee I interviewed who had once worked in a munitions factory in Hamhung City described in great detail to me his visits to the six large markets there that supplied the city. And aerial photographs of North Korea confirm the presence of vibrant farmers markets across the country.[32]

In contrast to the UNDP report's findings, the mid-year crop assessment released by the WFP and the FAO in June 1997 treated the alternate market system as a serious phenomenon:

> Severe food problems and the institutional and household inability to deal with supply constraints has also resulted in the de facto establishment of "private" food markets outside the public distribution system. These markets are now reported to exist in a number of areas where purchases of staples and other commodities can be made, albeit at phenomenally high prices which are beyond the reach of the majority of the population.[33]

The dynamics of supply and demand that operate in these farmers markets promise to be the best way for North Korea to feed itself over the long term, but only if the agricultural system is also privatized so market incentives lead to more food production. During the famine, North Korea functioned as a mixed system—the worst of all possible worlds—

with minimal food production because of socialist agricultural ineffi-
ciencies, yet high consumer prices. High demand, when mixed with regulatory and ideological constraints on imports and production, ensures high
food prices. The fact that party cadres and the secret police controlled
trading in the markets might also have ensured that prices remained high.

In what has to have been one of the most bizarre exchanges of the
entire famine, North and South Korean news agencies traded charges
and countercharges about the existence of the farmers markets in September 1999. South Korean news sources announced that the North
Korean government had shut down the farmers markets across the country in an attempt to recapture control of the economy and purge the
country of the rising class of small traders. None of the KBSM refugee
interviews conducted during 1999 could confirm this South Korean
news report. Interestingly, the North Korean official news agency said the
report was another South Korean fabrication—not because the government had not shut down the markets, but because the markets did not
exist in the first place, so there was nothing for the central authorities to
close. The agency admitted that some small markets existed and were
run by elderly people who engaged in modest trade, but it added that this
was inconsequential in the larger economic scheme of things.

FARMERS MARKETS AND FAMINE DEATHS

The increase in the price of food as a result of the rise of farmers markets
and the collapse of the PDS made food inaccessible to families that had no
way of paying the higher prices, particularly given the economic changes
that had reduced their purchasing power. As industrial production plum-
meted and factories were closed, salaries of urban workers and miners
were either reduced or entirely stopped. This occurred at the same time as
heavily subsidized food from the PDS was cut off. The average monthly
salary for industrial workers—if they received it, which most did not—
would buy enough rations of corn, the cheapest staple on the farmers
markets, to feed a family of five people for a mere five days.[34]

People died in the famine because they were unable to adjust to the
economic reality of these markets by producing some marketable product, labor, or service to exchange for food. Even if one excludes the farmers who grew their own food, the proportion of the population who

relied on the farmers markets still left a large number of families with no reliable system for feeding themselves other than by foraging for wild foods. In most famines, children under five, lactating mothers, elderly people, and the disabled and ill die first, but in North Korea these deaths were disproportionately large among the families of miners and urban workers in the transportation, industrial, and white-collar industries—that is, those with limited access to farmers markets.

PHASES OF THE FAMINE

Now that the elements of the political economy of the famine have been examined, it remains to put these seemingly disparate forces into a coherent chronology that makes sense of what happened between 1990 and 2000.

Phase I: Incipient Famine, the Reduction of Rations, and the Triage of the Northeastern Provinces (1990–94)

During the early stages of the famine, rations were gradually reduced for the nonprivileged classes as the availability of food declined. This reduction was first announced in a government propaganda campaign in 1992 in which citizens were urged to "eat two meals a day" and "contribute" their lost daily meal to the survival of the country.[35] The nutritional consequence of these early reductions in rations can be seen most clearly in the results of the nutritional survey conducted by the United Nations and released in December 1998. This study showed an 18 percent rate of acute malnutrition and wasting, the most severe level of malnutrition, and a 62 percent rate of stunting among children under nine years old.[36] This astonishingly high rate of stunting provides evidence of serious nutritional deprivation extending back to this phase of the famine and confirms the refugee reports of a continuing reduction in rations early in the 1990s.

The refugees I interviewed on the Chinese–North Korean frontier in September 1998 all confirmed that PDS rations were irregular between 1990 and 1994, after which they ended altogether for the nonprivileged classes. WFP field reports from 1995 onward warned each winter and spring of the imminent failure of the PDS, though their estimates of when this would happen each year were to a great degree dependent on suspect data provided by the central government.

On July 8, 1997, I testified at a Senate Foreign Relations Committee hearing that the regime had appeared to be placing the Northeast region of the country in triage as early as 1993, by depriving it of any food subsidies. I chose the word "triage" carefully as it referred to the medical practice of determining the order of treatment, particularly during war or catastrophe, when it is impossible to save every ill or injured survivor. The most severely injured are left to die so that medical care can be focused on those with greatest chance of survival.[37]

For most of the dynastic period, the Northeast had been the poorest and least developed region of the peninsula, and it remained so after the communists took over, though Kim Il Sung made some efforts to industrialize the region and raise living standards. In general, however, the region has been a drain on dwindling resources. According to several refugees, in good years the North Korean economic system exchanged surplus rice from the northwestern and southeastern regions of the country for industrial goods produced in the food-deficient Northeast.[38] As the economy contracted, what little remained of the rice surpluses, donor food aid, and commercial imports was directed to feeding the capital city, the party elites, the military, and laborers in essential industries.

In 1997, congressional staffer Mark Kirk asked Professor Hajime Izumi, one of the leading Japanese scholars on North Korea, about regional discrimination in distribution of relief food. Izumi described the historic rivalries between the northeastern region and the southern provinces, arguing that conditions were likely the worst in North Hamgyong, Yanggang, and Chagang. A Korean Japanese community leader told Kirk the famine was having unequal consequences, with northern mountainous areas and Hamhung City suffering the most.[39]

Local government officials and party cadres in the Northeast, who themselves appeared poorly fed, told Pomnyun they had lost members of their families to the great hunger. Hwang Jang Yop reported in his book that of the five hundred thousand famine deaths in 1995, fifty thousand of the victims were party members.[40] If anything is evidence of this regional triage strategy, it is the notion that even privileged party cadres were dying. None of the refugees from the Northeast reported seeing or receiving any donor relief food, though many claimed to have heard of its existence. The fact that more than 80 percent of the food refugees in the KBSM survey were from the Northeast may reflect not only the proximity of the ethnic Korean population in China, but also the devastation caused by the triage strategy. Even in a totalitarian regime, control breaks down under famine conditions and people vote with their feet.

The attitude of regime officials negotiating with the WFP over regional food allocations suggested they were pursuing a triage strategy. They assiduously resisted at every turn any WFP plans to allocate food to the Northeast. One NGO report from 1997 stated,

> The four [western] provinces [North and South Pyongan and North and South Hwanghae] are relatively better off as food supply is more regular . . . and almost all UN agencies and NGOs currently operating in North Korea are concentrating their activities on these four provinces. The WFP food coordinator, Mr. Anders Johannson, told us that he had received phone calls directly from the two northern provinces requesting that WFP take up some food for work projects in their areas. They wanted WFP to deal directly with them rather than going through the FDRC [Flood Control] officials at Pyongyang.[41]

For local officials to ask the United Nations for help suggests that the famine had reached such severe proportions there that officials were willing to circumvent the central authorities and the chain of command and thus to risk central censure. Only after unrelenting pressure did the central government finally agree to allow one food shipment in the summer of 1997.

The WFP announcement of new access agreements with the North Korean government on July 1, 1997, underscored the quarantine of the Northeast:

> A ship chartered by the World Food Programme has arrived in North Korea with urgently needed food aid for the northeast of the country where hunger is widespread, WFP reported today. The shipment will be the first food aid delivered directly to the hard-hit Northeast, where aid agencies have not previously been able to operate.

Thus, two and a half years after starvation began appearing in the Northeast, the central authorities finally allowed WFP aid shipments.[42] On top of anecdotal information, the denial of shipments to the Northeast clearly suggests that the regime had placed the region in triage.

None of the humanitarian food aid, whether bilateral or from the WFP, and no commercial imports were delivered to the northeastern provinces, or indeed to any eastern ports, from August 1995, when the floods first occurred until Tun Myat opened the Northeast in May 1997.[43] Even after the WFP forced open the eastern part of the country to food aid, the western provinces remained heavily favored in food shipments. During all of 1997 and 1998, just over 1.25 million MT of WFP and bilateral food aid were shipped to all ports; only 18 percent of that food was delivered to the eastern ports, even though these provinces constituted 33 percent of the prefamine population of the country.[44] The mountainous eastern provinces traditionally faced food deficits, and the harvests of 1996 and 1997 were among the worst since the Korean War. Moreover, eastern farmers hoarded much of what corn they produced. If food aid had been targeted where it was most needed historically, let alone in the disastrous years of 1996–97, the eastern provinces should have received much more than their proportionate share of 33 percent. Thus, the region was disadvantaged on two counts.

Now, the North Koreans could have claimed that much of the 2 million MT of Chinese food aid that arrived between 1995 and 1999 was sent to the eastern provinces; the WFP did not maintain Chinese shipping records by port. But Chinese ports bordered the northwestern corner of North Korea, and ships would logically have been sent to western rather than eastern ports. Logistically, donor government food should have been shipped to the eastern ports and Chinese food shipped to the western ports. Some bartered food from China was delivered by land across the Tumen River to the Northeast, but this was dwarfed in volume by ocean-borne shipments and rail shipments along the western train routes. The serious lack of fuel for trucks, as well as frequent shortages of electricity for a train system that was already in disrepair, meant that the land route remained problematic. Given this transportation crisis, and the fact that two-thirds of the population lives on the coast, it was unlikely that whatever was delivered to the ports would have been moved very far inland.[45]

In fact, Pyongyang made no such claim concerning the Chinese food aid. Rather, it made the specious argument that no ships were directed to northeastern ports simply because the Northeast did not need food aid. Floods had affected the Northeast as much as other areas of the country, but whereas the central authorities prevented any assessment from being conducted in the Northeast, they facilitated such assessments elsewhere.[46] In any case, the floods were not the principal cause of the food deficit, but merely a face-saving means by which Pyongyang could get aid. UN assessments claimed only 15 percent of the food deficit was caused by natural disaster; 85 percent was a function of the chronic dysfunction in the Stalinist agricultural system.[47] The Northeast was agriculturally poor and suffered food deficits even in years of bountiful harvests. It is said in Asia that where the rice paddies end, poverty begins, and the eastern provinces produce little rice. The corn-producing areas of the Northeast have traditionally produced lower yields per hectare than have other regions of North Korea; the Northeast was heavily dependent on corn, though even this was inadequate to feed the population.

The central government decided to reduce grain subsidies to the Northeast in the early 1990s and to stop them entirely in 1994. The triage of the Northeast therefore began well before the famine spread to the western provinces; mortality rates were much higher much earlier than in the rest of the country. The famine killed off the vulnerable population in the Northeast early in the famine, and since one can not die twice, the situation apparently stabilized as indigenously grown food and cross-border trade may have been sufficient to sustain the reduced population. The famine migrated to other regions of the country between 1995 and 1997, however, as the food crisis became more acute and drove up mortality rates in those regions too. Several refugees I interviewed from different provinces gave the same explanation for the movement of the famine from east to west.

The migration of famines is not a unique phenomenon. Ethiopian geographer Mesfin Wolde-Mariam has noted the movement of famines in Ethiopia in concentric circles around the initially affected area as merchants moved food from surplus areas into the famine areas when prices rose because of the crop failure. What were food surplus areas then became deficit areas because of this merchant activity, and death rates rose accordingly even as the death rates stabilized in the original locus of the famine.[48] Famine-affected areas would remain vulnerable because they would never quite recover from previous droughts before a new one would strike in a neighboring region, drawing food away. It is not a coincidence that farmers markets spread across North Korea just as the public distribution system was collapsing.

Phase II: The Collapse of the PDS, the Rise of Farmers Markets, and the Central Government's Effort to Stop the Collapse (1995–97)

The flooding of August 1995 pushed a teetering system over the edge and further reduced already declining food production, a loss that the country could ill afford given the sizable structural deficit that preceded the floods. Three natural disasters struck the country during each of the three years in this period and contributed to, but were not the cause of, the famine. The floods of 1995 and 1996 were followed by a severe drought in 1997 that reduced corn production by 50 percent beyond normal production levels.[49] Although the regime blamed flooding in 1998 for the food deficit, WFP and NGO assessments reported floods that year to be of negligible consequence. Indeed, the harvest in 1998 was thought to be among the best in five years, though it again produced a sizable food deficit.

The structural deficit and natural disasters forced Pyongyang to give North Korea's 211 county administrators authority over feeding their populations.[50] One report provided to the WFP stated,

> The food crisis appears to have given rise to a high degree of decentralization and regional autonomy. Contrary to prevailing perceptions about the highly centralized character of North Korea's economy, the magnitude of the food crisis has compelled the central government to give provincial authorities the license to fend for themselves. We found that local authorities were dealing directly with foreign commercial interests, bartering scrap iron and other locally produced raw materials for low-quality, broken rice or maize.[51]

Hilary Mackenzie, as well as NGO and UN relief workers, spoke well of the county administrators. As a class they seem to have been less driven by ideology and more by genuine duty to the people they were responsible for feeding. They showed some independence from the politics of the central government and negotiated around the bureaucratic obstacles that the central authorities had placed in their way.[52] Of course, some performed better than others; in counties with more skillful and energetic administrators, fewer people died, while in those with bureaucratic and lethargic administrators the impact of the famine was more devastating. It was primarily the county administrators, sometimes in cooperation with factory managers, who traded with China for food. They cut timber, harvested wild medicinal herbs and seaweed, cannibalized factory machinery for scrap metal, and caught seafood to barter in China.

This decentralization has caused disparities in food consumption between regions. Sue Lautze, in her North Korean food aid assessment prepared for the U.S. Agency for International Development (USAID), noted that

> the State appears to be abdicating its socialistic responsibility to equitably provide for the nation, thereby placing a great burden on local governments to maintain a system of socialism using only local resources. As a consequence, community survival currently depends upon the local availability of natural endowments and [the] skill of local administrators to barter goods for cereals. Wealthier areas are currently faring better at this than poorer areas, thereby increasing disparities in vulnerability and related capacity to survive until the next harvest. Trading rights . . . have further increased disparities.[53]

Hoarding and the Collapse of the PDS. Aggregate food production figures in themselves are insufficient to prove whether a famine has occurred, but they do influence donor contributions of food aid meant to respond to the famine and are thus of considerable importance. Many international agencies analyzed and estimated agricultural production during the North Korean famine, but nearly all the estimates included several presumptive mistakes. They all assumed that the PDS actually distributed all the food that was grown on the farms, confusing produced harvest with distributable harvest, a subject that will be discussed in chapter 8. When the population is under great nutritional stress, a great deal can happen between the time the harvest is gathered and the time people receive their food ration.

In his book on theories of famine, Stephen Devereux writes:

> In virtually every recorded famine, precautionary and speculative withholding of stocks has been blamed for magnifying food supply problems. Spitz (1985, p. 306) quotes Kuang Chung, First Minister to the Duke Huan of the Feudatory of Ch'i, who said in 650 B.C.: "That people are starving for lack of food is because there is grain hoarded in storehouses of the rich instead of [in] government granaries."[54]

Devereux goes on to explain the effect of hoarding on prices:

> Withholding food from the market is likely to increase as the price
> of food (or other commodities) rises, for many reasons. Large farm-
> ers will withhold their surpluses for speculative purposes, hoping
> for further price increases; small farmers will store food as a pre-
> cautionary measure against spiraling market prices; and general
> inflation might reduce the willingness of farmers to convert their
> produce into cash. Finally, if farmers are aiming to meet fixed finan-
> cial commitments (such as rent or taxes) rather than to maximize
> profits, the proportion of a crop which needs to be sold, as prices
> rise, will fall. The special feature of food which produces this
> vicious spiral of falling supply and rising prices stems from food's
> dual role as a source both of income and of necessary consumption
> to the producer.[55]

Although there was substantial evidence of widespread hoarding,
virtually none of the NGO, UN, or Red Cross analyses of the North
Korean famine acknowledged even the possibility, let alone reality, of this
phenomenon.

A country suffering through a sustained famine will likely experience
more hoarding as the psychology of permanent deprivation spreads out
among the population. This would cause enough diversion of food from
the national supply system that it could affect the country's agricultural
ledger balance. In a famine, hoarded food is more valuable than gold: a
fast route to profit and wealth. During the Somali famine in 1992, Fred
Cuny estimated that the warlords had hoarded 30,000 MT of donated
food that they had looted from relief convoys. As the manager of the
USAID famine relief effort, I followed one of Cuny's strategies and sold
donated food to Somali merchants in sufficient quantity to flood the market, driving the price down so much that the warlords would release the
food they had hoarded when prices were rising. During the Sudanese
drought of 1990–91, Cuny estimated that as much as 500,000 MT of
food was being hoarded by a half-dozen major grain merchants, food that
he predicted would be dumped onto the markets when the price had
peaked and begun to decline.

There were four separate reports of hoarding during the North
Korean famine. The first was Kim Jong Il's speech, which was quoted
earlier.[56] The second was the FAO/WFP report indicating that half the
corn harvest—amounting to 1.3 million MT in the autumn of 1996—

had disappeared before it was harvested.[57] The third report came from a defector who told me in Seoul that there were reports of the roofs of farmers' homes collapsing under the weight of the hoarded grain they had hidden there; and the fourth came from famine refugees who explained how and why they had hoarded grain. Some refugees told me they slept in their fields at night as the crop reached maturity, to guard against thievery, while others admitted to having stolen half-grown food from farms as a means of survival.

The scarcity of food and the rise in prices increased the level of corruption by party cadres who had the power to divert food to sell on the markets. The incidence of corruption in any system rises as the profit margin increases; people will risk punishment for violating the system if the potential profit is sufficiently high. Many former Eastern bloc diplomats who served for many years in Pyongyang reported a general increase in the incidence of official corruption after Kim Il Sung's death, in a system where it had previously been uncommon.

It is clear why the agricultural and industrial crisis drove up food prices and reduced household purchasing power, but it is not clear why the famine occurred at this particular time and not earlier or later. The four FAO/WFP crop assessments conducted in North Korea between 1995 and 1998 focused on the production, not distribution, of grain (see figure 2 above, p. 95). These assessments were typically made by estimating the amount of arable land, the varieties of crops grown on the land, and the amount of production per unit of land adjusted for climate, fertilizer use, pest problems, and seed and soil quality. Although this approach may be useful in determining agricultural production under ordinary circumstances, it is not useful in a famine. International food monitors told me they watched farmers surreptitiously diverting grain before having their "surplus" requisitioned by the PDS. In a nominally marxist agricultural system, this problem is compounded because the great bulk of the annual crop is cared for not by the individual farmer who produced it, but by the collective or state authorities. Thus, every farmer is a potential agent of diversion.

The catastrophic consequence of this widespread hoarding on the availability of food and on food prices paid by the North Korean people exponentially exaggerated the effects of the famine because of the particular effect it had on surpluses sold on the markets. As Devereux notes, "all other factors being equal, if 10 percent of a crop is sold as surplus, a 5 percent fall in yield would cause a 50 percent fall in surplus sold, after subsistence needs are met."[58]

What caused this widespread hoarding of crops? Farm families beginning in the fall of 1995 had their ration reduced by central edict to 50 percent of the minimum level needed to sustain life for an active adult. In the halcyon days of the late 1960s and 1970s, when harvests were bountiful, farm workers' rations had been an average of 200 kilograms per person per year. In the early 1990s, as the food shortages grew more severe, this was reduced to 167 kilograms, and in the autumn of 1995 it was further reduced to 107 kilograms.[59] At 167 kilograms the ration was 75 percent of the minimum adult requirement, while at 107 kilograms it was 50 percent of what was required. This reduction proved to be a disastrous decision by the central government. It changed overnight the economic incentives on the collectives, with three horrific consequences for the North Korean food system and the people who relied on it to survive.

The first consequence was that the state's decision broke the accepted social contract that farmers would grow food in exchange for industrial production from the urban and mining areas. Because of the economic downturn following the disappearance of Soviet oil and food subsidies, as well as the lack of maintenance and spare parts for industrial machinery and infrastructure, production declined precipitously in most factories producing agricultural inputs. Factories in the Northeast either functioned only a few days a month or shut down entirely. The collective farms were not being provided with the inputs needed for higher levels of production. Pyongyang decided to cut off the traditional interprovincial food transfers to the Northeast of rice surpluses grown in the southwestern plains. Henceforth, the only food distributed to cities and mining areas in the Northeast was locally grown corn, when it was available. These local surpluses disappeared by 1995 because of the collapse of inputs, the floods, and the droughts, which were followed by the disastrous decision to further reduce farm rations.

The WFP and the FAO noted cryptically in their 1998 crop forecast, "The significant fall in domestic food production over the last few years has also meant that there is greater resistance in the farming population to supply food to the urban population without sufficient compensation in goods and services."[60] This one understated sentence explains one of the major causes of the distribution crisis in 1996 and 1997 that led to the famine, though the WFP was several years late in acknowledging it.

The second consequence was that the reduction in farmers' rations encouraged farmers to divert production from the agricultural system before the harvest. By so rapidly and drastically reducing the farmers' rations, the state in essence gave farmers the choice of slowly letting their families starve or secretly collecting the harvest early—in other words, hoarding food and building up family stocks before the "real" harvest was actually taken. Kim Jong Il knew of and complained about this "pre-harvesting" in his December 1996 famine speech: "Cooperative farms and cooperative farmers hide a substantial amount of grain, using this or that excuse."[61]

As mentioned earlier, the FAO/WFP agricultural assessment in the autumn of 1996 acknowledged that half the corn harvest—nearly 1.3 million MT—was missing.[62] But the report did not explain this fact by acknowledging the traditional famine response of hoarding; rather, it argued that the corn was consumed green because people were so hungry. The weakness of this explanation becomes more apparent when one calculates the population's consumption requirements. At a minimal ration, 15,000 MT of grain will feed one million people per month, which means that 345,000 MT of grain would feed the entire country for a month, and 1.3 million MT would feed the entire country for nearly four months.

In fact, three distinct motives drove the early harvesting of crops. The first was the farmers' desire in the summer of 1996 to feed their families, which were already hungry because of the huge cut in rations the previous autumn.[63] The second motive was to hoard food in anticipation of future deprivation caused by either the food crisis or Pyongyang's decisions to reduce the farmers' rations further or stop them altogether.[64] And the third motive was to sell the hoarded, preharvested crops on the farmers markets at much higher prices than the PDS would pay.[65]

The third consequence of the reduction in rations was that it encouraged farmers to spend their most valuable and limited economic resources—their time and energy—on alternative food-producing activities. Thus farmers expended more efforts on private household plots the government had given them decades earlier and on cultivating secret plots of land in the mountains; both of these lay outside the control of the collective agricultural system. I suggested to a senior government official on my visit to North Korea in June 1997 that the size of the private plots be expanded, since they produced 30 percent to 40 percent more per unit of land than an equal amount of collective farmland.[66] The horrified official responded that the Agriculture Commission was having trouble with the amount of time the farmers were already spending working on their private plots, which would only get worse if the plots were increased in size. The secret plots, though illegal, could be seen everywhere —even on mountains so steep and infertile that it was difficult to imagine that anyone could work on them or that any crop could grow there. Yet I could see them arrayed across the mountainsides facing the Tumen River as Pomnyun and I drove along the riverbank in the autumn of 1998.

Refugee farmers told me that brush burning was the preferred system for clearing these mountainsides, a practice that had led to a substantial increase in forest fires throughout the mountainous regions of the country during the earlier phases of the famine.[67] Refugees reported that the authorities banned these "fire fields" because of the forest fire problem, but that the prohibition was widely ignored. Tun Myat, transportation director of the WFP, was the first expatriate relief official to be allowed into the Northeast. In May 1997 he took a twenty-nine-hour train ride from Pyongyang to Chongjin, and he said he was shocked by the number of forest fires he saw in the country's mountainous interior.[68] Farmers had so reduced if not ended their work on the corn-growing collectives in the mountain regions that the collectives had to be tended by soldiers and some urban volunteers. Soldiers and urban workers had always helped farmers plant and harvest the crops, but during the famine they appeared to have taken their place in the Northeast.[69]

North Korean farmers' response to the central government's reduction of their rations had historical precedent in the deprivation that peasants had suffered for centuries during the dynastic period and the Japanese colonial period. In previous centuries, when the level of state taxation increased to confiscatory levels or landlords increased the portion of the harvest they demanded of their tenants, peasants would simply leave their farms and secretly cultivate land high in the hills and mountainsides, outside the reach of landlords. This practice dates back to the early nineteenth century, but it was seen more recently in the reaction of the Koreans to the confiscatory harvest practices of Japanese and Korean landlords in the 1930s. As Andrew Nahm writes in *Korea: Tradition and Transformation*, "The landless peasants who refused to till the lands owned by absentee landlords, or those who live in areas where farmlands were scarce, became . . . cultivators of fire-fields. Fire-fields were created by burning wastelands and hillsides in order to plant corn, sweet potatoes, and millet."[70] A Japanese colonial government publication of 1935 stated that "these poor people are driven by hunger from place to place, making shelters in log cabins and keeping their bodies and souls together by planting grains and vegetables on the hillsides."[71] In many areas during the early 1930s, Korean landlords took 75 percent of the crop as rent and then sold it to the Japanese, leaving a starvation ration of 25 percent for the peasants to survive on until the next crop. Kim Jong Il's cadres had become the new landlords, confiscating the farmers' harvests and driving them off the collectives to fire-field farming.

The parallels between the dynastic and landlord oppression of the peasantry and that of the collective farming system under the Kim dynasty are striking. In neither case did the peasants own the land they cultivated, nor did they own the harvest they produced each year. In both cases the peasants reacted to confiscatory levels of taxation by circumventing the distant authorities over whom they exercised no control and had no hand in choosing. The consequences of the confiscatory policies were the same: levels of hunger and starvation rose, as did more extreme forms of coping mechanisms that allowed the farmers to deal with their deteriorating circumstances. Thus the long-suffering North Korean peasant borrowed a ready famine survival strategy from the memory of his parents and grandparents.

The Militarization of Agriculture. NGOs, UN workers, and refugees all reported that the central authorities by 1997 had ordered the military onto the farms to a much greater degree than in the past. During my trip to North Korea in June 1997 I noticed a strong presence of young soldiers, with their boots off and pants rolled up, planting seedlings in the rice paddies—a practice I was told was customary. The soldiers would again be ordered into the paddies to harvest the rice in late September. At 1.3 million men, the size of the standing army meant that a huge proportion of the workforce was being diverted into unproductive labor while the country starved, so it is not surprising that the central authorities ordered soldiers onto the farms. Moreover, Pyongyang appears to have further increased the military's "field presence" in 1998.

Some NGO colleagues who heard these same stories speculated that the farmers were so weakened by hunger that they did not have the energy to plant the crops alone, a plausible explanation. The North Korean deputy foreign minister, during his meeting with NGOs in Washington, D.C., in early 1997, expressed fears that unless more food aid was forthcoming from donors, the crop might not get fully planted.[72] Farmers weakened by hunger, he said, would not have the energy to till and plant the paddies, an effort that required great physical labor in the absence of fuel and spare parts for their antique tractor fleet.

But as mentioned earlier, the history of other famines suggests an alternate explanation for the presence of the military: to prevent the hoarding of food by the farmers as the famine swept across the country. The militarization of agriculture was Pyongyang's response to the breakdown of the social contract under which the obedient and compliant people exchanged their independence for a guarantee by the state to care for them from birth to burial. This contract had made North Korean society function, and it had worked either despite or because of the dark repression needed to enforce it.

The central government did not stand idly by while the farmers undertook the massive diversion of the 1996 harvest. It reacted in a very totalitarian way: by imposing command-and-control measures that, if anything, exacerbated the hoarding instead of diminishing it. According to defectors and refugees, in an effort to preclude this enormous diversion, Kim Jong Il dispatched soldiers—called corn guards—to protect the corn fields as the harvest matured. "He issued a direct order to give each soldier three rounds of ammunition, one for a warning shot and two rounds to kill the thief," reported one defector I interviewed.[73] But a refugee farmer explained why this tactic was of limited utility: farmers simply bribed the soldiers, who themselves were hungry because of a breakdown in the military food distribution system, and offered them meat and liquor if they joined them in the diversion. By the summer of 1998 in South Hamgyong province, the government had begun assigning two soldiers, instead of one, to protect each corn field against theft.[74] Farmers explained that it took a bit longer to bribe the two soldiers, who were supposed to be watching each other and the corn fields, than was the case when only one soldier was standing guard. But the grain shortages were causing problems for the military, which apparently was also suffering from hunger. Thus soldiers, converted by edict into an agricultural police force, had a motive to help farmers divert the harvest: they were hungry too.

On August 5, 1997, the North Korean Public Security Ministry issued a decree on hoarding and the theft of food: "Those who steal grain shall be executed by shooting. . . . Those who engage in trade using grain shall be executed by shooting."[75] Many KBSM reports and many of Jasper Becker's refugee interviews describe public executions in the villages for the crime of stealing food.

Kim Jong Il's solution to the hoarding problem, beyond arrests and executions, was to give more speeches and conduct political indoctrination. In March 1997 he said,

> Party functionaries must go among the cooperative farmers and say to them loud and clear: we are eating grain which international agencies provide because we have had bad harvests for three years in a row. No country intends to give us grain when the entire world screams it suffers from grain shortages. Our country faces the daunting problem of grain shortages. We are not able to send rice to the army because we do not have sufficient rice.[76]

Central government efforts to use force to gather hoarded food likely led to the deaths of many innocent people, but there is no extensive evidence of this, as the enforcing agents never really knew who was hoarding or how much had been hoarded. The agents likely collected more than they should have and ended up taking the last remaining starvation rations. During the period of Russian forced collectivization and the Chinese Great Leap Forward, enormous suffering resulted from arbitrary attempts by the central government to confiscate greater and greater portions of the declining harvests. The only effective method for reducing hoarding is to implement a pricing strategy in which the central government (or the United Nations or NGOs) steadily pushes more food onto the markets, thus driving prices down enough that those with the hoarded food, seeing the falling prices, release their food as well. But market strategies were not something the North Korean government understood.

In the case of the North Korean famine, the absence of any serious analysis by UN agencies and NGOs of microeconomic forces at work meant that the famine relief effort included no attempts to influence the black markets or the farmers markets. Even after having sanctioned the farmers markets, the central government remained thoroughly ignorant of basic microeconomic theory and saw hoarding as the problem instead of as a symptom. One UN economist was shocked when a senior North Korean finance official asked what the difference was between microeconomics and macroeconomics. North Korean leaders, understanding that their ignorance of economics would hinder their entry into the global economy, sent a few young men to study market economics in Australia in 1998 and 1999.

It was during this second transitional phase of the famine that death rates accelerated, peaking in the latter half of 1996 and the first half of 1997, a subject that will be treated in greater depth in later chapters. In brief, the poor harvest and the widespread diversion of grain in the eastern collective farms led the central authorities to panic in late 1996, so they made a further set of triage decisions beyond that of cutting off food subsidies to the Northeast. This second set of triage decisions focused remaining food stocks on those populations most important to the survival of the system: residents of the capital city, workers in critical industries such as functioning coal mines, and party cadres and the officers of the military and secret police. Thus, the people in the western provinces who did not fall into these categories either had their rations cut off entirely or saw them reduced to levels well below what was needed for survival.[77]

Phase III: The Emergence of a Fragile New Food Security System (1998–2000)

While the locus of the famine had been in urban areas, the famine struck earlier in the four eastern provinces—Yanggang, Kangwon, North Hamgyong, and South Hamgyong—which, before the famine, contained nearly seven million people. The other mountainous provinces of the country, such as Chagang and parts of North Pyongan and North Hwanghae, were also severely affected earlier in the famine.

According to a defector I interviewed who had access to information about the PDS management, the central authorities decided in January 1998 to make each family responsible for feeding itself.[78] This report was confirmed by South Korean press accounts a year later, in February 1999:

> Visitors to North Korea are saying that food distribution has stopped even in the capital of Pyongyang. According to once source, government agencies in Pyongyang were given official notice at the end of last year that they would soon have to either solve the problems as agencies or on their own as individuals because "from now on there will be no food distribution." The source said that he heard this directly from a North Korean government official.[79]

The central authorities thus appear to have made the deliberate decision to privatize the distribution system even further: from the county authorities who were given food distribution responsibility in Phase II of the famine, to a system of individual family responsibility in Phase III. It may be that this decision, though deliberate, simply recognized the evolving reality of where the system was moving—a movement that Kim Jong Il was powerless to stop. This new system reduced the control that the regime had over the people at a time when its grip on power had been weakening and its popular support eroding.

By the spring of 1998, the North Korean famine, as measured by high death rates, was over. This has been confirmed by anecdotal reports from refugees interviewed by the KBSM in early 1998; by data on monthly death rates in a mining city in the Northeast, which will be analyzed in a later chapter; and by the central government's attempts to reassert control over the exhausted population. The camps for internally displaced persons were systematically closed in the spring of 1999 and the prisoners moved to remote locations away from public view.[80] More guard houses were constructed along the Tumen and Yalu Rivers to stop population movements into China. The train cars and stations were purged of *kochibis* and new identification cards were issued in an attempt to reimpose the Stalinist internal population movement system. But despite the authorities' attempts to recreate a Stalinist state and resuscitate the moribund old order, the scars and horror of the great famine had permanently changed the country. It is unlikely that the regime can recreate the old order.

6

THE DIPLOMACY OF THE FAMINE

A S WAS TRUE OF ALL TWENTIETH-CENTURY FAMINES, the one that
descended on North Korea was preventable. For centuries analysts have known what factors combine to cause famine, what
the immediate warning signs are, and what measures may stop a famine
before death rates rise. In North Korea's case, its exhausted yet unyielding
economic and political ideology had impoverished the country's industrial workers and miners. But diplomatic interests prompted Western
governments, which traditionally led relief efforts, in this case to evis-
cerate them. These diplomatic complications delayed the response long
enough to ensure that when food aid did finally arrive it was too late,
delivered to the wrong areas of the country, and distributed so ineptly
that the regime was able to feed its elites and let the poor starve. This chapter first reviews the peculiar state of diplomatic relations that led to this
paralysis and then considers the North Korean response.

NORTH–SOUTH RELATIONS
DURING THE COLD WAR

For much of its existence, North Korea has been a rogue state, ignoring
even the most basic rules of international behavior. Its reputation for
mischief preceded the famine. During the 1970s and 1980s it engaged in
several terrorist attacks on South Korea. In 1974 an ethnic Japanese
Korean sympathetic to the North tried to murder South Korean president Park Chung Hee but ended up killing the president's wife instead;

some suspected that the assassin was an agent of Pyongyang.[1] During a 1983 state visit to Burma by South Korean president Chun Doo Hwan, North Korean agents planted a bomb that killed four South Korean cabinet members, two presidential advisers, and the ambassador to Burma. In November 1987 a bomb planted by North Korean operatives blew up Korean Air Flight 858, killing 115 people. In between these major events, dozens of smaller military incidents initiated by the North against the South fueled the poisoned state of relations. In response, the South demonized the North and its leaders with an invective nearly as inflammatory as that of the North toward the South. This made any possible outreach by the South toward the North during the famine much more difficult.

The clash of worldview and ideology between the two Koreas and the history of fifty years of unrelenting hostility between them led to terrible tragedies twice, both equally devastating in the loss of human life: first, the Korean War, and then the Great Famine. Chapter 5 discussed how the failure of the Stalinist economic model and the decline in Eastern bloc subsidies drove the economy to collapse. At the same time, South Korea was experiencing a two-decade-long economic boom that enabled it to modernize and expand its military forces and created a rising middle class. The latter successfully forced the previously autocratic Southern regime to initiate democratic reforms, giving South Korea an ideological credibility it had once lacked.

In other words, the North was failing just as the South was succeeding, and Pyongyang perceived Seoul as a much greater threat than it ever had been. In response to this threat, Pyongyang chose to spend its scarce resources on military production rather than shift its diminishing resources into agriculture and economic development to shore up its failing economy. In the 1980s and 1990s, the number of troops in all North Korean forces doubled in size, and with it the burden on the North Korean economy. Some analysts believe that 25 percent of North Korea's gross domestic product was devoted to military spending in the early 1990s.[2] Thus, a country of twenty-three million people maintained the fourth largest land army in Asia at a time when its population was suffering mass starvation.

Internationally, the end of the Cold War and the triumph of democracy led the South Korean system to win its decades-long battle with the North for diplomatic recognition from developing countries. By the early

1990s North Korea was increasingly isolated diplomatically as former developing and Eastern bloc countries established relations with South Korea and embraced democratic capitalism. North Korea's two closest allies, Russia and China, had aggravated the situation by ending their economic subsidization of the North Korean economy, but worse still from Pyongyang's perspective was their decision to establish diplomatic ties with Seoul. Even before the fall of the Soviet Union, Mikhail Gorbachev and his foreign minister, Eduard Shevardnadze, determined Soviet interests would be better served by the establishment of diplomatic relations with South Korea. Gorbachev dispatched Shevardnadze to break the news to his shocked North Korean counterpart, Kim Yong Nam, in September 1990. Then, in June 1991, China informed North Korea that it would not oppose the admission of South Korea to the United Nations; neither Korea had been a member since the international organization's founding. Although both Koreas joined the United Nations at the same time, the South's admission put it on equal footing with the North, something the North had assiduously tried to avoid for forty years. A year later Chinese foreign minister Qian Qichen quietly informed Kim Yong Nam that his government also intended to establish diplomatic relations with the South. Thus in one year the North lost its economic subsidies and the unwavering loyalty of its two closest allies.

The final blow to North Korea occurred with the release of Soviet archival material refuting some of North Korea's claims to historic legitimacy. The North had long insisted that Kim Il Sung's leadership in the guerrilla war against Japanese colonial occupation in the late 1930s rendered it the true heir to the legacy of Korean nationalism and independence. Northern propaganda further argued that North Korea had maintained its independence and opposed the American "occupation" of the South. The release of Russian archival material through the South Korean government irrefutably disproved the revisionist charge that the North was a victim of Southern aggression. Documents showed that the North had attacked the South with the support and approval of Stalin, whose permission Kim Il Sung had clearly received prior to the attack. Indeed, the archival evidence proved Stalin had personally chosen Kim Il Sung to lead North Korea after World War II, installed him in power, and ensured that he stayed there.[3] Thus the one remaining Northern claim of nationalist legitimacy was itself under twin assault, first by the opening

of the Russian archives, and second by the Southern embrace of democratic capitalism and its stunning economic success.

A TEMPORARY WARMING OF RELATIONS

As these events unfolded, or perhaps because of them, diplomatic relations
between the two Koreas began to warm. In October 1991, the North and
South Korean prime ministers met and made substantial progress on a set
of issues over which their two countries had been deadlocked for twenty
years. An accord was fashioned and signed by both sides in December
1991 recognizing each other's systems and renouncing the subversion of or
interference in each other's internal affairs. The accord also renounced the
countries' use of force against each other; created a process for negotiating
arms reductions; and called for family exchanges, new trade and transportation ties, the beginning of discussions toward a permanent peace
settlement, and the implementation of confidence-building measures.

The euphoria arising from this agreement lasted well into the
spring of 1993, after which four events intervened to poison the atmo-
sphere. First, Kim Young Sam, who was skeptical of the 1991 accords, won
South Korea's presidential election. Second, an ill-timed U.S.–South
Korean military exercise reignited Northern paranoia. Third, South Korea
arrested sixty-two people on charges of espionage for North Korea. And
fourth, a series of events led to confrontation with the United States in
1994 over the inspection of North Korean nuclear sites. This diplomatic
confrontation nearly led the United States to impose trade sanctions on
North Korea, which Pyongyang announced would be considered an act
of war. Former U.S. president Jimmy Carter's dramatic intervention and
visit to Pyongyang successfully defused the crisis and led the United States
to rethink its diplomatic strategy in dealing with the North.

Three weeks after Carter's departure from North Korea, however,
Kim Il Sung collapsed from a massive heart attack and died, throwing the
country into crisis. In any country the death of the sitting head of state
would be disruptive and perhaps destabilizing; in North Korea, given the
cult of personality surrounding the Great Leader, it was an apocalyptic
event. Although the party leadership blamed natural disasters for the
famine, the refugees I later interviewed all attributed it to Kim's death.

"If he were alive, we would not be dying," was the common refrain I heard from refugee after refugee.

Because this crisis had brought the peninsula close to war, the Clinton administration formulated what has come to be known as the "soft landing policy."[4] Leading advocates of this policy, which led to the 1994 Agreed Framework, included James Laney, then U.S. ambassador to South Korea, and Winston Lord, assistant secretary of state for East Asia and the Pacific. Through the Agreed Framework, the United States attempted to encourage the North Korean government toward more responsible international behavior and a negotiated end to fifty years of rhetorical attacks on and military threats toward South Korea. Laney, who had been president of Emory University prior to his appointment by President Clinton as ambassador to South Korea, knew Korean culture and politics well, as he and his wife had been Methodist missionaries in South Korea three decades earlier.

Opponents of the administration's policy advocated a hard landing, which had as its objective the collapse of the Northern regime. But avoiding war was one of the implied motivations behind the soft-landing approach, given the extraordinarily high casualty rates military planners were forecasting should war break out as the regime fell apart.

The Clinton administration pursued two elements of the soft-landing policy in negotiating the Agreed Framework. First, it attempted to dismantle existing North Korean nuclear power reactors, which could be used to produce nuclear weapons, and replace them with new reactors built with South Korean, European, and Japanese funding. The design of these new power plants would prevent them from being misused. While the new reactors were being built, the United States would provide North Korea with oil paid for with U.S. government funds. The North desperately needed oil for heating and fuel for transportation and industrial production. But conservatives in the U.S. Congress would later oppose the plan, arguing that the fuel could also be used to provision the North Korean military machine.

The second element of the Agreed Framework was an initiative to hold four-party talks. The Clinton administration believed that if it could get South and North Korea to the negotiating table, along with the United States and China—North Korea's most powerful remaining ally—diplomacy would take its course. The end goal was an agreement to diminish tensions on the peninsula.

In theory, the framework for a soft landing made good sense, given that the alternative hard-landing proposal risked war and a massive loss of life. The soft-landing policy's weakness was not its general idea, but its implementation; to succeed, it required a cooperative North Korea, but North Korea was characteristically uncooperative. Pyongyang saw the soft-landing policy as a means for achieving its own, very different, diplomatic objectives of avoiding the need to recognize South Korea publicly and of breaking apart the South Korean–U.S. alliance. In the autumn of 1997 the nuclear initiative began unraveling, as the Asian economic crisis led the South Korean economy to enter a tailspin. Seoul was no longer financially capable of sustaining the multibillion-dollar investment required to carry out the nuclear decommissioning and reconstruction program.[5]

KOREAN RELATIONS DURING THE FAMINE

North Korea has learned through negotiating with the United States that it can get what it wants without changing its behavior. Its objectives ought to have been clear from the start. First, although the famine was beginning to take its toll in the country, Pyongyang had no intention of weakening its commanding power and reforming its agricultural system to produce more food. Second, it intended to ensure the survival not just of the ruling elite, but of the essential elements of the marxist political and economic system in the country, regardless of how much this might cost its people. Thus, although the government did not contrive the famine that swept across the country in the mid-1990s, it clearly refused to modify its political objectives to save its own people. The North Korean government believed it could accomplish these formidable objectives by breaking up the U.S.–South Korean alliance, in the process leveling the military playing field between the North and the South. Pyongyang saw food aid not only as a way of sustaining itself and avoiding unrest, but more important as a way of pursuing its central political objectives.

The South Korean government, driven by contradictory motives, alternately supported, opposed, and then again supported food aid to North Korea. Over the course of the famine, the South Korean position on food aid was more a reaction to Northern provocation than a consistent policy. In 1995 the South Koreans and the Japanese ranked as the most generous contributors to the alleviation of North Korean suffering: Japan committed 450,000 MT of grain and the South Koreans donated 150,000 MT. But South Korea understandably feared that food aid might be diverted for use by the military, and, perhaps even more, it expected that denying the regime the food it needed might cause it to collapse. Thus, during the most destructive years of the famine—from the spring of 1996 through the summer of 1997—Seoul made only token food aid contributions. It also convinced several other governments not to contribute food. Kim Young Sam had hoped to achieve what every South Korean political figure had dreamed of for fifty years: the peaceful unification of the peninsula under the political and economic system of the South. He wished to be remembered as the Helmut Kohl of Korea.

The North Koreans knew that if the U.S. government supported aid and the South opposed it, the dispute might weaken the alliance. The North Korean calculation did not consider the salutary effect that news of the famine might have on public opinion in South Korea. As the famine's fury increased in the spring of 1997 and the South Korean media reported increasingly on the gruesome details of the Northern crisis, Seoul changed its policy to support the U.S. government's. Since the summer of 1996, Washington had been telling Pyongyang, "Come to the talks, negotiate seriously, and we will feed you." By the spring of 1997, Seoul pledged 50,000 MT of grain for the starving North.

Although Seoul had already pledged grain that spring, Kim Dae Jung's election as South Korean president in the autumn of 1997 meant a sea change in South Korean policy toward the North, because Kim pursued what became known as a "sunshine policy" of accommodation and reconciliation with the North. Pyongyang took more than two years to respond to Seoul's initiative, however, because it believed the new president was not fully in command of the national government—or at least this was its stated reason for maintaining its policy of orchestrated hostility.

President Kim had wanted to make a generous donation of food aid to the North, but his advisers strongly counseled against it. South Korea's economic crisis meant there were many hungry, unemployed South Koreans who might not have appreciated a massive food program for their Northern enemies. By mid-1998, however, South Korea's aid policy toward the North began to evolve into a more aggressive and generous approach. Instead of pledging large-scale food aid commitments as the United States was doing, South Korea chose to donate massive shipments of fertilizer, the single agricultural input that could substantially increase Northern food production in one agricultural season. To a great degree, the improved harvests of 1998 and 1999 were directly attributable to South Korean fertilizer aid, which along with U.S. government food aid effectively prevented a return of the famine.

Despite the support the South was providing, Northern provocations and hostile rhetoric continued, mostly for internal purposes. The North still believed its survival depended both on driving a diplomatic wedge between the United States and South Korea and on improving relations with Washington. The more likely motivations for Pyongyang's policy were two deep, related fears. First was the fear that any opening that allowed the South to see the North's wretched deprivation would cause Pyongyang to lose face. Second was the fear that, if North Koreans witnessed the prosperity and freedom in the South, they would rebel.

THE ROLE OF THE INTERNATIONAL DONOR COMMUNITY

Several conclusions may be drawn from the state of diplomatic affairs between the great powers and North Korea during the course of the famine. The regime's behavior alienated nearly all its potential food aid donors just at a time when it most needed their help. Japan and South Korea combined had in fact contributed more than 450,000 MT of food aid after the 1995 floods, but North Korea's inhospitable welcome of its adversaries' food ensured that this generosity was not repeated the following year when the famine reached its deadly climax. By initially delaying or later refusing to make food donations, China, Japan, the United States, and the European Union each played its own role in exacerbating the famine's effects. In each case, their responses were mitigated by domestic and foreign policy concerns.

China and North Korea

China and Japan were the two other stakeholders with significant interests in the North Korean famine. For China, North Korea was an obstinate and errant stepchild whose behavior in the international community made virtually anyone but Saddam Hussein and Muammar Qaddhafi look responsible by comparison. China surely did not object to the comparison: its liberalized economy, rapid modernization, and opening to the outside world made Chinese autocracy look pedestrian, and even successful, compared with North Korean totalitarianism. Throughout the famine the Chinese feared its potential consequences. Famines in autocratic regimes elsewhere have led to coups and popular unrest, which might well have occurred in North Korea. China recognized that the onset of a major refugee emergency would draw millions of starving North Koreans into China, an event that raised the specter of meddling NGOs and, worse still, international journalists seeking media access. A famine might also threaten the military balance of power on the Korean peninsula and risk a conflict that the Chinese had a pronounced interest in avoiding. A war between North and South, ignited by a famine raging out of control, would inevitably result in an increase in the size of the U.S. military commitment to South Korea, which already stood at thirty-seven thousand troops. It had long been an objective of Chinese policy to push U.S. military and political influence out of Asia so China could, among other things, prosecute its quarrel with Taiwan without U.S. interference. All of these factors gave the Chinese an interest in cooling the political tensions on the peninsula, which meant avoiding a famine by providing food aid. The problem was that Chinese internal financial problems meant that it could ill afford to waste budgetary resources on aid that might be needed indefinitely if North Korea did not reform its economy and agricultural system. And reform was something that so far Pyongyang had steadfastly refused to initiate.

The Chinese also wished to avoid having the North Korean problem interfere with Beijing's budding trade relationship with Seoul and the diplomatic leverage that this relationship gave Beijing over Taiwan. Taiwan had been an ally of South Korea during much of the Cold War, but the South Koreans broke relations with their former ally to establish them with China. Food aid from the Chinese might cool the raging famine and reduce the risk of instability, but this outcome would annoy many South Koreans. The Chinese ultimately saw it in their interest to contribute the food aid, though they did so without any enthusiasm. The Chinese food aid that did finally arrive was of generally substandard quality—mixed with rocks, corn cobs, and rodent remains—and may have reflected Chinese sentiments on the matter. It was as if they were telling the North Koreans, "Here, take the food, but you won't like what you get." By 1996, China was the largest single donor to North Korea, though it did not direct any of its food aid through the United Nations. Rather, the Chinese admitted to UN officials that they had given the North Koreans carte blanche and in fact encouraged them to keep their military well fed, to avoid a mutiny.

North Korean Aggression and Japan's Diminishing Desire to Help

Japanese aid policy was a very different matter. Its generous food aid in 1995 was followed by meager to nonexistent contributions from 1996 to 1999. Japanese abuses from 1905 to 1945, when the Korean peninsula was its colony, left deep wounds in the Korean psyche for which democratic Japan had long been asked by Koreans to atone. The famine might well have provided a good opportunity for Tokyo to do this, at least in the case of North Korea, but this would have had the opposite effect in South Korea. Japanese trade with Korea was considerable in the South but negligible with the bankrupt North. Trade figures between Japan and North Korea were impressive on their face, but they were superficially deceptive. Most "trade" consisted of contributions made by the million-member Korean Japanese community, which raised money through legalized pachenko parlors, primarily to subsidize otherwise dubious commercial investments in North Korea.

Like the Chinese, the Japanese had a clear interest in avoiding instability on the peninsula, as it would only threaten trade relations and regional security. Japan would inevitably be forced to take sides in any conflict between the North and the South, given that the United States would likely want to use air bases in Okinawa to support U.S. troops in Korea. One of the most prominent and powerful humanitarian figures in the world, UN high commissioner for refugees Sadako Ogata, was a Japanese citizen who was widely admired in Japan—as well as in the Western democracies—for the visibility and acclaim her good reputation brought her country. She and the United States at different points attempted to convince the Japanese government to support a major food aid effort. Both failed.

The decisive factors in Japan's parsimonious response were hardly geostrategic in nature; indeed, they appear strikingly unrelated to general Japanese foreign interests and more related to domestic politics. In February 1997 one of the most respected and influential newspapers in Japan reported that North Koreans had abducted ten Japanese citizens, mostly teenage girls, the first of whom was kidnapped in 1977. None of the women had been heard from since.[6] As bizarre as the story was, it was not new; it had appeared in the media for years. But renewed interest in the story was suspect, as it came just as the Japanese were about to make a commitment to the WFP appeal. Some questioned whether South Korean intelligence was somehow involved, trying to prevent Japan's aid commitment. But regardless of why the story once again made the news, the Japanese public was enraged by the reports and the Diet reflected this anger by ensuring the government would never make a major commitment of food aid. Then, on two separate occasions in May 1997, North Korean nationals were arrested while trying to smuggle illicit drugs into the country.[7] The abductions and drug smuggling operations were followed by news stories that as many as eighteen hundred Japanese women who had emigrated between 1959 and 1982 to marry North Korean men had not been heard from since. Pyongyang rebuffed Japanese demands to contact the kidnapped girls, claiming the kidnappings never occurred. The North Koreans enraged the Japanese even more by demanding food aid in exchange for the right to contact the eighteen hundred Japanese brides. To suggest that the release of these stories had a chilling effect on North Korean–Japanese relations would be an understatement: they produced an arctic freeze.

The tangible consequence that this diplomatic freeze had on the relief response soon became apparent. Members of the Japanese press corps in Washington told several representatives from humanitarian agencies that Tokyo was holding three million MT of old but still edible rice, unmarketable in Japan because of its age. This was twice the tonnage needed to end the famine. Transport costs and transit time to move the rice would have been minimal, given Japan's proximity to North Korea, but the rice was soon to be either dumped in the ocean or sold as pig food. Rep. Tony Hall (D–Ohio) traveled to Tokyo in an unsuccessful attempt to convince the Japanese government to send the surplus to

Pyongyang. The Foreign Ministry did not deny the existence of the rice, but simply informed Hall that the political controversy in the Diet, driven by media coverage and enflamed public opinion, was too intense to approve the contribution.[8] Had the North Korean regime apologized for the earlier incidents, attempted some accommodation to Japanese opinion, and allowed Japanese brides to return to Japan, however embarrassing their stories might have been, the Japanese would likely have reciprocated with a generous donation of food aid. But Japanese and North Korean political interests once again prevented a famine lifeline being thrown to the North Koreans.

North Korea's most serious postwar challenge to Japanese national interests occurred in August 1998, with the test launching of its new three-stage Taepodong missile over Japanese air space. In violation of accepted international practice, North Korea chose not to inform the Japanese that this missile launch would be traversing their territory, further infuriating the Japanese. The North Koreans, who appeared surprised by the angry reaction of neighboring countries and of the United States, quickly announced the missile was not carrying a weapon, only a satellite. What the missile carried was not particularly relevant, however, as future missiles could be made to carry weapons. Rather, it was the range of the missile that caused alarm, as it could reach all areas of Japan and the western and central region of the United States and Canada. Some observers argued that the North Koreans were attempting to alter radically the balance of strategic weaponry in East Asia.[9] The launch stirred a tidal wave of protests in Japan, further diminishing any potential for a serious Japanese food aid contribution. Indeed, the Japanese even protested a sizable food aid pledge the United States had made. As a result of the launch, the Japanese also temporarily withdrew from the Korean Peninsula Energy Development Organization (KEDO) accords. This withdrawal could have meant the demise of KEDO because of Japan's central importance as a financier of the power plant construction in North Korea, but Tokyo later rescinded its withdrawal under pressure from the United States.

Delayed Western Responses

As chapter 7 explains in greater detail, it was not until the summer of 1997 that the United States made any significant aid commitments to replace the dramatic reduction in Japanese and South Korean assistance. The aid itself did not arrive until late summer, after the famine had peaked and death rates were in decline. The European Union was also tardy in promising and providing aid, albeit for very different reasons.

In the case of the United States, once NGOs became aware of the extent of the famine, they organized an effort to force Washington to be more generous in its provision of food aid. An incident in September 1996 forced the abandonment of the entire advocacy effort. That month, a North Korean submarine, perhaps on an espionage mission, ran aground on the South Korean coast. The South Korean military hunted down and killed each of the North Koreans who escaped from the ditched vessel. After that, the South Korean embassy in Washington organized an energetic campaign in the U.S. Congress to counteract the NGOs' lobbying efforts. The embassy argued that, as the strongest Asian ally of the United States, South Korea should have veto power over any famine assistance to North Korea. Seoul was fully prepared to use such a veto, as it believed that any famine assistance would only be diverted to the North Korean military. Thereafter, each time the NGO community raised the food aid issue, congressional and administration opponents argued that the U.S. government must support its South Korean ally. When Kim Dae Jung announced the sunshine policy toward the North, however, neither Congress nor the administration followed with a change in U.S. policy. They continued to connect food aid to the Agreed Framework.

In most emergencies, U.S. leadership can make a remarkable difference in the behavior of the UN agencies, the funding of NGO responses, and the mobilization of international donor government support. This is particularly true when the emergency is either invisible or unappealing, even though many lives are at risk. Although the European Union tends to be more generous and has a larger budget for foreign aid than does the United States, its ability to act is much more constrained because it must balance the foreign interests of member-states. The European Union usually equals or exceeds many U.S. food aid commitments in a visible emergency, but it generally does so as a reaction to a U.S. government decision rather than on its own initiative. U.S. government opposition or disinterest can therefore depress responses to emergencies because the United States is the only stakeholder that can reliably move food in large amounts early, and because its diplomatic leverage is frequently required

to convince other governments to contribute. And in the case of North
Korea, U.S. geostrategic interests as defined by the Pentagon, State Department, and National Security Council staff were in conflict with the
humanitarian instincts of U.S. foreign policy. The European response to
the famine was late, erratic, and short lived.

HOW NORTH KOREA VIEWED THE CRISIS: KIM JONG IL'S DECEMBER 1996 SPEECH

North Korea's strategy in dealing with its food crisis was outlined in a
speech by Kim Jong Il to party cadres in December 1996 on the fiftieth
anniversary of the founding of his alma mater, Kim Il Sung University. A
recording of the speech was smuggled out of North Korea and the text
published in a respected South Korean journal, *Wolgan Chosun.* Unlike
other purported North Korean documents published in South Korea
that bear the disinformation marks of the South Korean Central Intelligence Agency, this speech appears to be genuine. The subtle and oblique
references to the famine reflect the experience of other countries and give
more credibility to the speech as a genuine North Korean document.

In the speech, Kim Jong Il seems obsessed by two central problems:
the famine, which he mentions nineteen times, and the incompetence of
the party elite in dealing with it. He says the "food problem is creating a
state of anarchy," which he blames on the party cadres. Kim bitterly attacks
these cadres for their lack of revolutionary enthusiasm, their effort to
protect themselves from criticism rather than to carry out their jobs,
their attempts to hide problems rather than to seek solutions, and their
attempts to get special privileges for family members.

His speech has enabled analysts to make several observations about
how the leadership viewed the crisis. First, North Korea's leaders clearly
knew they were in trouble and that a crisis could undermine the authority of the state, although in 1996 "anarchy" might have been an exaggeration. Second, they did not appear to know what to do about it. If they
had had an effective strategy, Kim would likely have disclosed some of it
to place his leadership in a somewhat favorable light. Third, Kim seeks
institutional solace in the military and labels it the only efficient and
functional institution in the country. He says the military is suffering
such serious food supply problems itself that the United States might be

encouraged to take advantage of North Korea's weakness and launch an attack. Interviews with refugees in China confirm that the military was having a serious problem, as new recruits appeared to be underweight and stunted. Finally, the entire speech appears to be an elaborate effort by Kim Jong Il to deny any personal responsibility for the cataclysmic events. He explains that his father told him not to involve himself in economic matters, so instead he focused on the military and party matters. It would seem that Kim read the transcripts of party meetings in Russia in 1933 and China in 1960, as his words echo those of Joseph Stalin and Mao Zedong in denying any responsibility for the famines they caused and transferring blame to the party cadres.[10]

The regime also regularly exaggerated the damage done by natural disasters—floods, cyclones, and droughts—in the hopes that this would elicit more international aid. In the floods of 1995 and 1996, the drought of 1997, and the cyclones of 1997 and 1998, Pyongyang exaggerated the hectares damaged, the decline in the harvest, and the number of people affected. When NGOs proposed food-for-work projects to repair damage done by the cyclones, the authorities greatly exaggerated the number of workers who needed food subsidies. The aid community quickly learned to counter with more modest numbers, thus bringing North Korean officials back to reality. The FAO/WFP crop assessments estimated that only 15 percent of the food deficit in the country could be attributed to natural disasters.

This scapegoating by the central government's propaganda organs was reminiscent of the Chinese government's reaction to the famine created by the Great Leap Forward. Mao Zedong, while blaming the Russians for collecting old debts, claimed that the famine was the result of "unprecedented natural calamities." According to one historian,

> China is a vast country, and bad weather causes food shortages somewhere every year. No one but the highest leaders had access to nationwide information about the weather. In fact, given the immobility of the population, few knew what happened in the next region, or even over the next mountain. Many thought then, and still think today, that the famine was caused by natural disasters.[11]

Jasper Becker, another historian of the Chinese famine, carefully reviewed meteorological data from the Great Leap Forward and concluded that no such disasters took place in China during the period of the famine.[12]

NORTH KOREA'S FAMINE RESPONSE AND INTERNATIONAL DIPLOMACY

When the leadership decided to ride out the famine by soliciting food aid rather than by initiating reform, it encouraged competition among ministries over how much food aid they could secure from donor governments. Pitting ministries against one another was a well-established practice that had been followed since North Korea's inception. Early in the crisis the NGOs and UN agencies discovered that each ministry received credit for pledges of assistance and would quarrel openly over who had secured the pledge. Each ministry kept careful records of each donation; if a shipment was late, never arrived, or did not equal the precise amount pledged, the ministry would confront the donor. My first extended conversation with diplomats in Pyongyang during my June 1997 visit centered on a detailed review of an inventory list of seed that World Vision had donated, as it was slightly different from the pledged proportions.

The Foreign Ministry informed NGOs that their staffs ought not to visit North Korea without bringing some donated commodity with them. NGOs would jump through logistical hoops to pledge commodities before departing and then arrange for delivery to occur exactly when they arrived for their visits. Pyongyang realized early in the crisis that field access was as important to NGOs as food aid and medicine were to the regime, so it used control over access to render the highest possible return in commodities. Entry visas, for example, apparently came with a price beyond the simple processing fee. NGOs reported that the regime required $500,000 worth of cash or commodity aid to be pledged for each visa application approval.[13] In an ironic twist, the NGOs and UN agencies providing aid to a mendicant regime had become the supplicants instead of the donors.

The North Korean government found one remarkably effective means of purchasing food and other goods at no cost from the private sector: it would buy goods on credit and then never pay the bill. Many businesses have reported a history of problems extracting payment from Pyongyang. Well before the famine officially began, North Korea defaulted on $76 million it owed for grain purchased between 1991 and 1994 from one U.S. company.[14] North Korea also owed Thailand $14 million for rice shipments, which led to severely strained trade relations between the two countries.[15] North Korea's strategy was effective for a few years, until businesses realized they were being abused and stopped selling to Pyongyang on credit.

In an arrangement carefully monitored by humanitarian agencies, in 1997 the regime negotiated an agreement to barter zinc ore for grain from Cargill, one of the largest U.S. grain companies. The deal collapsed even as the grain shipment was en route, because the zinc ore never left port. The poor condition of mining equipment prevented the extraction of the ore in time for the deal to be consummated. The North Koreans then claimed that the U.S. government had agreed to subsidize the agreement, when in fact it had only said it would facilitate the export license for Cargill.[16]

Chinese merchants complained even more bitterly about North Korean business practices. Trade with North Korea, one merchant related, is conducted on a barter basis only, because "if you send them goods they will never pay you."[17] Some Chinese businesses were driven to bankruptcy because of North Korea's refusal to pay its bills, which of course only exacerbated border tensions.[18]

The UN Development Program arranged for the Chinese to send a delegation of senior agricultural experts to Pyongyang in the spring of 1997. This delegation advised the North Koreans to "do a Deng Xiaoping" and adopt a Western model of market capitalism, particularly in their agricultural sector. The North Korean reaction was immediate and uncompromising: no reform would be considered. Deng, they replied, was a traitor to communism and would never be a model for North Korea. The North Korean reaction did not amuse the Chinese, who were tired of dealing with their inflexible and demanding neighbor, so the Chinese threatened to stop providing food aid. But the North Koreans skillfully leveraged what little remaining diplomatic influence they had by beginning negotiations with Taiwan for regular weekly airline flights between Taipei and Pyongyang, in exchange for which the Taiwanese government promised 500,000 MT of food. The Chinese were enraged to learn about the negotiations between their client state and their fifty-year nemesis, but they did make a substantial food aid commitment to North Korea, after which Pyongyang broke off the negotiations with Taipei.

North Korea may have appealed for food aid from the United Nations and donor governments, but it refused to behave according to its mendicant status. It would allow NGOs and UN agencies just enough access to the country to appear to satisfy donor government insistence on minimum accountability for distribution of food aid for public relations purposes. But it would not allow enough access for aid workers to determine how many people had died and where the need was most acute so that the relief agencies could target food distributions. The North Koreans ensured from the beginning of the relief effort that they, not outsiders, would control the distribution of the food aid.

Early in 2000 the North Korean government embarked on a diplomatic offensive to open new contacts with the outside world, a policy encouraged with aggressive U.S. coaxing. Thus North Korea established diplomatic relations with Italy, Kim Jong Il visited the Chinese embassy in Pyongyang, and then he met with Chinese leaders in Beijing, where some agreement was reached on economic reform measures the North Koreans might undertake. In July and August 2001 Kim Jong Il traveled by train across Russia to Moscow for talks with President Putin, the first talks between the two countries' leaders since the Soviet Union recognized South Korea. In June 2000, in what was widely applauded as a turning point in North–South relations, Kim Dae Jung made a three-day state visit to Kim Jong Il in Pyongyang. While little was concluded in the way of substantive agreements, the very meeting of the two leaders, the warm rhetoric, and the photographic opportunities suggested a turning point had been reached diplomatically. North Korean leaders may well have made the decision, with the famine behind them, to consider more aggressive reforms of their system. Alternatively, they may be pursuing the very same policy they followed during the famine, using diplomacy to increase international aid from China, South Korea, Japan, Russia, and the United States while assiduously resisting internal reform. Only time will confirm which interpretation turns out to be true.

THE POLITICS OF THE FAMINE: THE BATTLE IN WASHINGTON

I N AUGUST 1994, after a negotiating session on the nuclear issue, a member of the North Korean delegation asked Ken Quinones, a career State Department official, if the United States would provide North Korea with a million metric tons of food aid. Quinones, taken aback by the bold request, relayed the message to Washington, but the answer was an unequivocal no. The North Koreans nevertheless persisted in asking until State Department officials finally showed them the statutory requirements for food aid eligibility through Public Law 480, under which countries like North Korea are eligible to receive aid only if they are suffering from a disaster such as a famine. U.S. food aid policy toward North Korea dates back to this revealing incident, though few in Washington at the time understood the profound ramifications of this exchange.

A few months later, in response to reports of a cholera epidemic, Quinones arranged through private charitable channels for the shipment of five hundred thousand measures of cholera vaccine. He did this with the approval of his superior, Ambassador Robert Gallucci, who was leading the nuclear negotiations with the North Koreans. From the start, Gallucci argued for the provision of humanitarian aid to North Korea with no political strings attached, but he was alone among senior State Department officials outside the Bureau of Intelligence and Research. Gallucci and Quinones did notice that the provision of the vaccine had a salutary effect during the negotiations, building goodwill among their normally suspicious North Korean interlocutors.[1]

141

EMERGING EVIDENCE OF A
NORTH KOREAN FAMINE

Between 1992 and 1994, U.S. companies were engaged in brisk commercial trade with North Korea; a total of $120 million in corn and wheat
was exported to North Korea, an amount equal in tonnage to Soviet
shipments to North Korea. But U.S. shipments ended in 1994 when the
grain companies cut off North Korea's credit because it was not servic-
ing its $80 million debt. From this alone, the United States had evidence
a full year before the floods of 1995 that a food crisis might be imminent,
though the evidence was by no means definitive. But U.S. intelligence
also had reliable evidence of severe food shortages in North Korea during
the winter of 1991–92, the same year that the WFP had refused North
Korea's request for food aid.[2] The million-ton request to Quinones may
have been a reaction not only to the cutting off of Chinese and Soviet food
subsidies, but also to the termination of commercial shipments from the
United States and Canada.

Quinones returned to North Korea in the autumn of 1995, after the
floods, as part of a KEDO inspection team touring the northwestern
region. Quinones was surprised by the extent of flood damage in agricultural areas and by the clear signs of malnutrition and hunger among
the people. Even North Korean officials in his delegation appeared to be
lethargic; many slept half the day, a sign of reduced caloric intake. Upon
his return to Washington, Quinones reported that a food crisis appeared
to be under way—a report that was confirmed by Japanese and South
Korean intelligence officers who had evidence of starvation deaths. The
U.S. Central Intelligence Agency (CIA), the Defense Intelligence Agency
(DIA), and the Pentagon dismissed these reports as a cynical attempt by
North Korea to obtain humanitarian aid. According to these agencies,
the State Department had been "taken for a ride by the North Koreans."[3]

Quinones's reports touched off a debate over conditions in North
Korea that was not settled until the summer of 1996, when two trips into
the field made intelligence analysts change their assessment of the crisis.
First, the Office of Foreign Disaster Assistance (OFDA), the disaster
response unit within the U.S. Agency for International Development,
decided to send Sue Lautze to conduct a humanitarian assessment of the
nutritional situation in the spring of 1996. Her report, which will be

discussed in greater detail in chapter 8, concluded that a food emergency might in fact be under way. Second, as part of the ongoing KEDO inspections, Quinones again journeyed to the northwestern provinces, this time with a dozen U.S. military officers. The officers were shocked by what they saw: dead bodies on the sides of the roads, and emaciated people whose clothing hung on their sticklike bodies. A food crisis clearly seemed to be under way. When the officers returned with their stories, CIA and Pentagon skepticism faded. Interviews with defectors and refugees escaping into China confirmed Lautze's and Quinones's analyses. Even this growing consensus over the existence of a deadly famine did not stimulate a robust U.S. response.[4]

Interestingly, State Department spokesman Nicholas Burns did not refer to the food crisis in North Korea as a "famine" until more than a year later, on July 17, 1997, after the Clinton administration announced a pledge of 100,000 MT of food aid. In his press briefing that day, Burns reported, "there's a famine underway."[5] Before then, that "f" word was never used publicly—the preferred language was more gentle, more benign, and less alarming. It was as though the existence of a famine depended on how the United States responded to it. The State Department had reacted in much the same way to the Rwandan crisis, when "genocide" was not used to describe the killing of nearly a million Tutsis because it might have had uncomfortable implications under the provisions of the genocide convention.

THE POLITICS OF U.S. FOOD AID TO NORTH KOREA

Several factors constrained the U.S. government from offering anything other than token amounts of food aid in 1995 and 1996. The first was history. The entire U.S. foreign policy apparatus had grown up on the principle that North Korea was one of the country's most dangerous and irrational enemies, a proposition the North Korean regime did little to discourage and a great deal to confirm. Feeding one's enemies, regardless of how severe the crisis, would have required officials to disregard that principle. Thus, bureaucratic inertia and four decades of unrelenting hostility militated against a change in policy. Second, critics in the bureaucracy argued on a more mundane level that the food would be diverted for military purposes. This fear was repeatedly expressed by the Pentagon and by military officers at the National Security Council (NSC), as well as by members of Congress of both parties in letters to the administration. Finally, a high-level debate raged over the definition of a famine. A senior USAID official told me in the spring of 1997 that a famine could not occur from a structural food deficit, only from a natural disaster. Since the UN reports clearly indicated that 85 percent of North Korea's food deficit was structural, he said a famine could not be occurring. The same debate over the definition of famine was to occur within and among NGOs working in North Korea a year later.

Senior officers in the State Department's Office of Korean Affairs had previously opposed anything but token food aid, but beginning in the spring of 1996 they began revising their view as evidence of the crisis's severity accumulated. They made their recommendations not for humanitarian purposes but as a diplomatic carrot for use in political negotiations. In the summer of 1996, Chuck Kartman, then the principal deputy assistant secretary of state for East Asian and Pacific affairs, told UN officials that food aid was a central issue in the negotiations with the North Koreans. If the North Koreans agreed to participate in the four-party talks and progress was made, then they would get the food, and in addition the United States might encourage other reluctant donors to contribute toward the WFP appeal. If the North Koreans were not cooperative, however, they would receive no aid. Kartman was not the author of the policy, having inherited it from his predecessors in the Bureau of East Asian and Pacific Affairs. Pyongyang did not object to the use of food aid as a carrot; it simply wanted the carrot before it sat down and talked. The United States and South Korea, however, took the view that Pyongyang ought not to get its carrot until after it entered the talks and changed its behavior.

Successive presidents had insulated humanitarian food aid from the geopolitical strategic interests of the United States, so that the humanitarian imperative could operate relatively unimpeded. The ethical consequence of the policy should the North Korean government have refused to cooperate in the four-party talks was the starvation of the North Korean people. Punishing the common people in a totalitarian regime as a means of forcing their government to change its behavior has seldom been successful given that the people have no control over their government's behavior, and their government cares little what happens to them. The government officials eat and the people die.

This formulation, while full of ethical red flags, fit well into the traditional art of diplomacy. Diplomacy is after all an attempt to affect the behavior of another country by the use of incentives and disincentives. Diplomats pull various levers to influence this behavior, such as commitments of military and development assistance, the threat of military power or the promise of its protection, or the threat of economic sanctions. Other countries make decisions based on the promise or threat of these tools of diplomacy. In most situations these instruments of diplomacy are entirely appropriate, but not in a famine. The ethical dilemmas of this sort of diplomacy have fueled historic conflicts between the U.S. government and various NGOs and church groups. Since the time of St. Augustine, Catholic social teaching in the just war tradition has argued that the moral order constrains the use of force by the nation-state in the service of national interest. These same ethical constraints ought to limit the use of widespread human suffering as a means of affecting the behavior of other states.

The use of food aid as a weapon of diplomacy has a shorter history, given that food aid as one form of foreign assistance dates back only to the World War I; as an annual form of foreign assistance, only to the 1950s. The notion of denying food aid to a country in the midst of a famine became a public controversy during the Ethiopian crisis of 1984–85, when a million people died of starvation or starvation-related illnesses. The U.S. ambassador to the United Nations, Jeanne Kirkpatrick, and several staff of the National Security Council successfully opposed the commitment of food aid to Ethiopia, governed by one of the most brutal marxist dictators in Africa and one of the Soviet Union's premier client states in the developing world, based on an argument similar to the one members of Congress and the Clinton administration were making on North Korea: Why give aid to our enemies? A bureaucratic coalition led by USAID administrator Peter MacPherson and Gene Dewey, deputy assistant secretary of state for refugees, succeeded in overturning the policy by appealing to President Reagan, who announced the Reagan doctrine that "a hungry child knows no politics": famine assistance in the future would be based on need not on American geostrategic calculations.

Given the political sensitivity of sending any aid under any circumstances to one of the United States' greatest security threats, the decision to commit food aid to North Korea, with or without strings attached, fell to the White House. Catherine Bertini reported that State Department officials told her in 1996, "WFP's involvement in the DPRK has become the focus of very high level attention in the USG. This receives almost daily attention from the White House and the NSC."[6] President Bill Clinton did not announce a major shipment of food aid until July 1997, when it was too late. Although the administration had growing evidence of the famine's existence much earlier, White House staff I interviewed said Clinton was concerned about North Korea but did not act earlier because the contradictory evidence provided insufficient grounds for a major relief program.[7] In fact, U.S. intelligence estimates after Quinones's return in June 1996 showed that people were dying of starvation, a conclusion Japanese and South Korean intelligence had reached in the fall of 1995.[8] The White House had evidence of a famine a full year before any serious commitments of food aid were made. Historically, the only way the deeply held prejudices of the U.S. foreign policy apparatus could be overcome concerning an issue as provocative as food aid to North Korea was through presidential leadership or media pressure. Presidential leadership was not forthcoming, and the North Koreans steadfastly resisted graphic media coverage of the famine.

Without presidential attention, the natural instincts of the foreign affairs apparatus of the U.S. government—the Pentagon, USAID, the State Department, DIA, and the CIA—drive policy. An example of this occurred in May 1996 when Rep. Bill Richardson (D–N.Mex.) visited Pyongyang. With the approval of the NSC, Richardson offered the North Koreans 1 million MT of food aid annually in exchange for their participation in the four-party talks and their cooperation in returning the remains of U.S. soldiers who were missing in action from the Korean War. The North Korean officials accepted the offer. When Defense Department officials learned of the offer, they were irate. The NSC told Richardson to withdraw the offer.

As much as the NSC was constrained, USAID was even more limited. An independent agency that reports to the secretary of state, but not through State Department channels, USAID has been the traditional repository of the humanitarian instinct in foreign policy. Not surprisingly, its role has at times put it at odds with the State Department and the Defense Department. According to career USAID officials I interviewed, the agency had more political constraints placed on it by the State Department and the NSC in its dealings with North Korea than it had experienced in any famine since Ethiopia in 1985.[9] Beginning in January 1995 the State Department had been pressing for USAID's abolition and absorption, to provide the former with another lever of influence for conducting diplomacy. State had managed to have Senator Jesse Helms (R–NC) assume public responsibility for the effort to subsume USAID, even while the leadership of State worked to undermine the agency during the battle within the Clinton administration over the agency's future. Thus USAID was not well positioned in the fight over food for the famine. OFDA argued for the provision of food aid to North Korea in meetings during most of 1996 and succeeded in getting the NSC and State to approve modest purchases early on, before food became an instrument of negotiation. Brian Atwood, administrator of USAID, called NSC officials several times during the spring of 1997 in an attempt to stop Chuck Kartman from using food aid as a carrot in the four-party talks. He argued that since Nick Burns was publicly denying that the administration was using food aid as an instrument of negotiation, he ought not to be allowed to politicize the aid during the negotiations. The White House apparently took no action.[10]

One might attribute the critical absence of presidential leadership during the summer of 1996 to the presidential campaign, during which Republican candidate Robert Dole insisted that food aid be connected to U.S. national security interests. This could explain Clinton administration reluctance to act before the November elections, but this argument does not help explain the administration's refusal to provide aid after Clinton was reelected. Congressional pressure too could be blamed, but, despite four years of congressional threats to cut off aid, no legislation prohibiting food aid ever reached the White House. The fact remains that the White House knew well, yet chose to ignore, what was taking place. It refused to acknowledge publicly the existence of the famine, because it knew that pressure would have mounted for a humanitarian response, which in turn would have limited the State Department's ability to use food aid in diplomatic negotiations with North Korea. Thus, the White House placed the humanitarian imperative on the back burner for another crucial nine months just as the famine was peaking.

THE ROLE OF NGOS IN SHAPING U.S. POLICY

During 1996 and early 1997, NGO leaders were oblivious to the furious debate occurring within the U.S. government over the severity of the crisis, the amount of aid that should be given, and whether it should be contingent on participation in the four-party talks. Based on UN crop assessments and some NGO reports, it is clear that NGO leaders did know something was wrong and that a crisis might be developing, but they misunderstood its severity. The Office of Korean Affairs continued to tell NGO leaders that the intelligence estimates about the existence of the famine were ambiguous and murky, and that without evidence the United States would initiate no large-scale food program. Even as late as March 1997, senior State Department officials told the Venerable Pomnyun and me that evidence for the existence of the famine was ambiguous. They admitted that a food problem existed, but they said it had not yet become critical. Yet, that same month, an internal UN memorandum commented that the State Department

> estimates the starvation-related mortality rate in the region (the Northeastern and to a lesser extent Northwestern provinces) to be between 5 and 10 percent and says that current PDS ration levels (150 grams per day) have recently been restricted to men who perform hard labor. Women in the region are reportedly now receiving no ration at all. I was not told the source of the information, but State seems pretty confident of it.[11]

Clearly, the Office of Korean Affairs knew that a famine was under way, but it was not about to provide more ammunition to the NGOs' campaign to stop the famine with U.S. food aid.

Nevertheless, NGOs were to play a large role in shaping U.S. policy. In December 1996 Ellsworth Culver, vice president of Mercy Corps International, a well-respected, faith-based NGO of modest size, organized an off-the-record meeting of high-ranking individuals troubled by the warning signs of famine in North Korea. I attended the meeting as a representative of World Vision, the NGO for which I worked. Representatives of a dozen other NGOs also attended the meeting, which included presentations by diplomats from the North Korean mission to the United Nations in New York.

Culver and Mercy Corps were later to play an important role in the negotiations between the United States and North Korea over both the food aid issue and efforts to normalize relations between the North and South. Both the State Department and the North Korean Foreign Ministry regularly used Mercy Corps to deliver diplomatic messages between the two capitals, which did not have diplomatic relations. Culver's trustworthiness and gentle manner eased the otherwise suspicious and sometimes paranoid reaction of the North Koreans to the outside world. That an NGO could play this role was one more bit of evidence of the growing influence such organizations held in international affairs. The conference to which Culver invited me launched this rising role of Mercy Corps in the North Korean drama.

The conference was held in a historic setting: Musgrove Plantation, the country estate of the R. J. Reynolds family on the Georgia coast on Kiawah Island. The estate was made up of a set of elegant smaller stone guest houses, each used by different members of the Reynolds family, of 1920 vintage with high ceilings, fireplaces in each room, polished wide board floors, and idyllic views of the surrounding Georgian marshes. It was here in December 1976 that Jimmy Carter held the first meeting of his cabinet prior to his inauguration. Given my own conservative political prejudices, I was somewhat unnerved by the ideology of the funding organization for the conference: the R. J. Reynolds family trust, which focused on improving relationships between the United States and rogue regimes such as Cuba, Libya, and Iraq.

The Musgrove Conference turned out to be a seminal event in NGO efforts to combat the famine. It was at this conference that a State Department official for the first time indicated to NGOs that aid was being used as a carrot to induce the North Koreans into the four-party talks. It galvanized an unlikely coalition of organizations and people who shared one thing in common: the desire to prevent or relieve a famine in North Korea. The NGOs agreed that a major effort was needed to publicize the

North Korean crisis and to force an otherwise reluctant Congress and executive branch to send food aid before it was too late.

Among the only members of Congress to focus attention on the crisis were Bill Richardson and Tony Hall (D–Ohio). Hall had journeyed to North Korea in August 1996 to observe nutritional conditions and was stunned by the severity of the situation. He made six trips to the country between 1996 and 1999, many of which took him to parts of the country that no foreigners, not even UN staff members, had ever visited. His aggressive efforts to see the face of the famine at times grated on North Korean sensibilities. One diplomat asked whether all U.S. congressmen were as stubborn and demanding, and whether they all traveled abroad on U.S. Air Force planes; North Koreans probably suspected Hall and the air force were spying on them under the guise of a humanitarian mission. To increase the accuracy and depth of his reporting, Hall would take reporters, medical experts, and his own translators as often as the North Koreans would allow. Hall's opinion pieces in major newspapers, his trips, and his media appearances when he returned put North Korea on the front pages, but the NGO community was afraid that this was not enough to change administration policy.

Events in January 1997, one month after the Musgrove Conference, would profoundly affect the course of the coalition effort for the remainder of the year. To encourage North Korean participation in the four-party talks, State Department officials promised to meet with representatives of InterAction, a coalition of U.S. NGOs, and encourage increased private aid to North Korea. The meeting was attended by essentially the same group of NGOs that had participated in the Musgrove Conference, along with officials from the State Department, the NSC, and USAID. During the discussion, Chuck Kartman, the lead U.S. diplomat conducting negotiations with the North Koreans, suggested that U.S. policy toward the North Korean food emergency would be based on a carrot-and-stick approach, or, as he put it, a policy of "tough love." If the North Koreans were cooperative in the negotiations, then the United States would be cooperative with food aid. If they were not, the United States would not be, either.[12] The State Department had been quietly using food aid to entice the North Koreans into negotiations for eight months; this was the second time a senior administration official had so explicitly described the policy to NGO leaders.

Kartman's diplomatic formulation suddenly made clear to us why U.S. commitments for North Korean food aid had been so minimal. Traditionally, the U.S. government contributed at least one-third and sometimes up to three-fourths of the food needed to stop a famine. U.S. contributions to North Korea were token considering the food aid gap, the progress of the famine, and Washington's traditional generosity. At the time of our meeting with Kartman, the United States had committed less than 20,000 MT to North Korea: 6,400 MT in February 1996, and 13,000 MT in June 1996. In February 1997, Washington committed an additional 27,000 MT, followed in April 1997 by 50,000 MT, and in July 1997 by 100,000 MT. It was not until 1998 that food aid began to flow to North Korea to a degree commensurate with the severity of the crisis: at that time, the United States committed 500,000 MT. Yet, famine deaths had dropped substantially by the first six months of 1998; the famine was over before large-scale U.S. aid arrived.

Kartman's explicit statement of administration policy appalled the NGO representatives in the room. As the chairman of InterAction's Committee on Disaster Response, I reminded Kartman of the Reagan Doctrine, condemned its violation for the first time since 1985 as a dangerous precedent, and argued that denying food aid to North Korea was tantamount to using the mass starvation of poor people as a means for pressuring a totalitarian regime. Such a policy was ethically indefensible. Kartman appeared taken aback by my heated response. The conversation proceeded in more measured and cautious tones, but during the subsequent press conference—which included representatives from the *Washington Times* and the *Christian Science Monitor* but which was otherwise attended almost entirely by the Asian media—I continued my attack on the administration's policy.

It was apparent to me that my confrontation with Kartman was not about to change U.S. policy. I decided to advance the same argument in a newspaper commentary, only in greater detail. When I approached the *Washington Post*'s Sunday opinion page editor with my idea, he expressed great skepticism about the existence of the famine. He asked me how I knew there was a famine in North Korea, given there had been no media reports, and he wondered what evidence I had that the administration was in fact pursuing this policy. After an extended discussion about my own experience with famines, the evidence that NGOs had amassed on what was happening in North Korea, and Kartman's clear statement of administration policy, the editor agreed to run the article (reproduced here as an appendix, pp. 249–252). Its publication provoked a debate, albeit one limited to the foreign policy elite, about the conditions that should accompany humanitarian aid. According to one career diplomat, the secretary of state was quite angry about the column.

For much of the first half of 1997, the State Department spokesman regularly told reporters at the daily press briefings that the United States had actually been generous in supplying famine relief for the past year and a half and that it had been responsive to WFP appeals. His defense was misleading, as the appeal reflected the amount of food aid the WFP thought donor governments would really contribute, rather than what was actually needed. To call the U.S. response miserly would have been charitable. Associated Press reporter George Getta regularly asked Burns whether the administration was using food aid as a weapon during diplomatic negotiations, and Burns regularly denied it:

> QUESTION: "Are you establishing some sort of linkage between food contributions and these other issues?"
>
> MR. BURNS: "No, we have never had a linkage. . . . We do not link the food requests to other issues in our relationship."[13]

Burns's denial was not even an artful dodge; it was simply not true. The State Department was purchasing North Korean participation in the four-party talks with food aid, shipments being made just before each of the sessions.

It was becoming clear to the NGO community that the North Koreans did not appreciate hearing public critiques of their failed economic policies; many of us feared they would retaliate with greater restrictions on NGO field operations. Senior North Korean officials complained bitterly to World Vision representatives about public U.S. critiques of the famine. When the World Vision officials replied that North Korea would not have received any food aid had the NGOs not campaigned strongly for it, their hosts replied that they knew and appreciated that fact, but they said they did not want any more criticism accompanying the campaign. This tension reflected the classic conflict between effective advocacy on public policy and field operations on the ground: an NGO could not do both simultaneously without complications. Some of the more operationally driven NGOs with weak public policy mandates resisted explaining the reality of the famine to the Western public in an effort to avoid reprisals by the North Korean authorities. I argued in reply that NGO activities required resources and that no resources would be available unless media pressure succeeded in overcoming the paralysis of donor governments that should have been providing food aid. Private fund-raising efforts could never hope to produce enough money to buy enough food to end the famine.

The NGO advocacy effort had to be directed toward changing donor government policy, not toward private fund-raising. To that end, the Stop the Famine Committee was created in March 1997. It included the original coalition of NGOs that attended the Musgrove Conference, as well as the U.S. Conference of Catholic Bishops, the National Council of Churches, the Carter Center, and the Association of Evangelical Relief and Development Organizations, which included forty-two evangelical Christian NGOs. The committee had two principal objectives: increase public awareness of the existence of the famine, and then change U.S. government policy toward food aid for North Korea. World Vision had commissioned a national survey of U.S. public opinion about the famine in April 1997, and the committee used it to construct a strategy.[14] The survey asked whether people knew about the famine; despite the paucity of media coverage, 20 percent said they did. It asked whether they would support giving food aid to North Korea, which they were reminded was still a communist regime; they said they would, by a margin of 64.6 percent to 23.5 percent. And it asked whether they would still support food aid knowing that South Korea, a U.S. ally and North Korea's principal adversary, opposed famine aid; even then, a plurality continued to support famine relief by a margin of 48.5 percent to 34.3 percent. This survey suggested that Americans would not tolerate famine relief being used as a tool of diplomacy if they knew the famine was occurring, and that they would support a generous U.S. government response. We simply had to increase public awareness, an undertaking that did not prove simple at all.

For the first six months of the year, two World Vision media staff officers, Kathleen Brown and Sara Anderson, tried unsuccessfully to encourage the major U.S. media outlets to cover the famine. The Stop the Famine Committee in April began an unprecedented television advertising campaign proposed by the World Vision public relations staff. The three ads, broadcast in the greater Washington, D.C., area during national news programs, criticized the U.S. government for using food aid as a weapon of diplomacy in the North Korean famine. The ad campaign provided the committee with a great deal of free publicity as well, such as print and electronic media interviews of members of the coalition. These interviews stayed focused on one key idea: U.S. food aid to relieve the North Korean famine should not be contingent on any geostrategic calculation. In its written communications, Stop the Famine played up a theme I had struck in my *Washington Post* commentary: the United States would be endangering its thirty-seven thousand troops in South Korea if it let the famine take its course, given the unpredictable political and security consequences of famines. These communications concluded with an obligatory defense of food monitoring as a means of ensuring that the food aid went to the people in need and not to the military.

Careful cultivation of the media proved its worth in June 1997, when coverage of the famine finally exploded on the front pages of the major newspapers, radio and television news magazines, and talk shows. A *New York Times* article by Barbara Croesette proved decisive in convincing other media outlets of the legitimacy of the story.[15] But as the media coverage of the famine increased, so too did Washington's opposition to helping North Korea. Several powerful members of the House of Representatives sent a letter warning to the Clinton administration against providing any substantial food aid to North Korea unless four conditions were met, three of which, rigorously interpreted, were nearly impossible to satisfy. Among other things, the administration had to prove that none of the food was being diverted to the North Korean military. The letter was signed by the chairman of the House Foreign Affairs committee, Benjamin Gilman (R–N.Y.), along with the ranking Democrat on the committee, Lee Hamilton (D–Ind.), as well as by Doug Beureter (R–Kan.), who served as chairman of the House Committee on Agriculture, and by Senator Pat Roberts (R–Kansas). These four men were not traditional opponents of foreign assistance; Beureter, a moderate conservative, had for more than a decade been one of the strongest supporters of food aid and NGO work in the developing world. Their warnings made NGO efforts to change the policy of a reluctant administration even more difficult. Research reports by the House Republican Conference, led by Rep. Christopher Cox (R–Calif.), claimed that all the food aid being sent to North Korea was provisioning the country's military and ensuring the continuation of the regime. A House delegation of Democrats and Republicans from the Intelligence Committee traveled to North Korea and announced that the military was diverting food aid, though they could provide no evidence to support their claim.

On July 14, 1997, after months of sustained attacks by the NGO coalition, the Clinton administration announced that it would double its previous pledges of food assistance to North Korea with an additional 100,000 MT of mostly corn. It remains unclear why the administration was willing to pledge this additional food aid. Part of the decision may be attributed to the campaign waged by the NGO coalition and Congressman Hall's efforts to end the famine. The White House claimed that the WFP appeal in late June was the tacit explanation for the administration's decision. But perhaps more important may have been North Korea's assertion in the negotiations over the four-party talks that its participation was contingent on a further pledge of food aid. This element in the United States' decision cannot be ignored, given Pyongyang's previous success in getting its demands met.[16] Perhaps the NGO campaign provided the Clinton administration with a convenient defense to hard-line opposition in Washington. Whatever the reasons for the decision, however, more food aid was on the way.

The NGOs' victory celebration was short-lived, as opponents of food aid began to marshal their considerable forces against the administration's initiative. Congressman Cox, a member of the NSC during the Reagan administration, took advantage of congressional suspicions of the North Korean regime. He proposed an amendment to the foreign affairs budget that would stop all U.S. government food aid to North Korea, though it would leave untouched private food aid from the NGOs. In a letter sent in mid-July to his House colleagues, he argued that "this aid has been directed not to ordinary citizens but to the million-man military —the apparatus of repression that keeps Kim Jong Il in power."[17] This argument was similar to the one made by the research staff reports of the House Republican Conference that Cox chaired. But neither Cox nor the conference provided any evidence showing a diversion of food aid to the military.

The Stop the Famine Committee took two actions simultaneously. It sent a letter to members of Congress attacking the Cox amendment, arguing that food aid in a famine was the morally correct action to take however abusive the regime. The letter quoted the Reagan Doctrine that a hungry child knows no politics and added that food would stabilize a highly unpredictable situation that could endanger U.S. troops. The denial of food aid to North Korea would be the equivalent of "throwing a lit torch into a dry forest," the letter said. It assured members of Congress that the NGOs could take measures to ensure that food went to the intended beneficiaries and was not diverted by the military. The letter was signed by the sixteen members of the Stop the Famine Committee, most of whom had significant and identifiable constituencies. Like nearly every coalition action, the letter provoked an internal debate among the NGOs themselves. Several refused to sign because they found the letter too provocative and because they did not wish to annoy members of Congress, and still others continued to object to using the word "famine" to characterize the crisis.

On July 16, the North Koreans shelled a Southern guard post with artillery rounds, destroying it and injuring some South Korean soldiers. This incident only fueled the attack by congressional opponents of food aid. Unfortunately, it was not the only time that a North Korean government action would damage the efforts of those working to help the North Korean people. During each phase of the NGO advocacy campaign on behalf of the North Korean people, the North Korean regime could be expected to undermine the effort by some egregious political or military provocation. The effort to stop the Cox amendment was no exception to the North Korean regime's proclivity for self-destructive behavior. Indeed it became a standard line of dark humor among the NGOs that the North Korean military, which appeared to be behind the rash of incidents, were on the side of the State Department and NSC on food aid.

THE ROLE OF THE KOREAN AMERICAN COMMUNITY

Although Americans generally supported the efforts of the NGOs, they were not sufficiently motivated to write to their representatives in Congress to stop the Cox amendment. The only motivated group of voters intimately familiar with the devastation of the famine was the overwhelmingly anticommunist Korean American community, which the South Korean embassy and Congress had assumed was also opposed to aid. That opposition had diminished, though.

In the autumn of 1996, I had visited Rep. Jay Kim (R–Calif.) along with Doug Coutts, who was then the director of the WFP office at the United Nations in New York, and Russ Kerr, the World Vision vice president for humanitarian relief, to urge Kim's support for food aid. I did not look forward to the meeting. In a congressional hearing on the subject of North Korean aid, Kim had stridently attacked a UN official testifying before the committee for being a communist dupe. In our conversation, Kim voiced his strong opposition to food aid, which he was certain would be diverted to the military. After a long and difficult discussion, however, he began to listen to our side. I assured him that World Vision president Bob Seiple, a decorated Vietnam veteran, and I were similarly suspicious of North Korean intentions, but I asked whether he thought we should let poor people die because we opposed a government they never elected. By the conclusion of the conversation, Kim agreed to sponsor a bill to double the U.S. commitment to 60,000 MT, provided the North Koreans would allow him to visit some villages. He wanted to observe the food distributions and determine for himself whether there was a famine. Coutts agreed to raise Kim's request with the North Korean delegation to the United Nations, though we knew full well that Pyongyang would never consent to the visit of a Korean American of Kim's ideology.

Kim's position was not unusual; indeed, it reflected the Korean American community's two conflicting sentiments toward the issue of food aid to the North. Its members hated the communist regime for having provoked the Korean War, which had killed three million Koreans, and for its continued threats toward South Korea. But as stories of terrible suffering made their way into South Korean newspapers, to which the Korean American community had easy access, anger and hatred were overcome by fear. Korean Americans wished the regime would collapse as soon as possible, so they could see their long-lost relatives, but they were not prepared to allow their own families to die in a famine. Though it is difficult to confirm their estimates, several Korean Americans claim that 50 percent of their community still have relatives in North Korea.

I met with a prominent Korean American pastor in New York in the summer of 1997 who expressed some interest in having his congregation contribute to World Vision toward the relief effort in the North, though he had deep reservations about the potential for aid diversions. He explained that he had escaped from North Korea as the war began, joined the South Korean army, and rose in its ranks to become a battalion commander. He introduced me to his senior deacon, a man who managed the business affairs of this large church and who had served as the pastor's executive officer in the same battalion during the war. Not surprisingly, the pastor and deacon expressed palpable hatred toward the North. As the conversation proceeded, I explained the results of World Vision's research into mortality rates, based on interviews with North Korean refugees in China. I mentioned a particularly hard-hit city where 10 percent of the population may have died by the early months of 1997. The pastor hung his head in deep pain, covering his face with his hands: this city, he explained in a broken voice, was his hometown, where his entire family still lived, if indeed they were still alive. Whatever hatred he may have harbored toward the Pyongyang regime was at that instant overcome by the thought of what his family was enduring.

Our efforts to defeat the Cox amendment were thus focused on the Korean American public, particularly in California. We asked a prominent Presbyterian pastor in Seattle, himself Korean born, to call all of the Korean churches in Southern California to urge them to speak to Cox and express their strong opposition to his amendment. When the campaign concluded its work, more than three hundred pastors pledged to make the telephone calls and to mobilize their congregations to do the same. Thousands of church newsletters were mailed to congregations across the country, and a new humanitarian relief organization, the Korean American Sharing Movement (KASM), was formed in the Korean community to raise money to alleviate suffering in the famine. With the help of a KASM translator, I went on Korean radio in Los Angeles to urge people to call their legislators about the amendment. When Cox withdrew his amendment several days later and accepted benign compromise language proposed by Representative Hall, it became clear how successful the calling campaign had been, and more important how powerful the Korean American public could be on the food aid issue when it was organized and informed.

THE ROLE OF CONGRESS

Two events in rapid succession placed North Korea back on the U.S. policymaking agenda in the summer of 1998. Because of falling grain prices, a slow-moving agricultural economy, the Asian recession, and the approaching November elections, President Clinton—with the tacit support of the Republicans in Congress—announced that the federal government would purchase several million metric tons of grain to force up prices. The grain, the president promised, would go to feed the hungry in major emergencies around the world: Sudan, Kosovo, Indonesia, and North Korea. Within a few weeks, however, the administration without explanation quietly dropped North Korea from the list of beneficiaries of this wheat purchase. When a delegation of NGOs visited Len Rogers, the USAID deputy assistant administrator for emergency assistance, they found him uncharacteristically circumspect, even evasive, about North Korea's ambiguous position on the list.

Rumors began circulating in Congress that U.S. intelligence sources had revealed shocking new information about some undetermined construction activity in North Korea that would likely shut down the existing food program, let alone any additional commitments. Then the White House announced that aerial photographs showed a massive tunneling program was under way that intelligence analysts believed could be a facility for the production of nuclear weapons. An acrimonious debate ensued about the proper U.S. reaction to this construction effort. Defense Secretary William Cohen, the lone Republican member of the Clinton cabinet, announced that the construction did not violate the KEDO agreement. Members of Congress disagreed: they argued that the North Koreans were trashing the KEDO accords.

More than any other single act by the regime, however, the surprise launch of a Taepodong missile on August 31, 1998, alarmed the U.S. foreign policy establishment, because it directly threatened American soil. The reason for the launch may have been Kim Jong Il's desire to show his toughness and power to his own military and his hungry people and thus strengthen his internal hand. Whatever the internal rationale, however, the launch was yet another egregious affront reducing the incentive of the U.S. government to provide more food aid. House Republicans warned the North Korean foreign ministry that if further missile tests

were conducted, they would immediately impose a set of draconian sanctions against the regime. In response, the North Korean government
backed down; a promised second missile launch did not take place.

Congressman Gilman, one of the signatories of the July 1997 letter
to President Clinton opposing aid to North Korea unless certain conditions were met, quickly sent a bipartisan team of congressional staffers to
North Korea to determine whether the famine was over, how severe it
had been, and whether food aid was alleviating the suffering. If they
returned with the wrong answer to any of these questions, the food aid
program would be shut down. It appeared that a conservative revolt had
been under way but was temporarily driven underground during the debate over the Cox amendment the previous summer. The North Koreans
once again had undermined efforts to encourage more food aid.

Leading the delegation was Mark Kirk, Gilman's senior adviser on
the food aid issue (Kirk was elected to the House of Representatives in
November 2000). In North Korea, the delegation asked to see centers for
the handicapped, schools, and nurseries in remote areas that no relief
agency had yet visited. By then, agencies were reporting generally
improved conditions in schools and nurseries across the country, as the
WFP program of feeding all children under age seven had become fully
operational—that is, in the counties into which the agencies were allowed.
But Kirk and his delegation were taken to Chagang province, the center
of the military-industrial complex and an area strictly off-limits to any of
the relief agencies. Pomnyun's surveys reported that Chagang was suffering terribly from the famine, perhaps because it was both inaccessible
to transport and outside the WFP feeding program. Kirk found deplor-
able conditions and took pictures of terribly malnourished children. When
I saw the photographs on television as Kirk held his press conference in
Beijing, I thought I was seeing photos taken by Canadian journalist
Hilary Mackenzie in the summer of 1997, but they were in fact taken by
Kirk in August 1998. Clearly, either the North Koreans had deliberately
underfed these children to show Kirk what he needed for the electronic
media or, more likely, because Chagang province was off-limits to aid
agencies for security reasons, these children were not eating. The general
improvement in nutritional conditions for children across the rest of the
country was apparently not the case in the more isolated counties.

In meetings in the spring of 1998, long before Representative Gilman had ordered the trip, Pomnyun and I had repeatedly urged Kirk to visit the Chinese border area and listen to the testimony of North Korean refugees. He was polite but skeptical, but when given the order to visit the region, he promptly requested permission from the Chinese government to visit the border area. Beijing replied that NGO border activity was illegal and inappropriate and denied the request, but Kirk tried again, this time arguing that his delegation wanted to look into the prospects for U.S. business development in Manchuria. The Foreign Ministry approved this more mundane request.

While these business meetings along the border were taking place, members of the congressional delegation would excuse themselves from the meetings and go to a different room in the same hotel to videotape interviews of food refugees in a scheme worthy of a Tom Clancy novel. The Chinese thus saved official face, but they undoubtedly knew exactly what was happening. When the Americans returned to Beijing, they held a dramatic press conference and announced that they had been in contact with members of the North Korean exile community who had confirmed that between three hundred thousand and eight hundred thousand people had died in the famine in each of the previous three years. Kirk had in fact received these estimates from U.S. intelligence and had used his trip as a cover for disclosing the information, so as not to compromise U.S. sources. The conservatism of the intelligence community had given way to a more apocalyptic view of the severity of the food crisis: a great famine, not a food crisis, appeared to be raging. News flashes traveled around the globe as the electronic media recorded the first senior U.S. officials to confirm publicly the existence of high death rates. Upon their return to Washington, Kirk had the videotaped refugee interviews leaked to ABC News, but it decided against using them. Congressman Gilman confronted Kim Gae Gwon, North Korea's deputy foreign minister, about the mortality rates, but Kim, ever faithful to the party line, resolutely denied them.

A REVIEW OF THE U.S. RESPONSE

Despite substantial initial opposition in Washington from members of Congress, the White House, State, and the CIA, and despite the self-destructive and provocative behavior of the North Korean government, the food aid program had begun in earnest. After its modest beginnings, it expanded each year, but by the summer of 1997 the famine had already peaked, and by the spring of 1998 it was over. The food aid was off-cycle by two years, too late to stop the catastrophe.

Ultimately the U.S. government did the right thing, for the wrong reasons. It provided large amounts of food aid in 1998 to hungry people governed by a troglodytic government, but its motivation had little to do with ending the famine and a great deal to do with encouraging the regime to participate in the four-party talks. For the White House and the State Department, U.S. food aid was a sweet inducement for the North Koreans to accept Washington's bitter proposal for direct talks between the North and the South. Because the food was fundamentally serving a diplomatic rather than a humanitarian purpose, the State Department's concern for its distribution was subordinated to its concern for Pyongyang's diplomatic response to the talks. State's insistence on WFP and NGO monitoring of food aid distribution had everything to do with a desire to satisfy a critical Congress, and little to do with a desire to feed those most in need.[18] State would have had some difficulty in aggressively pressing the North Koreans on accountability and transparency as it was simultaneously urging them to negotiate with the South. The North Koreans recognized that the food aid was an inducement to talk, not an effort to end the famine, so they intended to use it as they wished. The complication was congressional insistence on high standards of accountability and transparency, itself motivated not by humanitarian zeal but by the desire to ensure that none of the food went to the military.

Humanitarian agencies urged that diplomatic interests be kept distinct from donor and recipient government humanitarian programs; however, notwithstanding the Reagan Doctrine, such a separation is not the normal state of affairs. Instinctively, diplomats, military officers, and political leaders use the instruments of power at their disposal to defend and protect the perceived national interests of the state they serve. Unfortunately, each time Western humanitarian agencies were at the brink of convincing their governments to make this fine distinction between interests and ideals, the North Korean government would engage in yet another outrageous act, thus ensuring that donor governments would reconnect food aid with geostrategic interests. The clash of these geostrategic interests with the humanitarian imperative to stop the famine caused the worst paralysis I have witnessed in any major relief effort since the close of the Cold War. Although food aid was ultimately pledged in the summer of 1997 and did arrive, it was two years too late, was sent to the wrong regions of the country, and had no rigorous controls on its internal distribution to prevent the elites from stealing it.

8

THE INTERNATIONAL AID EFFORT

J UST AFTER THE POOR 1990 HARVEST, senior North Korean government leaders asked to meet with Kim Jong Il to give him the bad
news. The party leadership told the premier's son that the steady de-
terioration of harvests, complicated by the precipitous decline in Soviet
subsidies beginning in 1989, had led to a large food deficit for 1990–1991.
The real deficit, different from the one publicly reported, would create
shortages in the public distribution system, Kim was warned, with serious
consequences for the population. They requested permission to appeal to
the WFP for food aid, though the request would be under the guise of
food aid in support of development projects, not to address a food shortage. Kim Jong Il approved the request but instructed the group not to
bother his father with the matter.[1]

The elder Kim's failing eyesight prohibited him from reading state
documents, so his son would read them to his father, a task that did not
hurt him in succession intrigue. As his father's health failed, Kim Jong Il
effectively assumed the duties of governing the country. When the *Washington Times* interviewed Kim Il Sung in April 1994 he commented on how
much he relied on his son to govern. "Because I have eyesight problems,
he has arranged for all reports to be recorded to save me from having to
spend hours reading them. I am very proud to have such a good son. He
is also concerned about my health."[2] Kim Jong Il was not a beloved figure among the public or the party leadership, but because he had his
father's support and held the reins of state power in his hand, his com-
mands were carried out without question.

If any other nation in the world appealed to the United Nations for food aid after a failed harvest, it would not seem peculiar, but for North Korea it was. It was a UN coalition led by the United States that had fought North Korea's attempted absorption of South Korea in 1950. North Koreans saw the United Nations as a thinly disguised instrument of U.S. power pointed at them. Although they had joined the multinational organization in 1991, they did so only because South Korea had become a member: much of the state bureaucracy remained deeply suspicious of the United Nations. The fear of a "common front" of democratic governments united against North Korea influenced much of Pyongyang's foreign policy for five decades. Given these misgivings, the request suggested some desperation.

In early 1991, in response to the North Korean request, the WFP promptly dispatched a team of four technical officers, three seconded from the FAO, to conduct a needs assessment. The assessment, filed away in the WFP archives, found no particular needs requiring a food aid response, and in fact it politely questioned why food aid had been requested at all, particularly given the government's claim of a 10 million MT harvest, no poor people, and no malnutrition.[3] The report concluded: "For a number of reasons . . . the mission has been unable to establish a case for food aid. It has not been unwilling to do so, but unable."[4]

The WFP assessment complained that the mission did not have access to the information it needed to complete its work. Little did the UN team know that its visit prompted a row within the senior leadership because Kim Il Sung, old and ill as he might have been, still kept his hand on the bureaucratic pulse and had discovered the presence of the assessment team. He angrily demanded to know from government leaders why food aid had been requested; he had not approved it, and from what he had been told the country obviously did not need it. The UN team had not received the information it needed because Kim Il Sung had countermanded his son's approval of the team's request.[5] The message from the Great Leader to the leadership was clear: donor food aid was not an option because the food shortage could not and therefore did not exist.

Little did WFP know at the time that it had played a starring role in an early scene of the famine drama. WFP understood better its emerging part in act two, which began with the floods of August 1995, but never completely because the murky and obscure nature of the system kept outsiders at a distance and in the dark.

In early 1992, Kang Song Son, a former prime minister and son of a guerrilla fighter against the Japanese in the late 1930s, gave Kim Il Sung a troubling account of the suffering and deprivation caused by economic decline in the border provinces where he served as governor. These accounts contrasted sharply with the glowing economic reports the elder Kim had been receiving from his son. Kim Il Sung's discovery of the precipitous decline in the economy led to his reengagement into the active affairs of the country. This conversation was not the end of the bad economic news he was to receive over the next two years.[6] As the officially nonexistent food crisis grew more severe from 1991 to 1994, Kim Jong Il ordered the regime to cut rations to the Northeast. As chapter 5 detailed, by 1995 the public distribution system had collapsed as a source of food for all but the privileged.

But Kim Il Sung was unaware of his son's orders, and he reportedly was shocked in 1994 to receive reports of starvation deaths in the remote provinces in the Northeast. When he visited North Hamgyong province to confirm the reports, he found people foraging for wild foods in the countryside and asked them what they were doing. "We are starving and trying to gather these wild foods to eat," he was told. When Kim returned to Pyongyang he called his staff together and demanded to know how people could be starving.[7] According to apocryphal stories circulating in Seoul, their excuses led to an angry confrontation between father and son over the son's mismanagement of the economy and his withholding of information from his father. This supposed confrontation did not stop Kim Jong Il from taking over the reins of power after his father died that July.

By late 1994 the North Korean leadership realized the country was in serious trouble: production from the harvest that autumn had been worse than the year before, exacerbated by hail storms during the summer. The ongoing food shortages would grow much more severe by the winter and spring of 1995. In early 1995 North Korea began making diplomatic overtures to Japan to purchase a million metric tons of rice at subsidized prices. The Japanese agreed to provide food of indefinite quantity, but only with South Korean concurrence and support. After secret negotiations in Beijing between the North and South Korean governments, an agreement was concluded under which the South would provide the North with 150,000 MT of rice. This allowed Japan to move swiftly in June 1995 to conclude an agreement with the North Koreans to provide 300,000 MT of rice: half to be donated through the Japanese Red Cross and the other half to be paid for over thirty years following a ten-year grace period.[8]

The Japanese and South Korean food provisions partially fed North Korea in the spring and summer of 1996, but the severe flooding that struck the country in August 1995 had destroyed large tracts of agricultural land. Facing another food shortfall, the North Korean government had little choice but to appeal to the United Nations once again for help. This time, however, the regime was able to admit the sorry state of its food stocks because it had an ideologically defensible explanation: a natural disaster over which it theoretically had no control. In fact, the floods of August 1995 had merely accelerated the decay of an already crumbling system. The FAO/WFP harvest assessment, though statistically not as gloomy as government figures, rang humanitarian alarm bells. The donor government response to the WFP appeal, however, was disappointing. Western governments showed no enthusiasm for contributing food to one of the most notorious rogue states in the world, and they made only token contributions.

WAS IT A FAMINE, A FOOD CRISIS, OR A CHRONIC FOOD SHORTAGE?

The central question gnawing at every expatriate worker, every visiting delegation, and every technical team sent in to design programs or assess the situation was this: had a famine struck the country or not? Was there a food crisis or was it a chronic shortage caused by the ubiquitous "structural deficit"? Although the U.S. government in the summer of 1996 had privately determined that a famine was under way, as it had proof of starvation deaths, NGOs had no access to this information and could not definitively answer this essential question. Thus the NGO relief effort suffered from the start. The frustrating search for a plain answer adversely influenced a host of decisions. Other donor governments were unable to determine how much food to pledge and where it should be targeted. UN agencies did not know how many staff members to divert from other crises to North Korea. NGOs had no idea what to ask their private contributors to support and why. And not a few editors had problems deciding whether to cover something that might merely be a nutritional fiction designed by a cynical government to get donor support for its failing economy.

When aid agency assessments fail, the best remedy is to debate definitions, which is what the NGOs began to do in the spring and summer of 1997. InterAction had seemingly endless discussions over how to define a famine. This same debate had taken place a full year earlier within the U.S. government.

In the spring of 1997, while I was involved with the NGO World Vision, I suggested half in jest and half from frustration that if there was that much confusion over the term, we should ask Amartya Sen, the renowned economist, to define a famine. Nancy Lindborg of Mercy Corps International, one of the most prominent NGOs working in North Korea, took the suggestion seriously and sent a letter to him. His response was wise, simple, and straightforward:

> I see no great reason to move away from the commonsense understanding that famines are situations of suddenly elevated mortality, related to hunger. The increased mortality includes not only people dying directly from starvation, but also of disease (often epidemics) which are unleashed by severe hunger, and the breakdown of sanitary and other arrangements and massive increase in short-term migration associated with the hunger. [9]

He urged us not to waste time on definitional disputes and focus instead on the real causes of the famine and what might be done to stop it. The same advice would have been applicable to the U.S. government debate. But determining whether a large number of people were dying was not as simple as it had been in other famines.

The language used in speaking publicly about the famine changed as the crisis evolved. In 1996, WFP officials explained that a famine had been averted because the public distribution system provided everyone with something, even though this contradicted the information that the U.S. government had given the United Nations in March 1997.[10] Although malnutrition was widespread, starvation was not, they claimed. By the spring of 1997, however, officials discarded this prosaic description and adopted a new and brilliantly conceived formulation: a "famine in slow motion" was spreading across North Korea.[11] This darkly evocative term coined by Tun Myat, the WFP director of transportation, as he returned from the first expatriate visit to the northeastern provinces, provided the WFP senior leadership with an elegant compromise to the contending sides in the debate over what was happening. The compromise satisfied everyone a little. For the U.S. NGOs that claimed a massive famine was ravaging the country, the operative word "famine" was used. For the European NGOs and the European Union, which were skeptical of the alarmist claims, the slow motion qualification allowed a measure of comfort. The term gave donors such as the U.S. government a defense against legislative branch and media criticism concerning the commitment of food aid to a repugnant regime; moreover, their modest aid commitments seemed more generous when the famine was described as being in slow motion. Most important, the moderated language diminished the anger of the North Korean government, humiliated by public disclosure of its internal problems. The term allowed some negotiating room for the nutritional scientists who themselves were engaged in a debate over what was occurring in front of their eyes, but which they were unable to see.[12] Clearly, people were in trouble and nutritional conditions were deteriorating, and yet expatriates saw no visible evidence of famine comparable to what they had seen in Somalia or Ethiopia.

During most of 1997, senior expatriate NGO and UN officials, congressional staff delegations, and diplomats descended on North Korea. The reclusive state welcomed them politely but with little enthusiasm. The visitors all made their own assessment of what they saw, even if they knew virtually nothing about famines, totalitarian states, or North Korea. The visits, combined with apocalyptic media reports and WFP statements about a slow-moving famine, served to confuse a now bewildered Western public.

Catherine Bertini, executive director of the WFP, had served as assistant secretary of agriculture during the Bush administration. The North Korean crisis was to try her considerable political talents as no other crisis had in her seven-year tenure at the WFP. Prior to her visit to North Korea in March 1997, Bertini had seen North Korea as another emergency to be managed. Her visit shocked her into a series of decisions that were to change the dynamic of the famine and the international aid response. What changed her view, according to senior WFP officials, was the appalling condition of hundreds of children she visited in children's centers across the country.

In the year preceding her visit, the Korea Office at the U.S. Department of State had cautioned Bertini not to be manipulated by North Korea's specious claims of imminent disaster. Moreover, congressional leaders warned her that any food aid to the North had better not end up in military hands. During the course of the year Bertini repeatedly requested briefings from the U.S. government on its information about the famine. After repeated disputes over the location of the briefing, it was presented to her at the U.S. Embassy in Beijing before her trip to North Korea. The briefing provided little insight or information, apparently because the U.S. officials had decided not to share more apocalyptic evidence they had of conditions inside the country from State Department analyst Ken Quinones's previous visits, defector and refugee interviews, and Japanese and South Korean intelligence.

Upon her return from North Korea, Bertini made three critical decisions based on the information she had collected. First, she pressed for a new appeal for more food aid from donor governments. Second, she insisted that Pyongyang allow an experienced journalist hired by WFP to visit the country, unfettered by official minders or political constraints, to photograph the human face of the famine. And third, she demanded that her most senior logistics expert, Tun Myat, be allowed to travel to the Northeast provinces, previously off limits to all expatriates, to conduct an assessment. The North Koreans, stung by the previously lethargic international response to their appeals for help, reluctantly agreed. They were later to regret their decision.

THE PUBLIC DISTRIBUTION SYSTEM: SOCIALIST EGALITARIANISM OR A PAPER TIGER?

In the spring of 1996, before the full fury of the famine raged across the country, the Office of Foreign Disaster Assistance at USAID sent Sue Lautze to North Korea to conduct a needs assessment. An experienced microeconomist of agriculture and famine, Lautze had previously worked with the USAID mission in Sudan overseeing the country's huge drought relief program. At the same time that Lautze was in North Korea, Trevor Page, the WFP national director for North Korea, had successfully pressed Save the Children UK to conduct a similar but independent assessment. The British NGO seconded one of its most senior food security experts, Lola Nathanail, to the WFP for this purpose. The differences in the two women's reports embody some of the profound interpretive disputes argued within the humanitarian and diplomatic communities during the famine. These disputes apparently influenced critical operational decisions made by donor governments. Perhaps more accurately, policymakers used one report or the other to justify decisions the NGO community suspected had already been made for political reasons.

The observations and conclusions of the two authors, both technical experts in their disciplines, visiting the same country at the same time, stand in remarkable contrast to one another. Lautze's report described families whose coping mechanisms had collapsed and a country in the early stages of famine, if not well into one. She concluded that preferential food distribution was taking place and argued against using the public distribution system because it was a politicized and thus untrustworthy mechanism for dispensing food aid. In a paper published by Tufts University's Feinstein International Famine Center in the summer of 1997, Lautze expanded on this argument. Totalitarian regimes, she said, control the public distribution of food to achieve political ends, one of which is not necessarily equitable redistribution of food, particularly when famine threatens the life of the regime.[13] In contrast, Nathanail observed some food stress but no acute malnutrition or need for supplementary feeding. She suggested that, "given the structural nature of the current food shortages in the DPRK, and the state's control of resources available (thereby promoting their equitable distribution), it is inappropriate to consider targeting the most vulnerable segments of the population only." She qualified this to some degree by proposing that the WFP target some assistance "through one of the State's distribution mechanisms: the nursery and kindergarten network," a recommendation the WFP was to adopt as the center of its program late in 1997.[14]

Lautze reported that the central government was engaged in preferential food distributions. Writing of farmers in the flood-affected areas, she concluded: "Contrary to DPRK reports claiming that flood-affected farmers had received one-half of their annual allocation of food (an estimated

90–100 kg/person), many farmers living on collective farms who lost their harvest received little or no annual allocations of cereals." Lautze's analysis indicated "that urban flood-affected areas (both farm and non-farm populations) have been prioritized to receive disproportionate quantities of limited emergency food assistance when compared to more remote rural areas." The cities were clearly more important to the regime than were the remote rural areas devastated by the autumn 1995 floods. She argued later in her OFDA report that those population groups with privileged access received relief food, while those without did not. Her conclusion was that the central government apparently used the floods to increase pledges of donor food aid that were later distributed to privileged populations mostly in the cities.[15]

Nathanail concluded that the country was effectively bankrupt and unable to import grain; Lautze argued exactly the opposite, that the country had currency reserves it could have used to purchase food but that it instead decided to purchase weapons. How either of these two writers could have been sure of their reporting when intelligence analysts did not know with any assurance what the situation was suggests that both were influenced by political constraints on their work. Nathanail's report reflects the North Korean regime's view of itself and the crisis it faced. She did not go to the border region in China (which Lautze did do) and did not interview any refugees. She occasionally gives interpretations that differ from the official North Korean versions, but for the most part she reports uncritically what she is told. Early on, the WFP and the FAO in their harvest estimates had made critical remarks about the North Korean agricultural system, but the North Koreans would not tolerate too much criticism. North Korean officials repeatedly told the WFP and the NGOs that a battle was under way within the government over the existence of the food program, with the military and internal security pressing to shut it down and expel the humanitarian agencies. Too much public criticism of their system, too many intrusive demands for access, or too many embarrassing reports about the famine to the world, officials warned, would lead the military and security apparatus to win the debate. The WFP and the NGOs were never sure whether this was a serious threat or simply a negotiating ploy to limit humanitarian presence in the country.[16]

Lautze's report is the more critical of the two and the one that has withstood the scrutiny of time, except for her observation that "the

DPRK still had the capacity to avert a disaster through political and economic measures. Its ability to cope with food crises should not be underestimated. Consequently, resolution of widespread food shortages remains
the sole responsibility of the DPRK."[17] Her conclusion here contradicts
both the tone and substance of much of the rest of the report. A senior
administration official told me the "State Department was upset with the
Lautze report and insisted it be revised before it was released. The State
Department and the National Security Council had put USAID on a
tighter leash than in any emergency in memory."[18]

Nathanail was not alone in admiring the egalitarian nature of the
public distribution system. Members of the Canadian Foodgrains Bank,
a consortium of Christian NGOs and churches in Canada, reported after
their visit of August 27–September 3, 1996,

> As predicted the people have suffered increasingly. Meanwhile, the
> public distribution system has divided the shortages over most of
> the Korean population, dividing available food judiciously. Chil-
> dren have been exceptionally protected by official priorities and by
> parents further reducing their own food intake, while youth and
> adults are visibly thinner. Therefore, even though the food shortage
> on a national basis is more severe than [in] Ethiopia in 1983–4, the
> shortage is being spread out over most of the population and there-
> fore has not yet produced widespread mortality.[19]

The WFP seems to have ignored the information on preferential
treatment, perhaps because its own experience contradicted the U.S.
intelligence report. At the same time, however, the WFP took the reports
on triage in the Northeast more seriously, perhaps because sources independent of the U.S. government had reached the same conclusion.
Lautze reported that no one had been allowed to assess flood damage in
the northeastern provinces near the Chinese border.[20] The three WFP
program directors in North Korea from August 1995 until May 1997 had
been rebuffed each time they requested permission for their staff to visit
the northeastern region and Chagang province.[21] NGO requests were
met with the same resistance. I still have a WFP map distributed at a UN
headquarters coordination meeting in the summer of 1997 showing their
areas of operation; the map carefully excluded the three northeastern
provinces. Some relief workers and analysts began to wonder whether
there was something the regime was hiding that could not be as easily

disguised as in other areas of the country. Catherine Bertini herself wondered why the regime was so insistent that no one visit the Northeast; she suspected that something was seriously wrong in the region.[22] Did the regime want to avoid pressure to divert food from other regions of the country by precluding any assessments of the Northeast, a prerequisite for food deliveries? What concerned me from the beginning of 1997 was that the central government might be using the humanitarian organizations' standards to their advantage, because the UN agencies and NGOs refused to deliver food to the areas where they were given no access. In fact, Western aid organizations were unknowing and unwilling pawns in executing the central authorities' triage strategy.

Bertini's post-trip decision to send Tun Myat to North Korea profoundly changed the direction of the famine response. Myat, a British-educated Burmese citizen, effective at working in Western and Asian cultures simultaneously, was a shrewd and resourceful negotiator. Upon his arrival, the North Koreans ignored their previous approval of the Bertini request and presented the same excuses as to why he could not visit the three northeastern provinces: there were transportation problems, weather conditions were poor, there was nothing worth seeing, and the region was generally inaccessible. Myat informed his hosts that the WFP would make no additional food aid appeals for North Korea unless he was allowed to travel there. His firmness appears to have changed their minds, as he was quickly placed on a train traveling to the port of Chongjin in North Hamgyong province. Myat's trip—the first by a foreign relief worker to the region since the start of the famine—provided the first authoritative evidence that the central government had written off the region to preserve the food supply for the western provinces.

Upon arrival in the city he asked to visit several homes unannounced that he, not the government officials, would choose. Unlike in other regions, where local officials assiduously resisted such requests, in North Hamgyong Myat was immediately taken where he asked to go. Indeed, all the provincial and city officials he met were more open, more friendly, less ideological, and more cooperative than any he had met in other regions of the country. The diet of the families he met was composed entirely of alternative foods: seaweed noodles, corn cob and rice root powder, and wild leaves. Local officials reported to Myat that the central authorities had told them in September 1996 that their allocation of food would be their last until September of 1997, the next harvest.[23]

It was Myat who provided the first clear evidence of mass internal population movements, which he later described at a press conference. His train ride to the Northeast took twenty-nine hours, and from his description of his accommodations en route, he had been given a party cadre cabin so he could not converse with the common people. While he could not easily see conditions on the other cars, at one point the train turned sharply around a mountain in such a way that the cars in the rear of the caravan faced the cars at the front. These rear trains were jammed with people on the move, all with bundles of what looked like food; the outside tops of the trains were packed with people in very precarious positions; people were jammed in the space between the trains. Most looked disheveled and dirty. Myat noted that at each of the train stops people would jump off the trains just before arrival, presumably so they could avoid internal security. The train traveled so slowly that this could be negotiated easily, and it meant that people could jump onto the train at remote villages along most of the journey even if the train did not stop. Myat's assessment trip provided another small piece of data to fit into the famine puzzle—it indicated food stress and confirmed in precise detail the refugee reports that NGOs had been receiving on the Chinese border.

Myat sent his WFP transportation staff to Chongjin in November and December 1997 to monitor food aid shipments. A Greek shipping captain who had just sailed up along the eastern coast to Chongjin reported that he was astonished to see thousands upon thousands of small boats fishing the waters along the entire coast.[24] Some of us had previously wondered why the fisheries had not been more widely used as a coping mechanism, but apparently they had been, on a massive scale. Lautze reports that villages would commission the one boat in the village to fish for the entire population. The limitation of this coping mechanism was that the coastal fisheries had been over-fished for some years and the remaining schools were well outside the range of small, hand-powered boats, which were all that could be used given the fuel shortage.

The Myat trip opened the Northeast to the relief effort; food aid began flowing to the region, and a steady stream of expatriate workers began to undertake assessments and begin programs. U.S. NGO efforts to target the Northeast for agricultural programs and food-for-work projects, though, continued to meet heavy resistance from officials in Pyongyang. The typical result was a compromise in which some resources went to the Northeast while the bulk went to the more politically sensitive western provinces. The effort to open the Northeast subtly affirmed Lautze's original insight: the public distribution system was not as benign and egalitarian as it appeared. It served the central authorities as an instrument for ensuring the survival of the politically powerful center by placing the poor mountainous regions in triage, so more food could be sent to the western provinces. It could be used at the whim of whoever controlled it, and that whim could result in the death of hundreds of thousands of people without power to protect themselves.

Refugee interviews conducted along the Chinese–North Korean border by John Pomfret of the *Washington Post* and representatives of Médecins Sans Frontières in 1998 and 1999 confirmed the suspicions expressed in Lautze's Tufts paper. Congressional testimony I had presented in June 1997 was also confirmed by these interviews. The public distribution system (PDS) was enforcing another set of triage decisions: the central authorities in late 1996 had decided to feed only the party cadres, workers in critical industries, officers in the military and security system, and people in the capital city.[25]

The WFP made a second decision at this stage, deliberately or not, that partially addressed the problem of preferential feeding. It abandoned the PDS as the principal means for distributing commodities, except for food-for-work projects conducted through the U.S. NGO consortium with U.S. government food. Instead, the WFP decided to feed all children under the age of seven through the public school system. Although this was an improvement over the PDS mechanism, it too suffered from weaknesses. Abandoned children on city streets, internally displaced people, and children of poor families that had withdrawn their children from schools were not covered by this new initiative. Even more seriously, corrupt party cadres and military officers continued to divert food and sell it in the farmers markets. For any family with enough income or wealth to buy from the markets, these diversions—however illicit—kept them alive. But the decision to feed school children made little difference to millions of families with no school-age children and no access to the markets.

THE POLITICS OF HARVEST FORECASTING

Donor governments use the data in UN appeals as a primary source of information to determine how much food aid they will pledge to emergencies. These appeals are based on field assessments conducted by the WFP and the FAO at each year's harvest. Because the North Korean harvest estimates affected the national security interests of so many donor nations, the arcane study of corn and rice production became a matter of considerable diplomatic and military interest. The number of harvest projections proliferated and, with them, the level of confusion over their accuracy.

Contestants in the clash between political and humanitarian agendas shamelessly manipulated harvest projections to prove or deny the existence of the famine. Chinese agricultural economists were the most pessimistic, followed by the WFP and the FAO and an independent think tank in South Korea, the Korea Rural Economic Institute. Unofficial Chinese estimates were similar to those of Hwang Jong Yop, the highest-level North Korean defector, who reported that the 1996 harvest was 2.1 million MT.[26] The WFP was reporting a harvest of 2.84 million MT, as 50 percent of the maize crop had been consumed prematurely in the summer of 1996 and thus was unavailable for the 1996–97 harvest.[27] This pessimistic estimate helped the WFP and FAO make their case for a large food aid program. In contrast, the U.S. Department of Agriculture (USDA) reported an optimistic figure of 3.1 million MT.[28] Opponents of food aid used the USDA and South Korean government's production figures to argue that the reports of famine were exaggerated. But Ken Quinones of the State Department's Bureau of Intelligence and Research disputed the USDA figures and published an article in the spring of 1997 with his own estimate.[29]

USDA estimates were based on what experts call the "all-source method," which simply means analysts combine remote sensing data from satellites with defector interviews, Chinese government statistics, and an on-the-ground assessment by their staff. These sources included extensive satellite photographs of cultivated areas in North Korea that the UN agencies could not access until 1998. Quinones in the spring of 1996 had been critical of the USDA's use of aerial photography for assessing crop production, because it confused cultivated areas with production areas. On one of his trips to North Korea he had brought back to Washington corn cobs and rice stocks from cultivated areas that from a distance looked healthy, though in fact they had no grain in them. The aerial photographs were deceiving yet were being used by intelligence experts to argue that the North Korean crops were more bountiful than they really were.[30] The FAO/WFP reports, on the other hand, were based on data from extensive on-the-ground field assessments conducted by staff experienced in harvest reporting during other famines.

The official North Korean crop estimates beginning with the flood year of 1995 were more pessimistic than any produced in decades because the regime wanted to make the case for food aid. This may not entirely explain their pessimistic forecasts. The extraordinarily sharp reported decline in food production may reflect something beyond the country's immediate need for food: the bureaucracy may have used the natural disasters of 1995–97 as a way of correcting the grossly inflated figures of earlier years. In a command-and-control agricultural system, farmers tend to exaggerate harvest production to make their superiors happy, as these superiors are under pressure to meet centrally prescribed production goals. Even Kim Il Sung recognized that the harvest figures reported by the collective farms were often seriously exaggerated. Thus, North Korean harvest reports cannot be trusted as objective and accurate. Hwang Jong Yop reports in his 1998 book that harvest estimates were regularly falsified.[31]

CALCULATING POST-HARVEST LOSSES

Above and beyond determining the size of the harvest, analysts must also consider post-harvest losses—that is, the amount of a harvest that is wasted through improper harvest, transportation, storage, and distribution. UN estimates of North Korean food production consistently underestimated post-harvest losses. Except for one private South Korean research institute, most of the other harvest estimates did not account for these losses. The North Korean agricultural system was designed and built around the Soviet model, which had experienced terrible post-harvest losses since forced collectivization in the early 1930s.[32] Soviet post-harvest loss rates in the late 1980s were between 20 percent and 30 percent, with losses for vegetables and potatoes sometimes as high as 40 percent to 50 percent.[33] Aristotle argued that anything held in common and thus

owned by everyone is not cared for by anyone.[34] What little incentive
North Korean farmers had to care for the harvest withered away after
the state reduced the farmers' rations as the famine progressed. Post-
harvest losses are a problem not only under socialist systems of agriculture, but under private market systems as well. Studies done by the FAO
of rice harvest losses in Asia show loss rates of 10 percent to 40 percent.[35] In Africa, post-harvest losses in subsistence agriculture approach
25 percent. A USDA study indicates grain and grain product losses from
harvest to consumption in the U.S. food system were 15.1 percent.[36]

The annual harvest assessments of the FAO and WFP estimated
North Korean losses to be nil in 1995, 6 percent in 1996, 12 percent in
1997, and 15 percent in 1998.[37] In the 1997 and 1998 assessments, UN
officials reported that the harvest loss problem had been growing more
severe owing to transportation problems: rice "was being left in the field
or roadside after harvest for longer periods than usual and often carried on
their back by people. In the case of maize, the losses would be similarly
larger in view of difficulties of post-harvest handling and other mechanical deficiencies."[38]

Some official North Korean documents hint at the post-harvest loss
problems. In a 1997 interview with a Korean Japanese newspaper, the
vice director of the North Korean Agricultural Commission, Choe Hyun
Su, said: "We are developing a campaign under the slogan 'Do not waste
even [a] single grain when you harvest in threshing crops.' . . . It is our
iron rule to carry the harvested maize to a threshing floor on the harvesting day. If they are left in the fields, they are damaged, resulting in reducing output."[39] One of the FAO harvest assessment teams told me that the
rice was often left in the paddy water after being harvested. This is an
acceptable practice, but after three days it begins to deteriorate. The team
members did not wait around to time the exposure of the harvest, but they
had the sense that the rice remained there much longer than three days.[40]

These loss rates were a chronic problem well before the famine;
Kim Il Sung himself complained in speeches in 1967 and again in 1970
that "large quantities of fruit, vegetables, and fish are left to rot simply
because we lack storage facilities."[41] And this was well before the transportation and logistics system fell into serious disrepair, which the
United Nations says increased loss rates.[42] Many anecdotal reports by

humanitarian aid workers confirm these serious problems in harvest storage and handling. Kim Young-Hoon of the Korea Rural Economic Institute (KREI), an independent South Korean think tank, told the House International Relations Committee's Mark Kirk that the "North Korean system probably wasted a large amount of grain in its outdated storage and distribution systems." KREI estimated the North Korean harvest to be a mere 2.8 million MT.[43]

Marina Ye Trigubenko, a Russian scholar who has written extensively on North Korea, reports that North Korean agricultural losses "are no less than 30 percent."[44] If her estimate is correct on this point alone, international agencies seriously miscalculated the size of the food deficit. If one takes the Trigubenko estimate and applies it to the UN estimates for agricultural production for the period 1995–98, the effect on harvest figures is devastating. Using her figures, total grain harvest figures during the peak famine period—from the summer of 1996 to the summer of 1997 —decline from 2.8 million MT to 1.81 million MT of rice and maize.

The politics of harvest estimates were at times entertaining or amusing, cynical or boring, and would all be quite irrelevant were it not for the fact that they were used as a principal defense of various stakeholders' views of the severity of the food crisis and how the international community should have responded to it. Total imports of grain from all sources were 1.17 million MT in 1996–97. If one adds to that Hwang Jong Yop's estimate of 2.1 million MT of milled rice and maize production that year, then 3.27 million MT of food was available for consumption in North Korea. This estimate of total food availability suggests a huge food gap that would set the stage for a famine. But if one adds the USDA production figure of 3.1 million MT, then the total rises to 4.27 million MT. Food stocks of this size would still be below the required tonnage of 4.7 million MT, including feed for the animal herds, but the crisis would at least have been manageable. The USDA figure, however, makes no allowance for massive post-harvest losses.

From the perspective of famine theory, however, this debate over harvest estimates may not be particularly instructive. Amartya Sen has shown that some famines have actually occurred during periods of rising harvests but rapidly falling wages. Food is available, but the poor cannot afford to buy enough of it to survive, so they starve to death.

DID THE FOOD AID END THE FAMINE?

Fred Cuny blazed a heroic path in humanitarian relief operations for nearly two decades until his murder during relief efforts in Chechnya in 1994. In his last book, published posthumously, Cuny reviewed various approaches to fighting famines.[45] For the years I knew him he argued that food aid was the least desirable, though sometimes only available, tool to defeat a famine. His prejudice reflected years of experience. He knew it was hard to ensure that food aid went to the right people, and that for logistical and political reasons it usually arrived after the famine had peaked, too late to help the dying. Economically, he said, food aid was the least efficient of the alternatives. The North Korean famine may well have proven Cuny's claim.

Donor governments, the news media, and the public inaccurately assume that food aid commitments are somehow equivalent to their de-livery. But the time lag between commitments and deliveries has plagued famine relief since its modern inception. Although the U.S. government usually delivers on its promises, some donor governments make com-mitments they do not keep. Others deliberately double count their pledges, thus making them look more generous than they are; this hap-pened regularly during the southern African drought in 1992. Sometimes paperwork and scheduling problems delay the delivery of food aid until six or eight months after it is pledged: the European Union has a partic-ular problem with this, because it depends on member-states to ship the food. U.S. food aid for North Korea would have been pledged from the Food for Peace budget within USAID, but it was purchased and shipped from the Midwest grain markets by the USDA, a process that takes two to three months. Thus, when the White House increased its food pledges in the spring and again in the summer of 1997, hungry North Koreans did not start eating the next day or week. For the purposes of this study, the food aid delivery date to North Korean ports is a more useful stan-dard than the date of the pledge when judging the effects of food aid. But even then the food had to be shipped to the receiving cities, which could take weeks given the feeble condition of the North Korean transporta-tion system.

Famines usually follow agricultural cycles and grow more severe as months pass after the harvest. Many subsistence farmers in countries with chronic food deficits call the months before the new harvest the "hungry season," because no food stocks remain from the last harvest and they must scavenge to survive. With the onset of the famine years in North Korea, the hungry season ran from March or April through to the harvest in late September and early October. NGOs introduced a spring barley crop, and potatoes and some vegetables harvested during the summer offered some relief for farm families with access to them, but they did not much help urban or mining families without resources to barter or buy them on the farmers markets.

Foreign food to overcome the gaping deficit in local production came from three sources. The WFP received and distributed food from donor governments; China provided commercial, bartered, and food aid; and donor governments, the International Red Cross, and NGOs provided bilateral food aid directly to the North Korean government. Shipments of all foreign food, humanitarian and commercial, showed a steady increase as the severity of the crisis increased, as can be seen in table 1.

It would be tempting to conclude that the macroeconomic national gap caused the famine, as the aggregated food data seem so compelling. But the data are only comparatively, not absolutely, compelling: 1995–98 were the worst years of availability for produced and imported food in decades. The country could have survived on 3.8 million MT if it had been evenly distributed to the entire population in the same proportions, with variations based only on age, and if all the domesticated animals had been left to die during the winter.[46] But production fell below this minimum requirement by 100,000 MT in 1995–96, by 500,000 MT in 1996–97, and by 300,000 MT in 1997–98. Had the ration even in these very lean years been evenly distributed among the entire population, people might have been able to use their coping mechanisms to avoid famine. Such an egalitarian ration, however, would have shaken the tenuous foundations of the state. It would have caused panic among the party cadres, internal security apparatus, and the military, who might have seen themselves starving as the rest of the population did, and it was on these three groups that the survival of the Kim dynasty depended.

For political reasons, the central authorities made some disastrous food distribution decisions in 1995 and 1996. As was explained in chapter 5, the first of these was the decision to cut off all food shipments into the eastern ports. For large regions of the country even outside the

Table 1. Domestic Grain Production and Total Food Aid and Commercial Imports (in Metric Tons), 1995–98 Harvest Years

Total Food Aid and Commercial Imports (Contributions) per Harvest Year	
1995–96	903,374
1996–97	1,171,665
1997–98	1,321,528[1]
Domestic Grain Production per Harvest Year (FAO/WFP estimate)	
1995–96	4.10 million
1996–97	2.84 million[2]
1997–98	2.66 million
1998–99	3.48 million[3]
Domestic Grain Production per Harvest Year (reduced by 30 percent owing to wastage, rot, and rodents)	
1995–96	2.87 million
1996–97	2.16 million
1997–98	2.19 million
1998–99	2.96 million

1. All figures taken from annual FAO/WFP crop assessments.

2. This figure excludes 50 percent of the corn crop that was harvested prematurely, some to be eaten and some hoarded in the rural areas as insurance against future shortages. It was thus not available for consumption in 1996–97.

3. FAO/WFP, *Crop and Food Supply Assessment Mission to DPRK: Special Report* (World Food Program, November 1998).

Northeast, the regime appears to have temporarily shut down the PDS following the disastrous 1996 harvest, though evidence for this is only circumstantial. On a trip to the Chinese border with North Korea in June 1997, Scott Snyder of the United States Institute of Peace collected anecdotal reports of sharply rising food prices and death rates for the three months following the 1996 harvest, when deaths and prices should have been declining.[47] The KBSM refugee surveys show a similar, sharp rise in death rates in the autumn of 1996, only a few months after the harvest had been collected. In theory, however, food should have been more available for distribution through the PDS and private sale in the farmers markets at lower prices following the harvest than during the hungry season.

One explanation for this phenomenon may be found in the response to a decision made by donor governments earlier that year. In February the deputy foreign ministers of South Korea and Japan met with the deputy U.S. secretary of state in Honolulu to discuss among other things the politics of food aid to North Korea. At that meeting, the United States and Japan acceded to South Korean demands that any further pledges of food aid be postponed at least until later that spring.[48] South Korea believed that the food crisis would lead to the collapse of the Northern government and therefore provided the best recent chance for the reunification of the country under South Korean control.

This ministerial announcement of a freeze on further aid was not a secret: it was covered in the Japanese and South Korean press and would have been known to the North Koreans. Thus the North Koreans had few reliable pledges of donor food aid by the autumn and winter of the 1996–97 agricultural year. To save the limited harvest, which appeared that it might be the country's only food supply for the year, the regime simply shut down the countrywide food delivery system. The only distributions that year went to the privileged and residents of Pyongyang. But such a decision could not have been more poorly timed: it was made just when the population would have been expecting higher rations following the harvest. Many families likely had consumed all their household stocks in anticipation of this new ration and were left utterly destitute. This may have caused the dramatic rise in deaths in the autumn of 1996.

A food aid program carefully targeted to people suffering most severely from the government's discontinuation of the PDS would have saved hundreds of thousands if not millions of lives. This is what a well-run relief program is designed to do. But determining who was vulnerable, who had been left out, and who was dying had been the great challenge from the beginning of the relief effort. The traditional diagnostic tools of the famine relief discipline would have provided this data instantly, but the regime would not allow any of them to be used. The food aid program clearly did not relieve the famine as it peaked, because the bulk of food shipments did not arrive until after deaths had begun to subside. The humanitarian agencies did not target food aid to the most vulnerable, as they did not know for certain who they were. The tripling of food aid shipments in the summer of 1997 ameliorated the suffering of the survivors, but it cannot be said to have ended the famine.

THE HUMANITARIAN CODE OF CONDUCT

Humanitarian relief agencies had faced similar challenges in other crises where food aid had been politically abused. Their unhappy experiences in Bosnia, Somalia, and Sudan led in 1993 to the drafting of a set of standards called the Code of Conduct,[49] widely accepted by relief agencies, designed to preclude or at least limit this abuse.[50] By the summer of 1997 relief agencies were privately wringing their collective hands that the North Korean government had trashed the Code of Conduct without the least protest by anyone. Of the ten principles in the code, only two were being fully followed, while the relief effort was in various degrees violating the rest, some quite blatantly. These violations were more systematic, more widespread, and more egregious than in any crisis since the code was written.

The code's principles may be summarized simply:

1. The humanitarian imperative comes first.
2. Relief aid is calculated, targeted, and delivered on the basis of need alone, regardless of race, creed, or nationality.
3. Aid will be independent of the foreign policies of donor or recipient governments.
4. Local culture and customs will be respected.
5. The relief response will cooperate with local institutions and involve joint planning and joint coordination.
6. Aid beneficiaries will be involved in the design and management of the relief program.
7. Relief aid should be programmed to reduce the vulnerability of the society to famines in the future and meet basic needs.
8. Aid will not further political or religious standpoints.

9.   Agencies will be accountable to the recipients and donors alike for their work.
10. Agency information to the media will treat the disaster victims as dignified human beings, not objects of pity.

No serious student of humanitarian relief work expects all of these principles to be completely followed in any response; the real world is too complex, conflicting interests too common, and local resistance to the principles sometimes too fierce. But some effort has to be made to comply, and these efforts usually improve the quality of the relief response. Nearly all of these principles require unimpeded access to victims, accountability of aid, and the complete transparency of relief operations, none of which existed in North Korea. The eligibility lists for receiving relief aid were compiled entirely by government officials; no one knew for sure who was on these lists, since NGOs were not allowed to have Korean speakers or readers in their delegations. The recipients could well have been party cadre and military families.

The established standard for monitoring food distributions also involve relief workers making unannounced visits to food warehouses and distribution centers at any time. Workers should also be free to make spontaneous visits to recipients' homes to check the fairness and accuracy of distribution lists without government minders or translators watching. In other words, workers should be able to monitor relief distributions from arrival at port to consumption in the home.[51] For this standard to have been followed in North Korea, food monitors would have had to live in the area they served, not in Pyongyang, where most were virtually imprisoned. No recipients were involved in programming relief aid, nor for that matter were the NGOs and UN agencies, which merely watched government officials manage the distributions. In other words, however much the agencies tried, the North Koreans resisted efforts to follow the procedures outlined in the code.

As should be obvious, the principles themselves conflict with each other. Respecting North Korea's local culture and traditions presumably translates into sensitivity to the country's five decades of isolation from the outside world and its totalitarian obsession with control over nearly every aspect of what happens in its society. In other words, such respect would have meant the subordination of every humanitarian principle to the political imperatives of the regime. As a totalitarian society, North Korea's state-enforced ideology was in fact entirely at odds with humanitarian principles. The state's policy for decades was to discriminate against class enemies[52] or, in the case of the Northeast, against regions that were not important militarily or politically. Thus, if agencies wanted to be faithful to the remaining nine humanitarian principles, they could not respect local culture at the same time.

Humanitarian agencies working in the country responded to these criticisms by claiming that progress on many of these principles had been made during their nearly four years of operations. In fact, with the participation of officials in Pyongyang, the agencies drafted a list of principles specifically written to address the shortcomings of the North Korean operation. But principles are useless if the participants share no common understanding of what the principles mean. A strong argument could be made that as famine deaths rose, peaked, and declined, the regime became more willing to comply with some of these modified principles. But it did so just as the importance of complying diminished, because the worst of the famine was over.

Rather than blame the humanitarian agencies, however, donor government critics of these egregious violations of the Code of Conduct need to look toward themselves when asking why this situation continued through the early and critical stage of relief operations. Quite simply, from the start of operations the humanitarian agencies did not have the political clout to insist on these principles. Donor government support and diplomatic intervention were nowhere near unified, and competing diplomatic and security agendas within donor governments took precedence over the famine effort. The United Nations has never had the political or military authority to insist on compliance with these or any other principles in any emergency. Principles are respected only when the donor governments are uniformly determined to support the United Nations in their enforcement over other geostrategic objectives. The foreign policies of North Korea, Japan, South Korea, the United States, and the European Union thus weighed heavily in the entire relief effort from beginning to end.

In October 1998, MSF stunned the North Korean government and other humanitarian agencies by announcing its withdrawal from the country. It argued that it did not have access to those most in need and could not ensure the accountability of relief commodities, and it then released twelve pages of interviews with famine refugees in China.[53] These interviews, described in earlier chapters, presented an unflattering view of the relief effort from the very people it was supposed to be helping. The NGO believed the regime had used it for political purposes in violation of the most basic of humanitarian principles: serving those in need. To quell public concern that their contributions were ending up being abused, other agencies scrambled to defend their management of relief commodities. As was the case with the World Vision and KBSM surveys, those relief workers who had not visited the border ridiculed and criticized the MSF refugee interviews. In fact, an acrimonious debate took place within MSF between the staff assigned to work inside the country, who disputed the refugee claims, and the staff who had interviewed the refugees in China and believed what they heard. It was the latter group who won the debate. Members of the U.S. Congress grumbled that the abuses they most feared had come to pass. This was not quite the case, as these refugees were describing pure and simple corruption, not diversion for military purposes. In fact, the interviews showed a breakdown of a system that Western observers generally agree had been relatively free of corruption prior to the famine.

THE CLASH OF ADVOCACY AND OPERATIONS

WFP executive director Catherine Bertini understood all too well these weaknesses in the international aid system; senior executives in humanitarian relief agencies spend much of their time compensating for these shortcomings. When Bertini returned to Rome from North Korea in March 1997, she realized that the only way she could increase food aid commitments was to publicize the famine and thus put pressure on donor governments. The Western public would not stand for a repetition of the 1985 Ethiopian famine, even if their governments might. This publicity could be accomplished only if photographs could be taken of the worst affected areas and released to the international media. Bertini asked Pyongyang officials to allow an experienced photojournalist to visit the country in the summer of 1997 and record the famine; their approval of her request is but one more bit of evidence that they were desperate to increase food aid.

The WFP hired Hilary Mackenzie, an experienced Washington correspondent for *Maclean's*, the Canadian newsmagazine. A Scot by birth, Canadian by citizenship, and an American by residence, Mackenzie was a powerful writer and an experienced photojournalist. She was to take the most provocative and alarming photographs of the famine. She surveyed and photographed the human wreckage of the famine from June 7 to August 17, 1997, in all of the provinces save one, Yanggang, reputedly the host of the prison camps where troublemakers and dissenters were historically exiled. She visited people in their homes unannounced, interviewed provincial and county officials in the disaffected Northeast, and was able to escape for long periods of time from the three minders assigned to her by the Pyongyang authorities. These minders sought to restrict her access, constrain her conversations, and limit her photographs and reporting, but her local minders and provincial hosts did exactly the opposite, much to her astonishment. They asked her if she knew just how bad conditions were in the Northeast. They brought her to hospitals full of dying people, to nurseries full of acutely malnourished children, and to families where elderly people collapsed in front of her from hunger. She passed dead bodies lying along roadsides. She photographed the face of the famine, aggressively and accurately. Mackenzie saw sights the food monitors were denied, but the price she and the WFP paid for this access was extraordinary.[54]

By mid-August the North Koreans had had enough of Mackenzie: they first exiled her to Pyongyang and then forced her onto a fast train to China. Her photographs had exposed to the entire world the abysmal failure of the North Korean government to feed its own people and had embarrassed the regime in a way no event in fifty years had done. A diplomat later told me that the North Koreans were convinced she was a spy and considered prosecuting her. The WFP was nearly expelled from North Korea over the Mackenzie episode. Its attempt to conduct humanitarian relief operations while running an advocacy campaign as provocative as this one did not work, however well intentioned and desperately needed.

RELIEF VERSUS DEVELOPMENT PROGRAMMING

Humanitarian relief efforts are invariably riven with intrigue and inter-agency conflict; North Korea was no exception. Some of the intrigue centered on long-standing institutional rivalries between NGOs competing for media coverage or scarce donor contributions, or on personality and mandate conflicts between UN agencies. These conflicts should not be minimized, as some reflected profound disagreements over the existence of the famine, its causes, and what needed to be done about it.

The famine relief discipline underwent substantial revision by scholars of disaster relief in the 1980s because it had, in practice, failed on three counts. Programs did not prepare the society to be again self-sufficient, they did not have built-in ways to protect the society from future disasters to which it was particularly vulnerable, and they did not further develop the society.[55] From this scholarship came the notion of the "relief-to-development continuum." This continuum in theory connects the disciplines of relief and development, but relief agencies and donor governments had a difficult time putting the concept into practical operation. Some of the agency disputes in North Korea reflected the failure of organizations to institutionalize the relief-to-development continuum, but for the most part they reflected donor intransigence in funding development programs in a troglodytic regime that resisted even the most elemental economic reform.

Under established doctrine, the United Nations Development Program resident representative in a country has the preeminent responsibility for coordinating the humanitarian response of all the UN agencies working there. But established doctrine is seldom followed, primarily because the UNDP has proven so poorly equipped to perform these duties; it seldom leads any emergency response. That has not stopped the agency from attempting to retake lost bureaucratic turf, however. In the case of North Korea, UNDP resistance prevented the appointment of the WFP country director as the general humanitarian coordinator. This intrigue led to a harsh exchange of letters between the two agencies, and the United Nations ended up having no humanitarian coordinator in the country until December 1997. American NGOs together firmly endorsed the choice of the WFP as the humanitarian coordinator, because the famine required an immediate food aid response as much as a developmental response. The UNDP, however, argued that the food emergency had been exaggerated. In private meetings, the UNDP and UNICEF claimed the North Korean response had unnecessarily withdrawn needed funds for more important development programs, such as to stop declining agricultural production and to deal with the acute health problems of the population. The UNICEF national director, Omawali Omawali, a distinguished nutritionist, even took the view that "food crisis" was too extreme a term; he preferred the term "food shortage" because it was less alarming. He argued that, instead of a famine, the country's collapsing public health system was the root of the problem. The crisis, he said, was caused by poor drinking water and sanitation which was spreading disease, driving up malnutrition rates. Omawali interpreted the cause of the alarming 1998 nutritional survey results to be these two factors rather than declining food intake by children.[56]

For centuries it has been known that epidemics accompany famines. For two main reasons, the body's immune system breaks down and vulnerability to communicable disease increases when a person becomes acutely malnourished. First, malnutrition reduces amino acids, which are the building blocks of proteins and thus critical to the development of antibodies to fight disease. Second, malnutrition damages the liver so that it no longer properly cleanses the body of noxious substances. Liver and kidney failure induced by acute malnutrition finally causes death from starvation.

Disease spreads more rapidly as sanitation and water quality deteriorate for people on the move in search of food during the later stages of famine.[57] No one familiar with famines would dispute this accepted wisdom; it is for this reason that, as famine approaches, most NGOs immunize all children under age five against major communicable diseases. The goal is to reduce the death rate among this very vulnerable population. It is UNICEF's mandate to deal with these consequences of famine: deteriorating sanitation, insufficient water supply, and the immunization of children against major diseases. Unfortunately, UNICEF also initially denied the existence of famine and later suggested that the deaths that were occurring were attributable not to hunger but to the failure of the public health system.

Most emergencies cause an intense rivalry among UN agencies for donor funding; during the North Korean famine more than any other, nearly all pledges were directed to one agency—the WFP. One could argue that the North Koreans repeatedly said they wanted food and nothing else, and that they requested medication much later in the famine and then only as an afterthought. Sue Lautze reported: "I was urged to understand that the current DPRK policy is [to] meet a singular and urgent need for food aid only. Any non-food assistance is viewed as an unwelcome waste of resources that otherwise could have been used to purchase emergency food aid."[58] Moreover, donor governments were reluctant to provide funding for any activities not directly perceived to be part of the famine response—such as UNICEF's medical programs—because there was so much political, diplomatic, and military opposition to providing any help for a rogue state like North Korea.

The UNDP had an even more difficult time than did UNICEF, as medication for children is much easier to justify to skeptical donors than long-term agricultural assistance. Christian Lamare, the UNDP resident representative, faced a formidable obstacle in his effort to move the North Koreans beyond the immediate crisis, as they insisted that their only agricultural problem was a lack of inputs—seed, fertilizer, herbicides, and pesticides. They claimed that if donors would only give them these inputs the famine would be over quickly, which while correct begged the sustainability question. If donors stopped the inputs, the famine would resume. Donor governments, led by the European Union, saw the solution to the North Korean crisis (which they initially denied existed) as a reform of the grossly distorted economic incentive structure, not the provision of inputs. They argued—correctly, in my view—that agriculture governed by North Korea's *juche* ideology was a disaster and should not be subsidized, but instead drastically reformed. Until these economic reforms were implemented, the European Union refused to give any assistance in agricultural development, and at one point in early 1998 it conditioned any further pledges of food aid on these reforms.

As has been said before, however, Pyongyang viewed reform as anathema and officials would explode at the mere mention of the word. Humanitarian agencies thus steered clear of using the term in their reporting or their program plans, or even in their casual conversation. As Lamare needed to secure North Korean agreement to a remarkably unpopular idea and then convince donor governments that Pyongyang had embraced and would execute something it found despicable, he presented modest reforms as "modernization," an ideologically acceptable term for ideologically acceptable change. Lamare and his staff successfully scoured Kim Il Sung's collected works to find some ideological defense of farmers markets. Considering the Great Leader's prodigious literary output, this was no small undertaking. The quotations they found helped them to introduce the notion of markets into the agricultural and food delivery systems. North Koreans may have taken the lessons from these expatriate-initiated economic reforms as an internal justification for the massive expansion of the farmers markets.

With EU support, the UNDP held two conferences on the topic of North Korean agriculture, in May and November 1998, so UN agencies, NGOs, and donor governments could discuss a modest program of small agricultural change with a very immodest price tag: $300 million.[59] The North Koreans agreed to the systemic changes proposed at the conferences: agricultural microcredit to expand local markets, increased household production, expansion of privately owned livestock, improved land use to stop erosion, an extended double-cropping initiative, and modernization of the country's two fertilizer factories. Acceptance of these changes was more than many Westerners had expected, given the resistance of the regime to reform, and it left the question open as to whether the regime intended to implement the changes, or whether it had agreed to the changes simply to get donor contributions. To say that the donor government response was tepid to the funding request for the UNDP program would be an extraordinary understatement.[60] Only one government had pledged $1 million by February 1999 and the UNDP added $1 million of its internal funds. Some of these same concepts were included in a $30 million agricultural development loan designed a year earlier by the International Fund for Agricultural Development (IFAD), which the United States decided neither to support nor to oppose when IFAD's board of directors voted on it. The IFAD loan project showed progress, but the international staff had no independent method for determining true compliance, which led the aid community to view the program with skepticism.

Marcus Noland, a senior fellow at the Institute for International Economics, argues that any internationally funded agricultural production schemes for North Korea make little economic sense, as agriculture will never be the country's strong economic suit.[61] Given the country's dearth of good land and its harsh climate and short growing season, investment in the industrial sector would seem a more logical choice, yet there the regime has been even more reluctant to implement liberalizing economic reforms. The point is well taken over the long term, but people must eat in the short term. The UNDP and IFAD agricultural development plans needed to be viewed as short-term solutions to the massive food deficits that the country faced.

THE WEAKNESSES OF THE FAMINE AID SYSTEM

The inherent weaknesses of the international humanitarian aid system became sadly apparent during the North Korean famine. The WFP has no food or money of its own to manage large-scale food aid programs; it is entirely dependent on Western governments with enough food surpluses to respond to UN appeals. The other part of the humanitarian response structure consists of the International Red Cross and NGOs, which issue appeals to private citizens.

Aid agencies have several limitations, which in the case of the North Korean famine proved particularly debilitating. In seeking private donations, both the Red Cross and NGOs depend on public knowledge of the crisis and sympathy for the people in need of help. If potential contributors are unaware of the crisis or, worse, have a negative impression of the country in need of help, their response will generally be lethargic. Media coverage must therefore be persistent over time, tell a consistent story, and make some appeal to one's emotions, or the public will not respond.

But whereas pictures of starving children on the evening news may motivate contributors to act, the fact that there are such photographs means the humanitarian response has already failed. Famines occur in stages; the earlier the stage, the more successful humanitarian aid is in preventing future stages. The kind of widespread, acute malnutrition that attracts photographic attention takes place in the final and irreversible stages of famine. Children in that condition, absent extraordinary medical attention seldom available in a famine, cannot be saved: the length of their remaining lives is measurable in days, not in months. The damage done to one's body in the final stages of famine is so severe that one cannot usually absorb food, even if it becomes available. More important, from the time it is pledged, food aid from Western governments takes two to three months—if not longer—to appear on a hungry person's table. People who are already suffering from acute malnutrition generally will not live that long. Waiting for the disaster to reach its full fury to get photographs makes no sense, and yet photographs of that fury are what force recalcitrant governments and distracted NGOs to act.

Unfortunately for hungry North Koreans, their government had an aversion to media coverage. In the spring of 1997 three senior NGO managers, myself included, accompanied Ambassador Jim Bishop, the humanitarian relief director for InterAction, on a visit to the North Korean mission to the United Nations to discuss the impending crisis. The North Korean diplomats made their formal appeals for food and medical help and asked politely when we could respond. I explained that the NGOs needed to educate the American people about the crisis so they might press the U.S. government to respond to the WFP appeals and contribute private money to NGOs. Only then could the NGOs respond to their list of needs. When I explained that educating the public required extensive media coverage, their facial expressions changed noticeably: their government would never agree to any media coverage and we should forget about it. They were particularly insistent about not allowing any photographs of any kind, which is exactly what we most needed.

These diplomats lived in New York City and undoubtedly had noticed the daily extravagance of Western electronic and print media, and the absence of any limits on coverage of even the most sacred subjects. The television programs I saw in Pyongyang could not have contrasted more dramatically: each night viewers are treated to Soviet-style propaganda films about the Korean War, patriotic songs sung by military choirs with occasional scenes of an idyllic countryside, and the North Korean version of the evening news. The thought of their country being subject to Western-style media coverage must have been frightening to the diplomats, but without it their country's survival was at risk.

Yet no publicity would have been necessary at all had donor governments acted on the intelligence data they had and made early and generous commitments of food aid to the WFP. The media did not focus concerted coverage on the famines and civil wars in Africa during the 1980s and 1990s, and yet the United States, Canada, and the European governments saved tens of millions of lives by their unpublicized generosity. The "CNN effect" that donor governments often mention as a necessary component of all disaster relief in fact is misunderstood and exaggerated. It is only essential when NGOs must raise private money, when military intervention is needed to stop massive loss of life, or when donor governments refuse to act for geostrategic reasons, as was the case in North Korea. Electronic media can change the decisions of paralyzed, distracted, or hostile governments over aid issues. North Korea was sadly one of these uncommon events where media coverage was essential but forbidden.[62]

THE SOVIET RELIEF EFFORT OF 1921 ## AS AN ALTERNATIVE MODEL

It would be tempting but wrong to conclude that one of the sad lessons of the North Korean crisis is that it is impossible to run a targeted relief and rehabilitation effort under a totalitarian political system. Herbert Hoover's legendary humanitarian relief effort during the Soviet famine of 1921–23, under conditions strikingly similar to those of North Korea in the 1990s, is proof that North Korea's fate was not foreordained.

Hoover had been the director of U.S. humanitarian relief efforts to save Belgium, and later the rest of Europe, from starvation caused by the economic and military devastation of World War I. His efforts dwarf the relief efforts carried on now, both in the size of their budgets and in the tonnage of food contributed. During the course of the war he shipped 56 million MT of food and clothing to Europe.[63] When famine swept across the Volga region of Russia in the early 1920s, Hoover was serving as secretary of commerce in Calvin Coolidge's administration. As perhaps the most admired humanitarian figure in the West, Hoover was able to correspond directly with Lenin and the new Bolshevik leadership.

A remarkable number of analogies can be made between Hoover's relief efforts then and those in North Korea in the 1990s. In both cases, the profound ideological antagonisms and conflicting worldviews colored all negotiations, all operations, and all personal relationships. In both cases, the famines threatened large populations and had the potential to undermine the foundations of the governments in power. Thus both regimes were under heavy stress, though in very different stages of historical development: one was a nascent revolutionary movement seeking a new world under a socialist banner, and the other was in its ideological death

throes. Both relief efforts were among the most politicized in this century. In the first, opponents within the Bolshevik government accused
Hoover of using the relief effort to undermine communism; this charge
was repeated by left-wing journals in the United States that were sympathetic to the Russian Revolution, such as *The Nation*. Hoover tried to
keep the relief effort neutral and distinct from trade and foreign policy
matters, though he well knew they could only be separated cosmetically.
Humanitarian relief, local politics, and diplomacy are inextricably inter-
woven. The politicization of the North Korean famine has, of course,
already been discussed in earlier chapters of this study.

On one critically important point, however, the two crises were
very different. Hoover intended to stop the famine and leave the country
after it was over, without engaging in any long-term development program. Lenin's collectivist agricultural policies, combined with weather
conditions, had caused the famine, and he was forced to retreat from his
policies because of their disastrous consequences. Once this happened
production improved and the crisis ended. The case of North Korea is
much more complex, as the country will never be self-sufficient agriculturally, and thus it must export mining and industrial products and import
food to stop the famine. If foreign food and concessional aid were to stop
and the NGOs were to leave North Korea as Hoover did Soviet Russia,
the famine would reemerge in all its fierce intensity.

The Republican right attacked Hoover's efforts because it believed
they ensured the survival of a malevolent regime. Congressional opponents of the relief effort in North Korea made the same charges. They
argued that the United States should use the relief effort to further its
diplomatic agenda in North Korea, that a purely humanitarian food aid
program might extend the life of a reprehensible regime, and that the
donated food might be diverted by the North Korean military. Those who
feared that the German military would divert food from the relief effort
had made a similar charge against Hoover's efforts in Belgium.[64]

In both cases other diplomatic issues complicated the relief effort
and how donors and recipients perceived it. In the case of North Korea
the diplomatic issues included the four-party talks and the Agreed Framework, and in the case of Bolshevik Russia they involved U.S. recognition
of the new government and the establishment of trade relations. In both
situations the severity of the famine became an issue—though in Russia,

the question was how many people were dying; in North Korea, the question was whether people were dying. Parallels exist even in the details of the relief effort. Stalin insisted on taxing the relief effort to gather revenue, though Hoover refused to pay, and the North Korean authorities charged outlandish rates to relief workers for everything they used in the country, and the aid agencies did pay. It is here that the similarities end and profound differences begin.

From the start of the Soviet relief effort, Herbert Hoover held unequivocal managerial authority in his hands and was only peripherally constrained by the Soviet government. He insisted that the effort be run privately through the American Relief Administration (ARA), of which he was the chief executive officer. The ARA was funded through one large U.S. government appropriation, so he did not have his attention diverted by fund-raising constraints. Hoover would not abide other relief organizations intervening with their modest staff and resources, for he feared that the Soviet government would play one organization against another—an activity at which the North Koreans became skilled.

Hoover also demanded complete control over the relief effort from start to finish. The ARA would determine who was eligible, which areas would be targeted based on need, who was appointed to local committees to oversee village distributions, and who was hired as local staff. The ARA would maintain control over food from delivery to consumption. At negotiations in Riga he obtained the Bolsheviks' reluctant approval of nearly all of his demands; when the agreements were violated, he would threaten to shut down the entire operation and go home. Hoover placed the ARA in charge of decision making over relief operations in the field and intervened on diplomatic and political issues impeding the relief effort only when his staff asked for help. Despite virulent opposition from figures as diverse as Leon Trotsky and Stalin, the Bolshevik government agreed to Hoover's intrusive terms. It wished to improve its relationship with the United States, just as the North Korean regime did more than seventy years later, and, moreover, Hoover pledged so much food during the negotiations that it could hardly refuse his offer.

Thus Hoover used his moral and managerial authority, enormous resources, and reputation for competence to take command of a huge undertaking in short order. More important than anything else, the ARA did the job well and was recognized across the Russian hinterland as the salvation of the proletariat and the peasants alike. Even Moscow recognized this fact, so, although it was annoyed by ARA tactics, it was thankful that the crisis had been overcome. Unlike in North Korea, the Soviet central authorities became admirers and facilitators of U.S. efforts and actions, but local Bolshevik officials unaccustomed to the burdens of governance were more obstructionist. In North Korea, the central authorities obstructed relief operations, whereas provincial and county officials facilitated them.

In short, the North Korean effort lacked Hoover's unity of command. No early, single source of huge resources existed with which to negotiate an agreement with Pyongyang. The many semi-autonomous NGOs, the Red Cross movement, and three UN agencies were unable to negotiate with the central authorities from a position of strength. The WFP was in no position to force a coherent strategy on this chaotic structure or to threaten to leave if the central government obstructed the relief effort. Some donors, such as the Chinese, the Red Cross, the European Union, the Japanese, and the South Koreans, chose to circumvent the WFP by providing bilateral shipments of food negotiated on separate terms. The WFP also had to contend with attacks by other UN agencies and the competing diplomatic agendas of donor governments for which the relief efforts were a distraction rather than a central objective. The United States did increase its food aid to North Korea substantially between 1996 and 1999, but the increase occurred so gradually that Washington squandered its leverage to insist, as Hoover did, on unambiguous standards of accountability and careful targeting.

9

A GREAT FAMINE?

A S THE NEWS MEDIA and NGOs accumulated public evidence of the existence of a famine in North Korea, even the most skeptical relief workers became convinced that there was a problem. By late 1998 and early 1999, even those who refused to use the contentious word "famine" to characterize the food crisis admitted there had been excess deaths. The question thus became not *whether* anyone had died from the "food shortages," but how many.

In the spring of 1998, on one of Pomnyun's visits to Washington, he and I were asked to speak to the Korea Society about the famine. We both argued in our remarks that the evidence we had accumulated suggested that between two and three million people had died. After our presentations a respected U.S. government intelligence analyst confronted me, upset by our calculations, and asked why we constantly insisted on trying to quantify the devastation of the famine.

Numbers count for several important reasons. They quantify the comparative devastation to inform the historical record. They help analysts determine the success or failure of a regime's response to it. Assessing a famine's severity before it ends can influence public, media, bureaucratic, and congressional opinion in donor countries on how robust the response should be. Finally, knowing the severity of a famine allows analysts to judge the success of the international relief effort.

Numbers are also important because exaggerating death rates in one crisis can kill disaster victims elsewhere by diverting life-saving resources. During the early 1990s, the United States, Canada, and the European Union—the principal donors—changed their agriculture policies and reduced national subsidies from domestic farmers to create theoretically an agricultural free market. These policy changes caused a deficit in the total level of food aid,[1] which in turn meant that committing too much food to one crisis would create a food aid deficit in others. Increasingly inadequate donor food aid reserves for famines and civil wars also caused donor governments to divert resources from long-term development programs in India and other developing countries with high malnutrition rates but no famine conditions, so emergencies elsewhere could be alleviated. For these reasons, some NGOs hesitated to declare North Korea's crisis a famine.

How many people died in the North Korean famine will not be entirely clear until there is a change of government, if then. Using what we know about death rates from border surveys and what scholars of the political system tell us about the nature of North Korean society, it is possible to make some estimates about the severity of the famine.

ANECDOTAL AND REAL EVIDENCE ABOUT DEATH RATES

As the famine was cresting in early 1997, anecdotal evidence began appearing that death rates were high, but it was not until 1998 that comprehensive and rigorous data could confirm these presumptions. Apocalyptic stories of massive death rates first appeared in some of the testimonies of refugees interviewed by the KBSM in September 1997. According to one refugee,

> Thirty percent of the population of Hamhung City have died. In [apartments in] Il-Hyong . . . all floors above the second floor have died. . . . people live only on the first floor. The large numbers of empty houses reveals the amount of people that have died. . . . A whole generation has died. A lot more people have died than during the Korean War. Starvation is more horrible than the war.[2]

However genuine this refugee's testimony may have been, there is no way of confirming the 30 percent figure, especially for a city the size of Hamhung with a prefamine population of seven hundred thousand. It is telling, though, that refugees from Hamhung City speak most often of apocalyptic death rates, compared to refugees from all other regions of the country.

A more authoritative witness to the famine was the defector Hwang Jong Yop, who as the third-ranking member of the North Korean Communist Party had access to state secrets such as those concerning the famine. Hwang, the president of Kim Il Sung University, defected in February 1997. Although reluctant to give specific information at first, in a speech before the Unification Council of South Korea on November 12, 1997, Hwang described starvation deaths even in the military-industrial complex in Chagang province:

> The[re] are many military factories in the North, but one in Chagang province was given no food rations for nine to ten months. According to a report from the related industry secretary at the meeting of secretariats, about 2,000 high-ranking engineers starved to death. He said that if the situation continues mass uprisings can be expected.[3]

Hwang claimed that 2.5 million people had died in the famine by the end of 1997. On one of his visits to the Chinese border in late 1997, Jasper Becker interviewed a well-dressed and well-fed North Korean who claimed her parents were senior party members. The woman told him that within party cadre meetings the figure being used for total deaths was one million.[4] Other refugees, however, told Becker that two million people had died.

In his 1998 book, *North Korea: Truth or Lies?*, Hwang describes a conversation he had with the director of the North Korean Office of Statistics:

> In November 1996, I was very concerned about the economy and asked a top official in charge of agricultural statistics and food how many people had starved to death. He replied: "In 1995, about five hundred thousand people starved to death including fifty thousand party cadres. In 1996, about one million people are estimated to have starved to death." He continued, "In 1997, about 2 million people would starve to death if no international aid were provided."[5]

Hwang also tells the story that in late 1996 Kim Jong Il called in six Central Worker's Party committee members and assigned them the sensitive task of contacting the provincial party committees and asking them to collect information on famine deaths in their areas. Their reports showed that, based on provincial estimates, three million people had died. Kim Jong Il's comments were twofold: First, he said, "The rich are becoming richer," perhaps a reference to that fact that the party cadres were profiting from the sale of diverted food. Second, he instructed the committee members, "Be tough. No uprising will be allowed. I will control military power. Have a strong heart. If the people revolt they will hang us, and if they don't [hang us] the South Koreans will."[6]

Western analysts often question the information provided by North Korean defectors, as they suspect that the South Korean Central Intelligence Agency (KCIA) instructs the defectors to conform to Seoul's view of the North Korean regime, or that the defectors on their own try to please their new hosts. Thus some questioned Hwang's credibility, despite his sources for the death rate data, his senior position in the government, the logic of the increase in death rates chronologically, and the similarity between Hwang's description of the regime's inner workings and descriptions offered by scholars.[7] Given that his book criticizes the South Korean government, however, it is likely that Hwang's comments represent his own views rather than those of the South Korean government. While many defectors do take the perspective of the South Korean government in their public statements about the North, Hwang is not just any defector. He is an old man of very high rank, infamous in South Korea as the founder of *juche* ideology, and a powerful figure in the North Korean hierarchy for several decades who would not be easily intimidated by anyone in the South, KCIA or otherwise. Moreover, at the time Hwang's book was published in 1997, the KCIA was consistently understating famine deaths and was publicly critical of anyone who claimed North Korea was experiencing high death rates.

By 1999, however, the KCIA had changed its position. In February that year, Seoul reported that the North Korean Public Security Ministry conducted a population survey before the July 1998 election of delegates for the North Korean parliament, the Supreme People's Assembly. The survey showed the population had fallen by between 2.5 million and 3 million.[8] Korea scholar Nicholas Eberstadt likewise notes that if one compares the number of delegates elected to the two national assemblies (1990 and 1998), three million people seem to be missing. Constitutionally, each delegate must represent thirty thousand people, and the population should have grown by three million people during those eight years, but the number of delegates remained exactly the same.[9]

Only one quasi-official North Korean statement admitted the existence of high death rates. In May 1999, Jon In Chan, an official from the

Foreign Ministry's Flood Damage Rehabilitation Committee, told a delegation of U.S., Australian, and European aid groups conducting a humanitarian assessment that 220,000 people had died between 1995 and 1998, "an increase of 37 percent."[10] Until this point no regime official had been willing to provide any hard numbers, except to say a few dozen or hundred children had died from malnutrition over the course of the entire crisis. In an earlier episode, an official said that 2.5 million people had perished, but the official news agency in Pyongyang produced an immediate correction, saying he had been misquoted. Jon's announcement in May 1999, however, was not followed by any official correction, which suggests that the regime intended for him to provide the data.[11] It is unclear from the press account the base against which the 37 percent increase was being measured. As with most North Korean statistical data, the announcement likely represents a political decision by the senior leadership that it was ideologically acceptable to admit the occurrence of famine deaths in order to increase donor food aid commitments. These death rates should be seen as political ammunition for the central government's survival strategy, not as empirical data upon which the famine's severity could be judged.

Jon's authoritative admission aside, one source of data on death rates was more precise than any other. A food refugee who traveled back and forth to China several times provided KBSM with monthly death rates from January 1995 to June 1998, which he obtained from the city hall of the mining city where he had worked.[12] According to these numbers, the famine claimed 19 percent of the city's population between January 1995 and June 1998. Yet the food refugee reported that the mortality data was understated rather than exaggerated, because 700 townspeople had died in a cholera epidemic exacerbated by the famine in the summer of 1995, whereas only 280 deaths were recorded. Also unrecorded were the deaths of internally displaced people and of food refugees in China. Mortality rates for the city reached their peak between May 1996 and August 1997, and they dropped precipitously between January and June 1998, as food availability increased and the number of mouths to feed had greatly decreased. More than any other statistic, the June 1998 turnout in the national elections in this city showed the famine's devastation: only 54.8 percent of the people voted in the elections, if one uses the 1994 population as a base. This suggests that beyond the recorded deaths,

26.25 percent of the city's residents had either left the town in search of food or had died and not had their deaths registered. If urban areas experienced death rates comparable to those in this mining city, total deaths could well have approached the number of deaths Hwang Jong Yop suggested.

Data from another unlikely source—county officials—suggests that there may have been high mortality rates in other regions of the country as well as in the urban centers. In planning food distributions, officials from the WFP took county population figures from the central government and, before shipping any food, attempted to confirm the data with the census records of county officials. Aid officials reported that in 60 percent of the cases, the figures from the central government were noticeably higher than those they received from the county administrators, and rarely if ever were they lower.[13] In an effort to confirm the WFP report data, an NGO public health expert obtained census data from two counties he visited in the summer of 1998. In these two northwestern counties, the population figures were 12 percent and 13 percent lower than stated in the central government census.[14]

These reports contradict what common sense would indicate that government officials' behavior should be. County administrators should have had a heavy incentive to exaggerate, not to understate, population estimates, so they could increase their allocation of fixed food aid resources for their hungry people. Central government officials, in contrast, should have had no such incentive, since donor governments pledge food aid based not on total population figures but on the food deficit of the country as a whole. Three possible explanations for this anomaly come to mind. First, one might think that the lower county figures reflect population movements induced by the famine, but, if so, then the figures should have increased in other counties, which they did not. Second, one could argue that these missing people were active-duty soldiers, but North Korean officials told the UN Population Fund that the military population is not included in the census figures.[15] The third and most likely explanation is that the census data discrepancy represents deaths. Perhaps it is only a coincidence, but a Johns Hopkins University study of death rates in North Hamgyong province in the Northeast (discussed later in this chapter) was 12.9 percent—the same as the population disparity in the two northwestern counties.

WHO WERE THE FAMINE'S VICTIMS?

From the analysis above, it is clear that the famine was devastating the entire country. But electronic media give the Western public the impression that famines cause universal misery, which is not true. Given the nature of the North Korean regime, its political objectives, and information provided by border surveys and other reporting, the question that must be answered is who was most vulnerable.

Public health conditions in North Korea had been deteriorating for a decade or more by the time the famine began. The hospitals I visited looked more like those in least developed countries than in middle-income countries such as Thailand, Taiwan, or Malaysia—a category to which North Korea had theoretically belonged in the 1970s. Tuberculosis, virtually unknown in Western countries, had reached epidemic levels by the 1990s, according to a Korean Chinese doctor I interviewed along the Chinese border who had treated many refugees over the course of several years. "Children are suffering from vitamin D deficiencies and have deformed bones and rickets," he said. "TB, hepatitis, and dysentery are common given the poor housing, inadequate heating, dirty water, very cold winter temperatures, and abysmal diet. Everyone in North Korea looks like a patient."[16]

What aggravated mortality rates in this famine more than most was the fact that it occurred in a northern climate with long, severe winters. People living in such cold climates need more calories to survive than do individuals in much warmer climates. The shortage of energy and fuel also meant that city apartments were insufficiently heated, if indeed they were heated at all. When temperatures reach as low as −30°F and heating is nonexistent, malnourished people do not survive for long. Although the extreme cold may have suppressed warm weather diseases such as malaria, it exacerbated upper respiratory illnesses. As one refugee reported, "I think the poorest people in North Korea are children and older people. The situation becomes more severe during the wintertime. People die not only from starvation, but also from cold weather because people cannot get coal."[17]

Refugees also reported several cholera epidemics. Because the water-purification systems had collapsed in the cities, drinking water was of poor quality and waterborne disease was common. In fact, most of the major communicable diseases unknown in Western countries were reported across the country even before the famine began.[18] These diseases took far more lives than the famine itself, a conclusion that the KBSM refugee surveys confirm. Amartya Sen writes that in "most of the famines I have studied, over 90 percent of the deaths have not been directly caused by pure starvation, but by diseases stimulated and spread by hunger and its associated correlates."[19]

Public health issues aside, however, some expert observers argued that Pyongyang was systematically using the famine to exterminate certain segments of the population. The Minnesota Lawyers' International Human Rights Committee and Human Rights Watch/Asia in 1988 published one of the few comprehensive studies of human rights in North Korea. Their study describes the organized system of state terror involving arbitrary arrest for the most innocuous violation of petty rules, regularized torture, and summary execution used by the North Korean regime to maintain control.[20] This repressive system is not equally applied to the entire population. Those in the upper ranks of the social structure are often not punished for serious infractions of the criminal law, unless the infractions imply disloyalty to the regime.[21]

Perceived loyalty to the state has long determined status in North Korea. In 1958 Kim Il Sung ordered the population divided into three categories: a core class fully trusted by and loyal to the regime (25 percent of the population), a "wavering" class (more than 55 percent), and a hostile class (20 percent). One percent of the population, or about two hundred thousand people, including the senior cadre and the extended Kim family, rules the country. Only the core class is allowed to live in Pyongyang, except for specially designated areas of the city where people of middle rank may live. Virtually the entire core class lives in cities and larger towns. Members of the wavering or uncertain class, who have something in their background or family history within the past three generations that makes them politically suspect, serve in lower-echelon cadre positions and certain professions and are not allowed to take any sensitive jobs. The hostile class is never seen by foreigners and is discriminated against in the provision of goods and services.[22] Many have been exiled to the remote Northeast.

The Heritage Foundation, a think tank in Washington, D.C., hosted a session in March 1998 with two defectors from North Korea, Col. Joo-Hwal Choi and a diplomat, Young-Hwan Ko. The two men talked about the food crisis, among other things, and claimed that the North Korean population was not at risk except for two groups of people. These groups included about two hundred thousand political prisoners and 3 percent to 4 percent of the population who were descended from precommunist capitalists or defectors who fled to South Korea during the war. Members of these groups had been sent into exile in remote mountainous areas and were not being fed, they said. But these two men defected in 1995 and 1991, respectively, so their information is questionable. Their reports contradicted much of the scholarship on the subject; most of the one thousand food refugees interviewed were from the coastal plain in the Northeast, not from the mountainous areas where the defectors said the politically suspect were in exile. Finally, the defectors' comments seemed to reflect KCIA views of North Korea more than anything else. They argued that the United States should be focusing on North Korean human rights violations, which they say are a much bigger problem than starvation is. Although they did not state as much, the theory that the state used the famine to exterminate problem elements in society— if true—would constitute one massive human rights abuse.

Indeed, if the weight of evidence supported this theory, it would have profound implications under international humanitarian law. I have used the term "food refugees" throughout this book to distinguish between the definition of refugee under international law and the people who crossed the border to get food for their families and then returned to North Korea. The latter were not true refugees protected by international conventions. The Geneva Convention states that a refugee must, among other things, be someone "with a well-founded fear of being persecuted for reasons . . . of membership of a particular social group or political opinion."[23] State-contrived starvation could reasonably be interpreted to be a form of persecution, more cruel than mass executions, since starvation takes so much longer to kill. If the central government was in fact using the famine as a means of liquidating politically suspect families, and the survivors were escaping into China, then they were true refugees and should have been afforded the legal protection they deserved. The genocide convention might even have obtained if a particular class of people had been marked for extermination by the authorities—even if by starvation rather than by outright execution.

Punitive rationing is not without precedent. In the Chinese famine of 1958–62, village families who descended from landlords either were not fed at all or were fed a lower ration than the poorer class of peasants.[24] Robert Conquest's research on the Ukrainian famine in the early 1930s proved that Stalin's objective was to liquidate the kulak class of farmers.[25] Similarly, U.S. government intelligence sources reported that as the public distribution system broke down, the North Korean authorities focused food supplies on three groups: members and immediate families of the military, of the party, and of workers in strategic industries such as mining.[26]

If differential feeding had occurred based on political classification, it should have been reflected in malnutrition data. The WFP, UNICEF, European Union, and Save the Children UK conducted a nutritional survey in the summer of 1998, a year after the peak of the famine. Technically, the survey had several weaknesses: the nature of the survey excluded 30 percent of the population from the database, including internally displaced people and refugees, and the survey teams relied on government translators throughout. Moreover, it was conducted after the famine had peaked and conditions had begun to improve. Nevertheless, it is the best extant assessment of nutritional conditions in the country.[27] The very high rates of malnutrition it reported suggest that society at the time was under severe nutritional stress: 75 percent of the children suffered from moderate to acute malnutrition. What is most instructive about the malnutrition rates, though, is that they are proximate in size to the three basic classes of political loyalty described in Kim Il Sung's 1958 speech (see table 2).[28]

The similarity of these numbers gives pause. If the theory of rationing according to political classification is correct, the malnutrition statistics should approximate the political classification proportions, and they do.

But this does not prove conclusively that political loyalty was used specifically to determine who ate and who did not; other related factors might have been responsible for the categories of malnutrition being the same size as the political classes. As was stated in an earlier chapter, the favored classes may simply have had more political power to command

Table 2. Classes of Political Loyalty and Rates of Malnutrition

Kim Il Sung's Classes of Loyalty (based on 1958 speech)		UN Nutritional Assessment Data (error rate of ±5 percent)	
Core class	25 percent	No malnutrition	32 percent
Wavering class	55 percent	Moderate malnutrition	62 percent
Hostile class	20 percent	Acute malnutrition	16 percent

food because of their status within the political system. Some anecdotal evidence exists that politically suspect elements of the population were faring no worse than other elements. The Johns Hopkins research teams conducted interviews on this very point: people interviewed did not believe that any deliberate attempt was being made to eliminate the hostile class.[29] Similarly, the KBSM survey suggests that the 27 percent mortality rate for food refugee families was actually a bit lower than the 29 percent rate for the population of the entire *han* from which the refugees came. If those people who crossed into China had been deliberately starved because they came from suspect families, the mortality rate in their families would likely have been much higher than that of the *han* as a whole. I asked one refugee in Jilin, whose father had been a soldier in the South Korean Army during the Korean War and had spent years in a prisoner of war camp before finally being released, whether he had been discriminated against. He told me that his efforts to move up into the ranks of the party were frustrated by his suspect background, but he dismissed suggestions that food was being denied him because of his father's history. He said all his neighbors were in the same position and they did not have the political problems he had had. Robert Scalapino reports that the many defectors he interviewed for his book on North Korean communism left because of their inability to move up the social and economic ladder, having descended from families with politically suspect backgrounds; this is not, however, the same as targeted destruction. Thus it may be that the most vulnerable elements of the population were not those whom the state somehow singled out for destruction, but those who lacked the political power or access to resources to protect themselves.

THE JOHNS HOPKINS STUDY OF NORTH KOREAN FAMINE DEATHS

The Johns Hopkins University's School of Public Health conducted the most rigorous analysis of death and birth rates in North Korea done since the beginning of the famine, based on interviews with 440 food refugees in China.[30] The Johns Hopkins survey took an unusual approach to correct for the criticism that many refugee surveys were not a random reflection of the entire population, a condition required to reach conclusions about national death rates. The Johns Hopkins researchers asked the refugees how many members of their families had died since the death of Kim Il Sung, a historic date all North Koreans would remember, until the day they left for China. By the very fact that they left their homes to escape to another country, however, refugees were a self-selecting segment of the population and therefore not random. For that reason, the researchers also asked the refugees how many members of their siblings' families had died. Since their siblings probably had not moved, this information provided a good basis for comparison and a more random representation of the general population. The researchers learned that siblings who stayed home in North Korea also experienced high family death rates, but not as high as those of the food refugees.

The study shows that from 1995 to 1997, annual death rates rose eightfold over the prefamine level, from 0.55 percent in the 1993 census to an average of 4.3 percent during each of the three years of the study. This 12.9 percent rate combines the higher death rate among food refugees with the lower rates of their siblings. During this same period the number of people who claimed that the public distribution system was their principal food supply declined from 61 percent to 6 percent. These numbers confirm earlier findings by the KBSM, Jasper Becker, and my own interviews. Births also declined by 50 percent over the survey's period, from 21.8 per thousand to 11, another famine indicator.

One failing of the Johns Hopkins study, like the KBSM surveys, is that it asks about deaths at home, not about deaths of people on the move. Thus both understate famine deaths.[31] As Alexander de Waal shows in his classic study of the Darfur famine in Sudan in the 1980s, the death rates of people escaping famine generally rise precipitously, because after they leave home, food refugees have lost their principal coping mechanisms—family, friends, neighbors, and familiar surroundings—and because their disease environment has increased the risk of infection.[32] In addition, travel demands more calories than does a sedentary life at home. The only exception to this are cases when migrants find humanitarian relief food near their homes or work to sustain themselves. In North Korea, however, food aid was not provided to displaced people or refugees, and as every region of the country suffered the ravages of economic meltdown, none could provide jobs for migrants.

As public health scientists (and thus wary of violating their analytical systems for predicting mortality), the Johns Hopkins researchers were hesitant to extrapolate their figures to the general North Korean population. But as 80 percent of the food refugees they interviewed were from North Hamgyong province, the researchers speculated on what the actual famine deaths would be among the provincial population as a whole. They write:

> [A]ssuming that the North Hamgyong population grew at the officially recorded rate of 1.4 percent in 1994 and then experienced a birth rate of 16 per 1000 and a death rate of 40 per 1000 from 1995 through 1997, deaths during the 3-year period would have numbered about 245,000, and would have exceeded births by 2.5 to one.[33]

To understand the relevance of the Johns Hopkins study to the population as a whole, one must ask how representative the province's experience was relative to that of the country as a whole. North Hamgyong does have three advantages not enjoyed by other provinces. First, it borders the Korean-speaking region of China. Hungry people could therefore visit their relatives in China to get money and food and others could find jobs and earn money to bring home. As one refugee from the northwestern province of North Pyongan, near the Chinese border, told the KBSM:

> There are so many people dying from starvation and diseases and so many people are crossing the border. There has been no ration for years now and the life is extremely difficult. People on the street sway as they walk as if they are just about to faint and there are a number of people who would actually faint and never get up. In

fact, quite a lot of people from my village have been to China and fetched resources. Probably that is how our village was able to survive until now. Most of the people who have passed away are those who have never been to China. . . . Over half of the people in our village left the village for food and the majority of those have crossed the border to China. They usually stay for two or three months or as long as six months. Most of them do return, especially if the family is waiting for them back in North Korea.[34]

Second, North Hamgyong had natural resources that could be traded for Chinese food provisions. One of the many striking visual images of my trip to the border was the difference between the mountain ranges along both sides of the Tumen River. On the Chinese side the mountains are densely covered with lush alpine forests of deep green pine and spruce, while on the North Korean side they have been denuded of any tree covering. Instead, the mountains near the cities are covered with new graveyards, secret agricultural plots, and low-lying brush. The once-plentiful North Korean forests now fuel Chinese lumber mills, furniture shops, and homebuilding projects.

Third, the farms along the Tumen River traditionally produced larger agricultural surpluses than did farms in North Korea's other mountainous eastern provinces, according to a map of agricultural production produced by the Office of Foreign Disaster Assistance at USAID.[35] North Hamgyong province likely experienced lower death rates than the other mountainous provinces that lacked these three coping mechanisms.

The famine was not limited to the Northeast or to North Hamgyong province, of course. The nutritional study by the WFP and UNICEF shows remarkably similar malnutrition rates in each of the locations surveyed across the country.[36] Also, the discrepancies between county and national census data mentioned earlier in this chapter were reported across the country, not just in the Northeast.

Anecdotal evidence also shows that the famine struck the entire country. A retired university professor from the southwestern province of South Hwanghae, who was visiting friends in China, told of famine deaths in the Southwest and Northwest. One of his former students had become a doctor in a hospital in a southwestern city and he reported that the bodies of the famine dead were regularly brought in to determine whether some would be suitable for use in the medical school's anatomy classes. Another of his former students worked in the statistics office of a huge industrial complex in North Pyongan province, in the Northwest, with about twenty thousand workers—a complex with "first priority for resource and food allocation." These workers and their families amounted to about one hundred thousand people. "At the height of the famine in the last half of 1996, 60 people, including family members, were dying each day, or about 1,800 a month."[37] The family clearly was not isolated to North Hamgyong or even to the four eastern provinces.

It is likely, then, that the Johns Hopkins death rates are a conservative estimate of the severity of the famine across the country. If anything, extrapolating the Johns Hopkins death rates to the country as a whole understates rather than exaggerates the famine's severity. Not including the 3 million people living in Pyongyang and the 1.2 million people in the military, applying the 12.9 percent Johns Hopkins mortality rate to the 19 million people remaining, the total number of famine deaths would equal 2.45 million, the same number of deaths Hwang reports. This number is also consistent with the death rates in the mining city described earlier, which when extrapolated to North Korea's urban population of 12 million totals nearly 2.5 million deaths.

10

THE POLITICAL AND SECURITY CONSEQUENCES OF THE FAMINE

I N THE EARLY AUTUMN OF 1995, Don Oberdorfer reports, the People's Army Sixth Corps, assigned to North Korea's northeastern region, was "disbanded, its leadership purged, and its units submerged into others, under circumstances suggesting disarray in the ranks."[1] Just after this incident the People's Army stopped its winter military exercises, two months earlier than usual, and began an intensive ideological education program for the troops. The two events were apparently a reaction by the central authorities to a planned coup that the secret police discovered before it could be carried out, according to information obtained by South Korean intelligence. A defector later told me that a corps-level army unit had been planning a coup in Hamhung City that autumn. The North Korean secret police apparently discovered the plan three days after senior officers met to assign future cabinet positions to the coup leaders; the officers were arrested and executed. The defector said a colleague of his who happened to be in Hamhung City when the arrests were being made watched the officers being marched out of military headquarters, bound.[2]

In his speech to party cadres at Kim Il Sung University a year later, Kim Jong Il referred to the food shortages causing "anarchy," which could be an oblique reference to this military unrest. In fact, it would not be difficult to conclude that the attempted coup was induced by the famine sweeping through the province. North Korea's senior-most defector, Hwang Jong Yop, reports that five hundred thousand people died from famine in 1995, most between the late spring and early autumn as food stocks ran out—the same time as the coup plot was unfolding. As the capital of Hamgyong province, the region with the largest food deficit, Hamhung City suffered greatly in the famine. According to refugee accounts and surveys conducted by the KBSM, Hamhung was the worst-hit city in the country, the second-most-populated and largest industrialized city in North Korea. Hamhung had the highest proportion of factory workers and, perhaps not coincidentally, was the headquarters of the corps-level unit that planned the coup.

In March 1998, diplomats in Beijing reported that martial law had been imposed in North Korea, that a power struggle was under way, and that purges had begun. Foreign residents in Pyongyang heard shooting between police and soldiers on March 5, and later the same week a curfew was imposed in the city. At the same time, Kim Cong-u, a senior party leader and chairman of the Committee on External Relations, was arrested. His portfolio included the Najin-Sonbong special economic zone in the Northeast,[3] and he had been a leading advocate of economic reform. His arrest was seen as a blow to any hopes for systemic change; most analysts and diplomats I have asked about the incident believe he was later executed. A defector confirmed for me Kim Cong-u's arrest on fabricated corruption charges, which he interpreted as one more effort by Kim Jong Il to terrorize the senior cadres and maintain his control over a party apparatus increasingly disaffected by the famine.[4] Jasper Becker reported that the official Chinese media, for the first time since the crisis began, started reporting both the scale of the famine and these military incidents. Becker argued that this suggested a shift in Chinese government policy, perhaps to prepare the population for an anticipated change of regime in North Korea.

Clearly, some—perhaps many—North Koreans were growing frustrated with the regime's response to the famine, and the regime was clamping down. NGO representatives traveling along the Chinese border during the summer of 1998 reported having seen Kim Il Sung buttons for sale in shops, which meant that merchants had purchased them from food refugees. Wearing these buttons is seen in North Korea as a form of religious devotion to the Great Leader; the configuration of the button also defines the wearer's rank in North Korean society.[5] One could interpret their sale as a famine-coping mechanism to get cash to buy food, but it may also have represented an act of symbolic disavowal of the regime on the part of the food refugees.[6]

In fact, perhaps the most provocative question in the KBSM surveys—a question that would indicate public support or opposition to the central government—asked food refugees about the causes of the famine. In the 1997–99 surveys, 60 percent or more of the refugees attributed the famine to a failure of leadership, absence of economic reform, bureaucratic misrule by the party cadre, too much spending on the military, bad policy, or the lack of an open door to the outside world. Only a fourth of the respondents attributed the catastrophe to natural disaster, which was Pyongyang's official explanation. The KBSM notes that the percentage of people who blamed the regime in one way or another rose substantially between 1996 and 1997.[7] This change may have had less to do with a shift in opinion than with an increase in people's willingness to express their opinion because the crisis had reached such a catastrophic level. Still, it is difficult to interpret this facet of the survey. On the one hand, these views, if held by enough people, could destroy the popular base of support for the regime. On the other hand, one could say that the statistics were skewed, because this particular question asked the opinion of the refugees themselves, not of their family members or of neighbors in their *bans*. After all, people who would take the risk of leaving the country had to have been highly dissatisfied with their circumstances.

One fact is unquestionable, though: the famine was manifesting itself politically. A defector told me that Pyongyang officials in 1997 were warned not to wear their ties to or from work, as infuriated citizens might identify them and take their revenge. Angry citizens stoned an official automobile one night in the capital. People in Pyongyang froze in the cold winter months because of a lack of fuel that, combined with substantially reduced food rations among a population accustomed to better treatment, was having a devastating effect on the population's morale. I met one refugee from Pyongyang on the logging roads around Mt. Paekdu near Changbai, China, who said that starvation rations even in Pyongyang drove him to escape to China. Another food refugee, a former factory worker, admitted to having poured sand into a machine in his factory to destroy it. Another said he had helped to derail a train. Both workers said their acts were protests against the central authorities, whom they blamed for their suffering during the famine.[8]

Three refugee interviews indicate that order was breaking down as the famine bore down on the crumbling society. One food refugee noted,

One has to adapt oneself to the environment in order to survive. The only thing I could do as a young man to save my wife's and my own life was stealing. I stole pigs. I ran away from prison. I became a wanderer. There are many group gangs in Chosun. Their bases are at the mountain caves and their rules are severe. Most of them are condemned criminals or escaped prisoners. They have strong fists, rectitude, and discipline. There are women among them. They don't use fire for cooking for fear of being noticed, but they are equipped with artificial generators. They attack the homes of rich officials for personal vengeance.[9]

Another refugee from the same region said, "Last March they shot 13 people to death who ate humans or cows in Wonsan. The criminals were dangled high up and people were forced to come and look at them. What an unimaginable tragedy! At the present time, Chosun is hell on earth."[10] Such public acts of discipline were not uncommon, according to a third refugee. In his town, he said, "there were no public executions during the Kim Il Sung era, but these days we see them often. Nine were executed on May 6, 1997. One of them [had eaten] a human, another cut electric lines and sold them, one ate a cow, and another ate the seed corn grains."[11]

Kim Jong Il may have inherited his father's position, but the population clearly has never held him in the same esteem it did his father. With the exception of one teenage boy, all refugees I interviewed said disparaging things about the "Dear Leader," claiming that if his father were still ruling they would not be suffering so terribly. One merchant and party cadre member I interviewed reported, "The only person who supports Kim Jong Il's policies is Kim Jong Il." Both Jasper Becker's reporting and the refugee interviews conducted by Médecins Sans Frontières show the same attitude. A fifteen-year-old food refugee in a Chinese border city said students in her high school in Hamhung City openly criticized Kim Jong Il. Her teachers warned her and her friends to keep their silence or they would get into serious trouble. The fact that the refugees were distinguishing between the performances of father and son suggests that they had not rejected the legacy of the father, only that the son was now being held accountable, whereas the father had been immune from criticism. It was Kim Jong Il's misfortune to have assumed power just as the famine began sweeping across the country.

THE FOOD AID DILEMMA: THE POISONED CARROT

Kim also failed to manage effectively the state's anemic response to the famine, as previous chapters have shown. North Korean military leaders opposed the food aid program after the 1995 floods because they feared its political effects inside the country.[12] The larger question is whether the food program kept the North Korean government in power, as Western opponents of food aid claimed it would. Kim Jong Il clearly did not like the aid program and attacked it publicly in an official speech: "The imperialist 'aid' is a noose of plunder and subjugation aimed at robbing ten and even a hundred things for one thing that is given."[13] His hostility was warranted: if anything, the food aid program undermined the state rather than propped up the system. As Paul Bracken noted in a prescient essay written in 1993, Western aid was a "poisoned carrot."[14] Bracken argued that the more connections North Koreans at all levels had with the outside world, such as through aid programs, the more the discontinuities would become apparent between the regime's broken promises and the economic and political reality in the outside world. This realization over time would increase the likelihood of social revolution. This is certainly one reason that Kim Jong Il publicly denounced the subversive effects of the food aid program.

Since the Biafran civil war in 1967–70, analysts and policymakers have known that food aid can be used as a powerful weapon in war or as a key instrument of diplomacy in negotiations. The more severe the food crisis, the greater the power of food aid to influence the behavior of those who need it. The Bosnian civil war and the Great Lakes catastrophe in central Africa both taught discomforting lessons about the misuse of humanitarian aid by donors and recipients alike. It is difficult to predict accurately the effect of introducing huge amounts of humanitarian aid into a highly charged political crisis with terrible human suffering and high death rates. Sometimes humanitarian aid is so destructive—as was the case in the Goma refugee camps in Zaire following the Rwandan genocide, where the Hutu militias were stealing food and selling it to buy weapons —that the only ethically defensible course is to stop providing aid.

In other cases aid has had unintended and profound political and security consequences.[15] This certainly was the case in Somalia, where food aid unprotected from clan diversion exacerbated clan conflicts and increased the level of violence. It was also certainly true of the aid program in North Korea, which donors intended as an inducement for the North Koreans to reach a political settlement with South Korea and bring stability to the peninsula. But the aid also had several unanticipated, positive outcomes, from a Western point of view.

First, the diversion of humanitarian food aid stimulated the size and robustness of the urban markets, a form of unplanned privatization that the central authorities deplored but seemed unwilling or unable to stop. Because people were no longer dependent on the state for their food supply, Pyongyang lost a principal means of control. One refugee I interviewed had been to local markets in six northeastern cities and found the bulk of the grain for sale in them was maize and rice from donor governments: it was still stored in its original bags. The maize for sale in the northern border markets in cities along the Tumen River was Chinese, but rice in the southwestern urban markets appeared to have been locally grown, according to other refugee interviews I conducted in September 1998. MSF border interviews confirmed the presence of donor food aid on the farmers markets.[16]

Second, the donations—and their diversion onto the farmers markets—led to a stabilization and reduction in food prices. For two years, from 1997 to 1999, the KBSM kept careful track of food price fluctuations. According to the KBSM surveys and interviews I conducted, the price of food on the private markets dropped by 25 percent to 35 percent between March and September 1998, when the price should have been increasing. But the steadily increasing supply of Chinese maize and the amount of donor food aid diverted to the markets provided a source of food just when the 1997 harvest had run out. The volume of food on the markets reduced the price sufficiently so that families with limited assets could purchase or barter for food.[17] Thus the declining grain prices driven by stolen food saved lives.

Third, Western aid undermined regime propaganda about the United States and South Korea. Many refugees from South Hamgyong province knew that Western countries, including Japan and South Korea, were donating food aid. As one refugee from Hamhung City told me,

"We were taught all these years that the South Koreans and Americans were our enemies. Now we see they are trying to feed us. We are wondering who our real enemies are." When the first shipment of U.S. food aid arrived on the east coast in May 1997, North Korean central authorities did not want the U.S. ship to arrive in Chongjin flying the American flag. They feared the incendiary message it would send the local population, whom they had abandoned to famine and starvation. After a row over the issue the ship lowered its flag and the grain was delivered, but the WFP logistics staff on duty in the city at the time told me that everyone in Chongjin knew the food came from America (Congress instructed the administration to mark all bags of food aid in Korean as a "Gift of the American People"). The political message inherent in the grain donation could not have been more devastating to fifty years of central government propaganda.

Fourth, diversions of food undermined public support for the central government. Refugees told the KBSM that corrupt cadres were stealing the food and selling it on the markets for their own profit while the people starved. A refugee from Hamhung City reported, "The party cadres with authority possess the food aid, and sell it to markets through merchants at high prices. . . . Bags [of grain in the markets] are labeled as Chinese maize, Chinese flour or Korean flour, or 'A gift from the USA' or 'Republic of Korea.'"[18] The inability of the regime to feed its population and the presence of food aid in the markets undermined Pyongyang's popular support. In a totalitarian system in which people had been conditioned over fifty years to be entirely dependent on the state for all their necessities, the breakdown of the distribution system, increasing corruption, and the diversion of food by the cadres made public anger and disaffection even more severe. This public dissatisfaction may not have been reflected in overt opposition, given the efficiency of the secret police, but it manifested itself in increasing corruption, black market activities, and other antisystem behavior that reflected public cynicism and anger. As one refugee told KBSM, he learned about the international aid donations only after he reached China, as he had never seen them in North Korea. "I don't understand where all the food aid went; our people are starving—starving to death—and the government does not interfere. Those who lead us to death and drive us into such devastating situations must all be punished. The army of the people does not administer the welfare of the people. On the contrary, it is now pointing its guns toward the people. This is a sign that the country will soon come to its ruin."[19]

Fifth, the food aid program brought the outside world into North Korea, undermining the *juche* ideology of self-reliance and Kim Jong Il's promises. For two years beginning in mid-1997, North Korea was "invaded" by humanitarian relief workers, though contact was limited to the party cadres and local officials. Nearly one hundred expatriate relief workers from UN agencies and a dozen major NGOs toured the country at any given time, and two aid agencies even set up offices in regional cities. Although the aid workers' travel was controlled and managed by the security police, this intrusion was painful to a country that prided itself on its self-sufficiency, relative isolation, and ideological purity.

Sixth, these foreigners introduced new ideas that conflicted directly with *juche:* humanitarian ethical norms and operating systems followed by NGOs and by humanitarian institutions within the United Nations such as UNICEF and the WFP. In those areas suffering most from the famine, where aid workers reported that local and provincial officials were much more accommodating, and less rigid and ideological, these new ideas likely fell on fertile ground, given the level of anger among local people over their abandonment by the central government.

Finally, food aid improved the nutritional condition of children, at least marginally. The one intended effect of the food aid program was to reduce the malnutrition rates among children under age nine still attending school. This was the focus of the WFP distributions that began in late 1997. Although even some of that food was diverted onto the markets, a significant amount was properly distributed in the public schools. This undoubtedly stabilized the nutritional condition of the country's children, but from the nutritional surveys conducted in late 1998 rates of malnutrition remained alarmingly high.

THE ROOTS OF DISSATISFACTION

During the five years of the famine, North Korea sustained more destabilizing change than it had over the previous forty years combined. Kim Il Sung's death in 1994 was followed the next year by his son's ambiguous accession to power. Very high death rates in the urban and mining areas followed the replacement of the public distribution system with farmers markets as the principal means by which people obtained their food supply. Mass population movements within the country and to China both led to and followed the erosion of the travel permit system. The virtual collapse of the water, sewer, and health care systems led to the spread of communicable disease and the poor health of the population. Urban unemployment rates rose dramatically, the industrial infrastructure of the country was cannibalized to barter for food in China, and political authorities in Pyongyang decentralized control over non-security-related matters to county officials. Perhaps more disturbing to the internal security police was the influx of humanitarian relief workers from countries the population had long been told were their enemies. These enormous changes put the creaking old regime under severe stress.

A small number of politically powerful people took advantage of and exacerbated the regime's problems. Some used the famine to enrich themselves either by turning their influence into cash through bribes or by going into business through the farmers markets or secretly on the black market. In fact, the markets were fueled by the dramatic rise of widespread corruption among the cadres who hoarded food intended for the public distribution system. Most people, however, were not so fortunate, and they suffered terribly during the crisis: family members starved, and those who survived were hungry and seemed without hope or plans for the future. Jasper Becker described the country as one great prison camp. Similarly, a food refugee told KBSM interviewers, "Now, many intellectual people in North Korea are often saying North Korea is a kind of big prison. Many people complain about Kim Jong Il, but they cannot express such things in public."[20] Those who were suffering saw the few who were prospering, which inevitably encouraged resentment and anger. In a purportedly marxist society, the rapid growth of a dispossessed and destitute mass of common people alongside a new class of people on the make—crony capitalists and predatory entrepreneurs—not surprisingly caused seething public discontent.

People experiencing such intense suffering as that caused by famines ask angry questions about who is responsible and why the authorities are not acting to help them. Confrontation with death encourages otherwise docile people to take risks and to speak, think, and do the unthinkable. Even a totalitarian state with astonishing control over its population begins to break down after years of intense suffering and social trauma. This was happening in North Korea as the famine progressed, despite the regime's aggressive efforts to prevent it. That breakdown led otherwise hidden information to seep through the fissures in the crumbling totalitarian edifice. An American on a visiting delegation in 1998 asked his guide and translator, a senior North Korean official, what effect year after year of food shortages, starvation deaths, and malnutrition was having on the general population. The usually circumspect North Korean paused and said, "Much of the population is exhausted and suffering from severe depression."[21]

Similar levels of discontent arose among the destitute during the seventeenth- and eighteenth-century English and French famines and in India and China in the nineteenth century. This resentment led to dramatic increases in crime rates, food riots, and pilfering of crops before they were harvested.[22] Moreover, when central governments fail through ineptitude or insensitivity to deal with famine, they are short-lived. Bad harvests in 1787–89 in France brought the worst food shortages and the sharpest rise in food prices in decades. By mid-1789 wheat prices had doubled and reached record levels across France, which was one of the causes of the French Revolution later that year.[23] In earlier eras in imperial China, the emperors properly managed the cycle of famines, thereby increasing the power of the state. The Chinese created public works projects, irrigation schemes, flood control efforts, and an elaborate system of government granaries that fed the population when the crop failed—and all of these programs required state management. The Chinese rulers' success in famine relief and prevention efforts is one of the reasons for the extraordinary longevity of Chinese dynasties. The emperors well knew they could be swept away in a peasant revolt if they failed to respond to a famine, so they took their humanitarian duties very seriously.[24]

David Arnold describes the stress on societies being traumatized by famine:

> [A]s society fractured and split under famine's pressure, so collective action and protest gave way to more individualistic acts of violence and theft. Grain was filched from fields, jewelry snatched from those foolish enough to parade it. Strangers were murdered for a few rupees or a crust of bread. Worse still, families turned against each other. Husbands and wives killed one another or murdered their offspring rather than have to share a last spoonful of gruel.

From whatever cause and by whatever means, crimes against property and persons soared. Many of them, reports attest, were committed by people "not ordinarily criminal," and increasingly, as protest waned or became ineffectual, it was a case of the poor robbing the poor. Even in Ireland, where wholesale looting and the organized robbery of grain stores were, it seems, rare, food stealing, mainly at night from the fields of those who still had a few potatoes or turnips, was reportedly common; and crimes against property increased threefold in 1846 over the previous (prefamine) year. Although the Bengal Commission of 1944 noted a surprising absence of violence and looting, in general in India years of dearth were years of exceptional levels of crime. The Orissa famine of 1866 and the Madras famine of 1876–78 produced the highest rates of agrarian crime reported in those provinces over the entire period from the 1850s to the Second World War.[25]

And so it was in North Korea as the famine ravaged a society where crime and corruption had been previously uncommon. During the famine years, acts of corruption and theft dramatically increased, according to defectors, refugees, and merchants; KBSM accounts are filled with reports of executions in village squares for corruption and thievery. Husbands and wives had to guard their secret plots at night or they would be robbed of their only supply of food. One woman told me she had planted a garden next to her home and repeatedly had all her hard-earned produce stolen, so she gave up having a garden. One man told me that a truck driver explained to him that all North Koreans had become thieves to survive the great famine.

POPULATION MOVEMENTS AND POPULAR DISAFFECTION

At the same time that the food aid program brought Westerners into North Korea, the failure of the public distribution system led many North Koreans to leave the country in search of food. Aside from hunger and starvation, the mass population movements caused by the famine have had the most politically insidious consequences for the regime's survival, for they exposed food refugees to the realities of the outside world. Pyongyang likely recognized these consequences and thus fiercely opposed these population movements. One refugee from Hamhung City put it well: "Our first border crossing is a grammar school degree, the second time you visit China is a high school diploma, and the third and fourth trips are college and graduate degrees in reality. The cadres have been lying to us all these years."[26] For years party propaganda had claimed that, despite their problems, people in North Korea were better off than those in China, where civil war, epidemic, and famine raged—a credible claim during the Great Leap Forward and Cultural Revolution in the late 1950s and 1960s. But the refugee movements across the border into China gave lie to this claim, as the prosperity created by Deng Xiaoping's capitalist market reforms is evident everywhere. Food refugees in China were able to confirm rumors they had heard in North Korea, that their South Korean, European, and American "enemies" had donated food aid and medical supplies to relieve their suffering.

These "lessons" learned by food refugees help to explain why attempting to escape North Korea was a crime punishable by death. Yet even that punishment, over time, ceased to be as rigidly enforced.[27] Perhaps the massive number of people crossing the border made execution impractical or infeasible. Hungry border guards readily took bribes, according to dozens of KBSM refugee interviews. The famine and systemic crisis had destroyed the regime's previously unyielding discipline.

Possibly because it recognized the dangers of widespread population movements, Pyongyang announced in June 1998 that it would issue new identification cards in connection with the national election. This announcement led many food refugees to return to North Korea from China.[28] Ironically, Pyongyang's decision to encourage this reverse migration unwittingly undermined the prospects for its own survival. Suddenly, a large group of angry and cynical refugees schooled in economic and political reality were returning to their home villages to tell their families and friends what they had just learned. The returning refugees continually confirmed Kim's fears by spreading their new worldview and their cynicism about the regime's claims. As one refugee told the KBSM,

> Through this famine, many of us have come to realize that we have been ignorant of the real world. I now know that people in China are well fed and clothed and South Koreans are far wealthier than the well-fed and -clothed Chinese. . . . Everywhere you go [in North Korea], all of the commercial areas are barren, closed and deserted, and schools closed. Only starving, emaciated bodies are in

sight. Who can save this country from our misery, who will pay the price for this? Those who are pushing the innocent into the grave must be punished.[29]

A year and a half earlier, Kim Jong Il had complained about the increasing inability of the party organization to generate results through political indoctrination, a failure he blamed on the party cadres' lack of enthusiasm:

> In order to demonstrate this superiority [of socialism], party functionaries should be with the masses to conduct political work. In difficult times, it is more important for party functionaries to conduct political work among the masses. Party functionaries currently are not properly carrying out political work. When they do, they do it perfunctorily, generating no results. Many party functionaries do not go out to the masses, but linger in their offices. . . . They only give orders, like a boss [and] merely mobilize agents from the Ministry of Public Security and functionaries from other dictatorial agencies to clamp down on them [the masses] according to law. . . . If we do not endlessly conduct political works among the people, their ideological and spiritual condition will become poor.[30]

The food refugees' return in June 1998 merely contributed to the further erosion of the regime's base of popular support, making Pyongyang's efforts to mobilize the population through propaganda and political education campaigns increasingly more futile.

PROSPECTS FOR THE FUTURE

As North Korea's internal crisis grew more acute and the stresses on the collapsing system grew more severe, Western analysts' speculation on the country's future prospects increased. Nicholas Eberstadt argued in his book *The End of North Korea* that the collapse of the system had proceeded so far as to be irreversible.[31] In contrast, Marcus Noland suggested that North Korea had muddled through the catastrophe and would survive, limping along.[32] Scenario development and analysis became a growth industry among scholars. The great famine will undoubtedly have political consequences; the problem lies in attempting to predict what they may be.

As the famine waned and the regime remained in power, the party cadre and leadership tried to reconstitute the state of Kim Il Sung and the highly centralized, totalitarian structure that existed before the catastrophe struck. In September 1997 the regime ordered the creation of displaced persons camps, designed to shut down population movements and restore order. Beginning in the winter of 1997–98, the number of border guards was increased, so they patrolled a smaller area, and getting to China became much more difficult. One well-traveled refugee reported a general attempt by the internal security forces beginning in the summer of 1998 to reimpose order in the transportation system. Internally displaced people were no longer allowed onto the trains without a travel permit and a paid ticket. This had not been the case since 1995. The refugee suggested that security was "six times more severe" than he had experienced since the start of the crisis.[33] Railroad stations were cleared of internally displaced people. The new identification cards issued in the summer of 1998 had the effect of voiding older, forged cards and eliminating the ability of displaced persons to claim that they had lost their cards. The state's transport of arrested internally displaced persons earlier in the famine had occurred under lax security procedures, and many escaped on the journey home; by late 1998 the prisoners were chained or bound together for the return home, making it difficult to escape. One fifteen-year-old boy who had been captured four times and escaped said security measures during his last arrest and incarceration were much more strict than during his first three.[34] Other refugee interviews confirmed his story. All this amounted to an attempt by the central authorities to recapture control of a society in "anarchy," as Kim Jong Il put it.

Chances are remote that this strategy will succeed. North Korea sustained a massive drop in gross national product, a substantial disaffection of the people from their government, and a precipitous drop in living standards even for party members. Although Noland has been right, at least thus far, that the regime will remain in power, how much longer it will remain in power is much more ambiguous. The notion that the old order can be fully restored and the historical clock turned back is specious. The scars of the famine are too deep, the embitterment of the population too widespread, and the changes in the economy too profound for the old order to be restored.

If the regime persists in avoiding reform and resisting evolution, it will eventually collapse. What will happen then will depend on how the collapse occurs. In one possible scenario, the Kim dynasty could be deposed in a successful coup d'état, which is how Nicolae Ceausescu met his demise in Romania. In another, an initially successful military coup could fail because of factional infighting within the command structure and thus be unable to assume power despite bringing down the leadership. The country would then descend into civil war extending over many years, as has been the case in Afghanistan, Liberia, and Somalia.

The potential for a coup in North Korea should not be ignored. In Africa, famines have often produced coups. Following the great West African famine of 1968–74, every government in the region fell to a coup save that of Senegal, which was least affected by the famine.[35] Ethiopian emperor Haile Selassie's fifty-year reign was brought to a bloody end by a military coup, the leaders of which blamed his government for the famine of 1972–74, which killed several hundred thousand people. Less than twenty years later, two rebel movements overthrew Selassie's successor, Mengistu Haile Mariam, citing his responsibility for, among others things, the 1985 famine that killed a million people and his use of food aid as a weapon against civil populations during the civil war.[36] If the death rates in North Korea are as substantial as was argued earlier, a significant portion of urban families have seen members die. Popular discontent in cities is a much greater risk to the stability of any government than is unrest in the countryside isolated from vital media outlets, communications and transport systems, military and political nerve centers, and population concentrations. A demonstration against political authority in a remote mountain village is not necessarily heard; the same demonstration in a city is another matter.

Given the attempted coup the previous year, Kim Jong Il not surprisingly expressed a certain unease about the loyalty of the military in his December 1996 speech: "Socialism fell in many countries because their parties degenerated and failed to control the army. In order for the party to control the army, the party's leadership over the army should be guaranteed."[37] Kim's desire to ensure the military's support may explain why nearly all of his public appearances, according to his published schedule, were before military units.

But whereas the newly promoted general officer corps may be loyal to Kim Jong Il, it is not clear that field- and company-grade officers share the same loyalty. A large, popularly based military is much more vulnerable to discipline problems during and after a famine than is a career, elite military long separated from homes and families. And as Nicholas Eberstadt and Judith Banister reported in the early 1990s, nearly 40 percent of the sixteen- to twenty-four-year-old population of the country was in the military—6 percent of North Korea's total population.[38] Under more prosperous circumstances, this number of people under arms would provide a strong base of popular support for the military and a high level of political mobilization in the society. Under famine conditions, however, the reverse is often true. A large proportion of troops saw relatives die, as it would have been logistically and practically impossible to ensure that all military families were fed, and it is likely that many held the regime at fault. In other words, the regime has a large number of young men with weapons, and although they are in a highly controlled and disciplined organizational structure, many are quite likely unhappy about deaths in their families. As Jasper Becker wrote in his book on the Chinese famine, a People's Liberation Army report "expressed strong fears that the loyalty of the army was in doubt because some of the troops were openly blaming Mao [Zedong] for the deaths of their relatives."[39]

The potentially explosive effect of famine deaths among military family members gives credence to a U.S. intelligence report given to the WFP in April 1997. According to the report, immediate members of military families were one of the three groups to which the public distribution system was still attempting to provide food. This would likely not have solved the regime's problem. In Korean culture, daughters generally care for their elderly relatives, so with food rations going to relatives of the predominantly male troops, the elderly from military families were still not protected by the system's preferential treatment.

But the regime also faced another, entirely different, military problem. The famine may have undermined military morale in a way that could be threatening to the state, but it also devastated the combat readiness of the once formidable North Korean military. According to the WFP nutritional survey done in 1998, 75 percent of children under age nine who had been measured were suffering from malnutrition and stunting caused by prolonged malnutrition. Given that serious food shortages were reported as early as 1988,[40] the current generation of recruits into the North Korean military are remarkably smaller than were their counterparts in the 1970s. Reports from food refugees on the border mention that before new recruits are inducted, they have to go through a fattening-up period to improve their health and physical condition and make them combat-worthy. Several of the refugees I interviewed said that the military was full of soldiers who survived by begging for food from civilians. In areas where discipline broke down, soldiers stole food from civilians at gun-point.[41] In rural areas military units occasionally organized raids of farming areas. Thus in some areas the once-revered People's Army became a predatory symbol of a utopian-state-turned-nightmare. None of this could have helped military morale.

The food distribution system in North Korea has been de facto privatized, the regime's revolutionary fervor has cooled over time if for no other reason than because of the famine, and Pyongyang has no allies left to intervene to save it in the event of a military coup. Given the likely level of anger in the military over the number of famine deaths, it is a coup that most threatens the survival of Kim Jong Il's government, and it is the military that Kim Jong Il must now fear. Perhaps that is why, according to U.S. government sources, during the famine he avoided visiting military units conducting exercises using live ammunition.[42]

THE LONG-TERM CONSEQUENCES OF THE FAMINE

The future preferred by North Korea's allies and adversaries alike is a soft landing in which the country gradually evolves into a more open and less aggressive state while adopting Chinese-style market reforms that permit it to feed its hungry population without international aid. This reform and evolution scenario has been the conceptual cornerstone of U.S. policy. For the common people of North Korea, however, the landing has been far from soft; it has been as catastrophic as the Korean War in terms of the number of deaths and the level of widespread suffering. Nearly three-fourths of the current generation of surviving children are stunted and many of the elderly have died. While the soft-landing approach may be working diplomatically and politically, there is little evidence that serious economic reform measures are being implemented within the regime, which means that North Korea will continue to rely on aid for the immediate future.

In his formidable work on the Chinese famine during the Great Leap Forward, Dali Yang argues that the receptivity of the Chinese peasantry to later privatization reforms of the agricultural system in the 1980s was directly proportional to the regional severity of the famine. In those provinces in which the famine was most severe, the peasants were much more willing to accept radical agricultural reform.[43] Yang writes: "The Great Leap famine changed the outlook of the peasants and basic-level cadres and provided the incentives for peasants allied with those cadres to seek institutional change."[44] The Chinese peasantry has traditionally tended to be quite conservative, resisting change in its approach to agriculture because it involved too much risk. The famine changed the peasants' incentives to embrace major reform to avoid a return to the catastrophe they experienced between 1958 and 1962.

The historical record provides a remarkable lesson for North Korea. The northern mountain provinces have long had an unsettled relationship with the central government. During the Yi Dynasty, for example, royal officials discriminated against both the northwestern (North and South Pyongan) and the northeastern provinces (North and South Hamgyong) because of their reputation for opposing the regime.[45] Loyalty to the center has always been weakest in the Northeast, which is undoubtedly why Kim Jong Il decided this region was expendable. All this is to say that these provinces may be more disposed toward reform and independent action. The international aid effort should have been concentrated there in all of its manifestations—relief, rehabilitation, and reconstruction. Humanitarian need and the political objectives of the United States, Japan, South Korea, and the Europeans in encouraging reform and evolution would have been perfectly coincidental. The Northeast was the worst-hit region earliest in the famine and the most embittered toward the central authorities. A well-designed relief and rehabilitation program in the region might have begun an irreversible process of reform and evolution. Not surprisingly, the central authorities strongly resisted aid being sent there.

One could easily argue that the eastern coastal cities pose the greatest threat to the survival of the central government. If the Chinese example described by Dali Yang plays itself out in North Korea, then well before the rest of the country, these cities will embrace economic reform; if such reform is unavailable, perhaps they will embrace political change. Although the northeastern provinces have not at this writing become hotbeds of sedition and rebellion, they may well be one day, given the opportunity. Home to seven million people, these provinces comprise nearly a third of the prefamine population of the country; further, the population includes party elite, provincial and county officials, and military stationed in the region—people about whom Kim Jong Il should be deeply concerned.

11

WHAT IS TO BE DONE?

A S EARLIER CHAPTERS HAVE SHOWN, substantial evidence pointed to
the existence of a devastating famine in North Korea, even though
the government tried to hide its severity from the outside
world. Inside the country, aid workers from NGOs and UN agencies
witnessed the pervasiveness of famine indicators such as the hoarding of
grain and the mass movement of populations. Outside the country's
borders, other NGO representatives interviewed thousands of famine
refugees who had fled to China in search of food. Once the evidence was
clear that a famine was under way in North Korea, the policy question
facing Washington and other Western donor governments was what, both
ethically and strategically, should be done about the crisis.

This question needs to be asked because, although they did not cause
the famine, donor governments did have the power and resources to prevent it. Had they been generous in early 1996, perhaps the risk-averse government in Pyongyang might not have continued to pursue its disastrous
triage strategy, which was partially motivated by the fear that the poor
1996 harvest would be the country's only food for the next year. Donor
governments could have demanded a much more regionally balanced
and socially equitable distribution of food aid as a condition for its delivery, and they could have demanded that the distribution be managed and
monitored by a large expatriate staff with expatriate Korean translators.

But although donor governments could have avoided the tragedy
by early action, the famine clearly and emphatically was caused by the
decisions of North Korea's leaders. They must accept responsibility for
the massive number of deaths of their own people. Their refusal to take

the risk of internal reform, their provocations toward Japan and the United States, and their refusal to embrace political accommodation with the South caused the death of millions of innocent people.

THE ETHICAL DILEMMA

Some analysts implicitly argued that the United States should have starved the North Korean regime into collapse. Soon after my commentary ran in the *Washington Post* in February 1997, arguing that the United States needed to separate aid from politics, Robert Manning of the Progressive Policy Institute and James Przystup of the Heritage Foundation wrote a rebuttal of sorts that also ran in the *Post*. They argued that North Korea was a clear threat to U.S. interests and that food aid should be conditioned on North Korea's diplomatic behavior. "Generous economic help for North Korea should be forthcoming to the degree [that the regime] reduces its military threat and opens its economy. Pyongyang should be offered the choice of keeping its guns or its tin cup. But to allow it to have both is sheer folly."[1] They also suggested that "food aid is fungible. No matter how scrupulously the delivery of food aid is monitored, one cannot escape basic arithmetic: more food aid to feed civilians means more domestic production can go to keep the military well fed." Karen Elliott House made a similar argument in the *Wall Street Journal*,[2] as did Charles Krauthammer in a *Washington Post* column later that spring.[3] Finally, in testimony before the Senate Intelligence Committee in July 1997, Marcus Noland of the Institute for International Economics also argued that food aid is fungible.[4]

The fungibility argument misses the point. These writers may be correct that aid helped Pyongyang in the short run, but in the long run it weakened the regime's control over its citizens, as the last chapter argues. In fact, food aid was not fungible if the regime was triaging some groups and aid was targeted by donors to those groups. Had the United States separated humanitarian aid from geostrategic politics and implemented an aid program along the lines of Herbert Hoover's aid to the Soviet Union in the early 1920s, it could have helped the neediest North Koreans in a way that would have precluded Pyongyang from taking any benefit. In the same Senate committee hearing, I argued, in response to Noland's comments, that if food aid were delivered to the eastern ports of the country, it could not easily be rerouted to the western ports because the internal transport system was so paralyzed. Where food was delivered, I said, it would likely stay until consumed. Had the international community known then that the Northeast had been placed in triage, this argument would have been even stronger. Food delivered to the Northeast would not have been fungible in the way these critics argued, because people in that region were not receiving any rations in the first place; Pyongyang had nothing to gain from such aid deliveries, which is why it prevented the shipments in the first place. In fact, it did not allow food to be shipped to these eastern ports until more than two years after the floods that initiated the WFP effort.

Some might argue that the famine has been over since 1998, and perhaps 10 percent or more of the population starved to death, and yet the regime has remained stubbornly in power. As Jasper Becker has written, no totalitarian government has been overturned during or after a famine, though authoritarian governments with much less control over their populations have been frequently replaced by coups or popular revolts after famines.[5] Similarly, as Marcus Noland wrote in an article in *Foreign Affairs,* the Romanian people's terrible suffering under Nicolae Ceausescu's brutal dictatorship did not lead to his overthrow for a decade.[6] But the record on totalitarian famines—in the Soviet Union, China, Ethiopia, and Cambodia—may not be all that applicable to North Korea, as those regimes were just beginning when famine struck. Revolutionary fervor was heartier, and the regimes maintained tight control of the food distribution system so dissenters would starve. The likelihood of Pyongyang clinging to power indefinitely is low, and it is even less likely that it will be able to do so without undertaking a radical departure from its current economic policy. The weight of evidence suggests that the government will fall, be overturned in a coup by an angry military, or transform itself by adopting the Chinese model of economic reform. It cannot long survive on its current course without the final destruction of the old order, likely through a chain of events of unpredictable violence and chaos.

The food aid program exists to this day, and the question remains whether it should be continued, shut down, or redesigned and reexecuted in a different direction. The answer depends in part on how analysts and policymakers judge the program's success or failure. If it is determined that the donations are not going to needy people or are systematically diverted by the central government to feed the military, then a cutoff

would be justified on a humanitarian basis. There are always other countries in need of food aid. Shutting down a country's food program for this
humanitarian reason is very different from doing so because aid opponents
argue that the program is politically unjustified because it supports a
dangerous and irresponsible regime. Essentially, however, the question
remains as to whether the U.S. government could ethically justify a decision to allow the deaths of two to three million innocent people to accelerate the regime's collapse.

If one answers yes, following the ethical argument to its logical
conclusion produces some odd policy prescriptions.

On the one hand, if policymakers intended to undermine the
regime's base of support, then the flawed food aid program as it unfolded
from 1995 through 1999 should have been continued without reform,
because it facilitated privatization through the expansion of the farmers
markets. This is not to say, however, that the food aid program was a great
success in humanitarian terms; it was not. As the last chapter argued,
diversions of food meant the aid program did not reach those most in
need. Although it did reduce prices on the farmers markets for those
who had some money, the most destitute by definition had no resources
and thus no access to the markets, and so they died. But one can hardly
deny that the philosophical underpinnings of and support for this regime
have been weakened.

If, on the other hand, policymakers wished to save the starving North
Korean underclass, then Herbert Hoover's approach as described in earlier chapters would have been the only one that could have prevented
catastrophe. Food aid distributed under this approach would not have
been used for diplomatic purposes, but by ensuring that food was delivered to those most in need, this approach would have reduced the ability
of the elite to divert the aid to farmers markets and their own tables. Thus
good humanitarian principles applied rigorously would have guaranteed
that the poor would be fed. But by propping up the system, they would
have simultaneously diminished the threat to the regime that arose from
aid being diverted onto farmers markets.

This most realistic alternate approach would have focused the aid
precisely where the central government had prevented it from going: to
the eastern mountainous provinces and to the politically powerless people
at the lowest level of North Korean society, whom the regime had placed

in a sort of triage. The North Koreans would have agreed to these distributions only if they had had no alternative source of food aid. This would have required broad agreement among all donor governments to this single strategy and objective, as well as a large commitment of food aid. Food aid could easily have been targeted to the northeastern region simply by delivering it to eastern ports. Aid could not easily have been moved from these ports because of the collapse of the transportation system and lack of fuel.

In any case, the ethical question remains as to whether it is an acceptable policy decision to force the regime into collapse by using famine victims as humanitarian hostages. I think it a repulsive presumption that the deaths of two to three million innocent people, most of them elderly people and young children, is an acceptable price to pay to rid the world of this regime. The regime remains in place, two and a half million people are dead, and the food aid program was unable to save them because of its timing and because of weak accountability systems governing its distribution. All famines in the twentieth century occurred under autocratic or totalitarian political systems, so following a policy that says humanitarian relief efforts should be foregone to avoid strengthening a repulsive government would mean that Western nations would never respond to human suffering in famines. The ends do not justify the means, particularly when the means are so horrible and the ends so problematic.

THE STRATEGIC DILEMMA: TOWARD A WESTERN RESPONSE TO THE FAMINE

Humanitarian relief efforts to end this famine made eminently good sense not only from a moral perspective, but also from a security strategy and political perspective. As described in chapter 10, even the most ineffective relief efforts in North Korea encouraged contact with the outside world, in the process weakening the effects of regime propaganda about external "enemies," and they unintentionally stimulated the private farmers markets through food aid diversion. These diversions in turn have seriously undermined support for the regime among the population who see the donated food in the markets and realize why it is there. The illicit sale of donor food aid on the markets also reduced prices so more people can afford to buy more food, thus reducing hunger—albeit not as

much as proper distribution would have done. Kim Jong Il's public statements reported in official sources clearly show that he viewed donor food
aid as fundamentally subversive to his government. He was right. But he
took the risk of acquiring it because the situation was so desperate.

This is not to suggest that a food aid program, even if skillfully designed and shrewdly managed, can substitute for a coherent diplomatic
strategy for dealing with North Korea. Understanding the dynamics of
the famine can inform diplomacy and can explain some of the regime's
seemingly bizarre diplomatic and military behavior. As the famine progressed, the regime began directing its confrontational tactics, its deliberate and managed irrationality, and its aggressive demands toward new
ends. During the 1970s and 1980s these tactics had been designed to
keep the South Korean, Japanese, and U.S. governments on the defensive
and frighten them into concessions over political and security issues. As
the famine grew more severe, however, the same tactics were employed to
get more food for the starving population. Western diplomats inaccurately assumed that if the tactics remained the same so must the objectives
toward which the tactics had been employed. This was not necessarily
the case.

Analysts and scholars generally agree that the North Korean regime's
central objective is survival. Given that the greatest threats to the regime's
survival were the food crisis and a military mutiny that the crisis could
have induced, it is not surprising that the regime should have used its traditional tactics in an effort to obtain food aid. Two incidents in 1998 and
1999 support this view. North Korea's launching of the Taepodong missile
over Japan, which since 1995 had been parsimonious in its commitment
of food aid, was designed among other things to threaten Japan into
being more generous. Pyongyang clearly did not expect the enraged
Japanese response. In the same year, U.S. aerial photographs indicated
the regime was constructing a massive underground facility that U.S.
intelligence believed housed a nuclear weapons production plant. When
the facility was finally inspected in May 1999, after the U.S. government
pledged its largest commitment of food aid since the start of the crisis in
order to get access to the underground area, U.S. inspectors found nothing
but an empty cavern. It would have been impossible, U.S. intelligence
argued, for the North Koreans to have surreptitiously removed equipment from the facility without detection. The facility was built, among

other reasons, as a bargaining chip to obtain more food aid; the Taepodong missile was launched for similar reasons.

Western countries found their worst fears about North Korean behavior realized as the regime played on these fears to get more food. The politicization of food aid by Western countries simply taught the North Koreans to reverse the tactic and likewise play politics to encourage larger donations. In this the North Koreans have been remarkably successful. Had the humanitarian aid effort been run as a traditional aid effort, and had Pyongyang been convinced that donor governments' pledges were genuinely delinked from diplomatic negotiations, then perhaps the North's aggressive behavior would have at least diminished in frequency. Politically driven food aid became a perverse diplomatic incentive for bad North Korean behavior. After South Korean president Kim Dae Jung's historic trip to Pyongyang, North Korean efforts to support a warming of political relations on the peninsula were rewarded once again by a U.S. shipment of food aid. Once again, food aid was used as a carrot for diplomatic action rather than to encourage what North Korea needs most: economic reform.

To prevent such irrational North Korean responses, donor governments should have insisted that accountability conditions be attached to food aid pledges, and the aid program should have been delinked from negotiations over security and political matters. This decoupling could have been done by timing the announcement of food aid pledges after the harvest assessment each year and at no other time. Food aid should not have been used as a bargaining chip in diplomatic negotiations. Implicitly and explicitly, it should only be used as a bargaining chip in humanitarian negotiations on access and accountability.

Now that the famine is over, the United States, Japan, the European Union, and South Korea might want to consider an agreement to link aid with economic change. They might agree to supply North Korea with food aid if Pyongyang were to agree to Chinese-style market reforms to privatize its agricultural and industrial economy. Currently, the regime fears that if it attempts reform and the reforms are either slow in coming or fail, as they have in the Soviet Union, the resulting crisis would be worse than what it now faces. The regime certainly can no longer fear losing control over the population because of the collapse of the public distribution system, since that system is virtually defunct now except for the capital city, party cadres, internal security forces, and the military. But a guarantee of food aid could potentially provide the insurance the regime needs to undertake economic reforms.

Such a strategy would have several ameliorative outcomes. It would eventually reduce North Korea's heavy dependence on international aid from Tokyo, Washington, and Seoul, the provision of which over time is unsustainable. Contrary to the pretensions of *juche* ideology, North Korea has always relied on external aid to support itself; the only difference is that in the past its aid came from Pyongyang's ideological brethren. North Korea is now in the utterly unique, if extraordinarily tenuous, predicament of having the enemies it has demonized for nearly fifty years —Japan, South Korea, and the United States—feeding its hungry population. But these countries cannot continue their food contributions indefinitely. The longer North Korea's dependency continues, the greater is the potential for the regime to misbehave in the mistaken presumption that it can intimidate its adversaries into providing a permanent subsidy. The rapprochement between North and South Korea in the summer of 2000 may well have been driven by Kim Jong Il's need to diversify the sources of North Korea's aid subsidies, particularly given the change in the U.S. administration. By encouraging economic reforms, the West would reduce the likelihood of disruptive population movements toward South Korea after reunification or during a civil conflict, disruptions over which the South Koreans have shown increasing anxiety as they contemplate the extraordinary gap between a starving North and their own prosperity.

Although the four-party talks appear to have been a diplomatic success at this writing, North Korea's central objectives may not have changed much. There is little evidence that the regime is attempting any sort of economic reform. But even if the political thaw does evolve into a permanent spring and economic reforms actually are implemented, these successes will have been purchased at an enormous cost. Delaying humanitarian food aid to spur the talks that led to these changes allowed several million people to perish, most of them small children, pregnant women, disabled people, and the elderly. I do not believe such a policy can be defended ethically, regardless of its apparent "success."

U.S. foreign policy should not be driven by moral principle, but rather by a set of policies that protect U.S. interests broadly defined. But in a civilized society, moral principle does constrain the defense of those interests. In pursuing political objectives in North Korea, however desirable or even successful, to the exclusion of all other goals, Washington wandered well outside the fundamental moral limits constraining foreign policy.

CONCLUSION: TOWARD A NORTH KOREAN RESPONSE TO THE FAMINE

The Great North Korean famine has finished its destructive and malevolent work—for now. But the conditions that created it have not much changed. The new food system feeding the population remains extraordinarily fragile. It is exceptionally vulnerable to small disruptions in the market price of corn from China, to changes in North Korea's mendicant status, and to climatic disruptions in the country's anemic agricultural system. North Korea has no buffer stocks, no insurance policy, and no long-term plan to feed itself with its own resources. What's more, because of a severe drought the 2001 harvest is predicted to be worse than any during the famine years of the 1990s.

Against Pyongyang's will, the system is changing ever so slowly, in modest ways. But every moment that Pyongyang resists needed reform, it increases the risk that events beyond its control may well drag the country into another crisis to which it cannot respond. The regime should be racing against time to remake itself to avoid a second apocalypse, but it is not racing anywhere. It is crawling. Moreover, it has no Deng Xiaoping to guide it through the thicket of economic reform and liberalization.

One thing seems certain: should the fragile food system unravel because of a crop failure, the population is not going to react to a second famine as it did to the first. The people who survived the famine did so by abandoning the old order that had already abandoned them. They survived on their own, a relatively new experience for a population previously supported from cradle to grave by the state's beneficence. Population movements to China and back taught food refugees the truth about official propaganda, about the outside world, about North Korea's enemies, and about the supposed deprivation of North Korea's neighbors. The devastation of the famine has scarred the country for generations in ways the outside world understands only dimly, if at all. Regardless of how centralized and hierarchical the system may be, popular rage will express itself, perhaps not through a popular uprising as such, but through military unrest: a mutiny, a coup, or an assassination attempt. The people will have their revenge one day.

In Confucian China, emperors and the scholar-gentry who governed the country nervously observed weather conditions, harvests, and the level of hunger and destitution among the peasantry to determine whether popular discontent was rising. They feared that the mandate of heaven, which Chinese culture conferred on rulers when they governed well and people's stomachs were full, could be at any time assaulted by an angry and indignant peasantry suffering from a famine attributable to the emperor's misadministration of state affairs. When this took place the mandate of heaven was replaced by the revenge of heaven, and the emperor was removed by peasant revolt. North Korea remains a remarkably Confucian society despite fifty years of Kim Il Sung, or perhaps because of it. The Kim dynasty's mandate to govern may yet be revoked by an angry, suffering people. Only time will tell whether Confucius will take his revenge.

From what analysts and aid workers in North Korea can gather, and from what history has borne out, that revenge may be on the horizon. In January 1992, Fred Cuny and a team of famine experts visited Russia to determine whether the food crisis was threatening Russia. In Murmansk, Cuny visited a home for the elderly to which the United States was then supplying food rations. His translator asked a withered old man, "What do you think of these Americans feeding us now when just yesterday they were our enemies?" The elderly man's face lit up in anger. "Young man, the Americans may have been your enemy, but they were never mine. This is the third time in my long life they have fed me when I was hungry. As a young child they saved me and my family from the great famine of 1921 and then again after the Great Patriotic War [World War II] and now they come to our rescue again. They were never my enemy; they have been my friend and the salvation of my family."[7] Popular opinion may be of little consequence to a successful totalitarian regime, but should the regime begin to unravel, the public's view of the outside world—including its former enemies in Japan, South Korea, and the United States—may matter a great deal. Memories of a famine's horror are long and undying, but so too is the appreciation for those who end the nightmare. And unlike the Soviet Union in 1921 or 1945, North Korea is not at its beginning years but at its dismal and depressing end.

Some Western policymakers opposed the aid program because they feared it would be used to help the massive North Korean military that threatened South Korea and the U.S. troops stationed there during the 1990s. The fact is, however, that the famine relief effort in no way exacerbated the threat; rather, in some important ways it helped to reduce it. The entire effort, seriously flawed though it may have been, sent a startling message to the mid-level party cadres and field officers who were also victimized by the famine and who lost friends and family members to it. The people whom they had long been taught to view as their enemies were feeding them, while their government was not. If a coup d'état should eventually end the regime and a military government come to power, it is likely that the relief effort will have played some role. Moreover, it will have sent a striking message to the new leadership of the country: their so-called enemies may not have been as threatening or as malevolent as they had been taught all their lives. This is not a bad message to be sending under such unstable and unpredictable circumstances. Generosity and decency on occasion can have attractive geostrategic consequences.

APPENDIX

The following op-ed by the author appeared in the *Washington Post*, February 9, 1997, C1 and C4.

FEED NORTH KOREA

Don't Play Politics with Hunger

The White House and the Congress are engaging in a potentially deadly game of famine roulette with North Korea and South Korea. U.S. government relief officials have been prohibited from any serious effort to address the famine now spreading across North Korea. The consequence could be the mass starvation of hundreds of thousands of people who have no political or military power.

The government's inaction, cloaked under the guise of great power diplomacy, eviscerates the policy put in place by Ronald Reagan during the Ethiopia famine when he overruled his advisers and ordered food shipments. "A hungry child knows no politics," Reagan said, declaring that we would not use food as a weapon. He thus reaffirmed the moral high ground the United States has held on famine relief since Herbert Hoover helped feed Europe after World War I.

There is good reason for the United States to remain on that ground. Though it may be in our interest to deplore a particular government, as we certainly did the Stalinist regime which ran Ethiopia in the 1980s, I have yet to see a member of the political elite or the military die

249

in a famine anywhere. The sequence of death follows a pattern: first the children under five, then pregnant women and nursing mothers, the sick, the elderly, and sometimes healthy adults.

In at least half a dozen instances during the Reagan and Bush administrations, aid was provided to people in countries with which we had strained or no diplomatic relations, including Iraq immediately following the Persian Gulf War; Angola during its civil war (in which the United States actively supported a rebel faction over the central government); and Vietnam. Even Sen. Jesse Helms, who initially objected to several of these efforts, offered his support after the policy was explained and safeguards established. But in the case of North Korea, no effort has been made by the Clinton administration to go to Congress and build a bipartisan consensus.

Certainly the politics of the Korean situation are complex. The reclusive and hostile communists of the North damage chances for their own survival at every turn, while the South—a crucial U.S. ally—senses the impending collapse of its mortal enemy. The crisis comes at a time when the United States is trying to get the North Koreans to begin negotiations on a new peace agreement.

And the threat of a crisis has been raised before. There were dire predictions this time last year after much of the North's harvest was wiped out by floods, but the North Koreans coped. Estimates of the death rate from the food shortages in 1996 range from several thousand to the tens of thousands. No one knows for sure because North Korea is a police state that bars most reporters and relief workers. Officials there had refused even to admit the severity of their problems until this week when, in a significant departure from their dogma of self-reliance, they said they have less than half the food they need (a number that was confirmed by the acting CIA director, George Tenet, in congressional testimony last week). The North Koreans also linked talks with the United States and South Korea to immediate food aid.

I do not believe that they are being deceptive. During the Bush administration, I ran the government's famine relief efforts in two dozen places. I know a famine when I see one and North Korea is facing famine. The evidence is incontestable; the only disagreement is how massive the crisis will be.

It is generally in the second year of food crises that mass starvation appears as families' personal survival strategies run out. The next harvest in North Korea is not until late September and only three months of stocks remain, which is about the amount of time needed for U.S. government aid to be ordered, shipped and distributed.

In other famines I have witnessed, people go through identical stages of trying to cope with food shortages. Aid workers who have been in the country tell me that families in North Korea are now following these sad but familiar patterns. They are foraging in the countryside for wild foods—which will reduce the pain of hunger but have limited caloric value to stop the wasting of the body. They are selling their household articles, such as furniture and kitchen implements, along the roadsides. There are few domesticated animals in the farm fields, suggesting they've already been eaten.

The limited official data confirm the situation. An internal study by the U.S. Department of Agriculture last fall, based on satellite imagery, showed record-low corn production and further extensive flood damage. Half of that crop was prematurely harvested and eaten in August when the cobs were still green, according to the December report of the World Food Program and Food and Agriculture Organization of the United Nations.

The evidence is clear that North Korea is looking at a shortage significantly more severe than the one that led to the deaths of a million people in Ethiopia in 1984–85.

Of course, North Korea has long been its own worst enemy. It is a pariah state with one of the largest land armies in Asia and a dismal history of making threats to annihilate South Korea, of continuing extravagant rhetorical attacks against the United States, of producing weapons of mass destruction and selling them without restraint.

Stubborn adherence to failed Soviet-style agricultural policies has caused declining food production since 1984. The Soviet collapse meant the end of food subsidies and began a spiral into nutritional oblivion which turned calamitous after two years of floods.

Yet when South Korea sent humanitarian food north after the first floods, North Korea arrested the crew of the transport as spies. Last September, just as aid was again being discussed, and U.S. congressional opposition had softened, the North dispatched a submarine to the coast of South Korea on a clumsy espionage mission, provoking international outrage. While the unusual North Korean apology has allowed for the possibility of negotiations, many wonder what surprise is next.

The North's only recourse to feed itself has been a series of business deals, the most desperate of which is an agreement with Taiwan to dispose of 200,000 barrels of low-level nuclear waste. Over a number of years the deal is supposed to yield $200 million in scarce foreign exchange, but not in time to resolve this crisis.

Meanwhile, the South Koreans have been busily lobbying to prevent food aid from reaching the North—and having great success convincing even moderate Republican and liberal Democratic members of Congress with a history of supporting foreign aid to oppose famine relief. They argue that the food would be diverted to the military, and that in any event, it would prop up a regime that is close to imploding. (These are the same arguments that were used by National Security Council staff that stonewalled the relief response in Ethiopia.)

U.S. inaction has also kept other sources of relief on the sidelines. In ordinary circumstances the U.S. government—through the Agency for International Development—would have initiated a major famine aid program, usually matched by the Canadians and Europeans. In virtually every famine since Ethiopia, the United States has contributed one-third of the total food requirement—frequently more.

That is what we should be doing now. We can find other ways of getting the North to the bargaining table. And our contribution must be substantial, not the token 20,000 to 30,000 tons we gave last year.

It is in the interests of Japan and South Korea to contribute even more generously. Because apart from the moral issue, there is a pragmatic one as well. Subordinating the famine to a muddled diplomatic agenda does a great disservice to the cause of peace in the region. Famines are cataclysmic events with unpredictable consequences. Even if policy makers are unmoved by the ethical problem of using the threat of mass starvation to force the North to negotiate, they should worry about the profoundly destabilizing effects famines can have. Already, hungry families are escaping across the border into South Korea; far more could follow. What will the South Koreans do? What will the Chinese do?

And if the famine initiates a chain of explosive events, our diplomacy may be putting another group of people at risk—the 37,000 American troops in South Korea.

NOTES

As noted in the introductory chapter of this book, I have chosen not to identify by name NGO workers, officials, and refugees when to do so might be to risk their harassment by North Korean officials. I have also provided sparing details of the source of information given to me by officials of various governments on the condition of anonymity.

INTRODUCTION

1. Frederick C. Cuny (with Richard Hill), *Famine, Conflict, and Response: A Basic Guide* (West Hartford, Conn.: Kumarian Press, 1999), 16.

2. David Arnold, *Famine: Social Crisis and Historical Change* (Oxford: Basil Blackwell, 1988), 12.

1. ROOTS OF THE CRISIS

1. Dali L. Yang, *Calamity and Reform in China: State Rural Society and Institutional Change since the Great Leap Forward Famine* (Stanford, Calif.: Stanford University Press, 1996), vii.

2. Jean Dreze and Amartya Sen, *Hunger and Public Action* (Oxford: Clarendon Press, 1989), 275–279.

3. Edwin O. Reischauer and John Fairbanks, *East Asia: The Great Tradition* (Boston: Houghton Mifflin, 1960), 2:446.

4. Andrew C. Nahm, *Korea: Tradition and Transformation, a History of the Korean People* (Elizabeth, N.J.: Hollym, 1988), 124–125.

5. Takashi Hatada, *A History of Korea*, ed. and trans. Warren W. Smith, Jr., and Benjamin H. Hazard (Santa Barbara, Calif.: ABC-Clio, 1969), 86–87.

6. Ibid.

7. Ibid.

8. Bruce Cumings, *Korea's Place in the Sun: A Modern History* (New York: W. W. Norton, 1997), 83.

9. Nahm, *Korea: Tradition and Transformation*, 132.

10. Hatada, *A History of Korea*, 88.

11. Nahm, *Korea: Tradition and Transformation*, 239.

12. Ibid., 238.

13. Don Oberdorfer, *The Two Koreas: A Contemporary History* (Reading, Mass.: Addison-Wesley, 1997), 218.

14. Robert Scalapino, *North Korea at a Crossroads* (Stanford, Calif.: Stanford University Press, 1997), 2.

15. See Hy-Sang Lee, "Supply and Demand for Grains in North Korea: A Historical Movement Model for 1966–1993," *Korea and World Affairs* 18, no. 3 (fall 1994): 509–553. According to Nicholas Eberstadt, oil imports from Russia in 1991 were 10 percent of what they had been in 1990; see *Korea Approaches Reunification* (Armonk, N.Y.: M. E. Sharpe, 1995), 134.

16. *World Resources: A Guide to the Global Environment, 1996–97* (Oxford: Oxford University Press, 1996), 240–241.

17. Robert A. Scalapino and Chong-Sik Lee, *Communism in Korea* (Berkeley: University of California Press, 1972), 1026.

18. Ibid., 1103–1106.

19. Ibid., 1034–1035.

20. United Nations Development Program (UNDP), "Thematic Roundtable on Agricultural Recovery and Environmental Protection in DPR Korea, Geneva, Switzerland, May 28–29, 1998" (photocopy), 17.

21. Scalapino and Lee, *Communism in Korea*, 1120.

22. Democratic People's Republic of Korea (DPRK) and UN Food and Agriculture Organization (FAO), *Agricultural Recovery and Environmental Protection (AREP) Programme: Identification of Investment Opportunities*, vol. 2, Report no. 98/093–UNDP/DPRK (November 20, 1998).

23. NGO agricultural economist, interview by author, January 1998, Washington, D.C.

24. Scalapino and Lee, *Communism in Korea*, 1030.

25. Ibid., 1099–1100.

26. North Korean defector in Seoul, interview by author, September 1998.

27. Based on interviews by author of a Chinese agronomist and of North Korean refugees in Tumen City, China, September 1998.

28. Sadao Murakami, "Forty Years of Japanese–North Korean Trade Relations: Unknown Episodes Told by Insider," *FBIS Daily Report*, FBIS-EAS-96-161, May 1, 1996.

29. Robert Hauser, director of the World Food Program (WFP) in North Korea, April–September 1996, interview by author in Rome, January 1999.

30. Eberstadt, *Korea Approaches Reunification*.

31. The bicycles were needed when gas-powered transportation ground to a halt after the U.S. Congress refused to provide any more oil under the Agreed Framework negotiated in 1994. This framework stipulated that North Korea would agree not to produce the fissionable materials needed to make nuclear weapons. In exchange, a consortium of South Korean, Japanese, and European firms would build light-water reactors to provide power for the country— reactors that by their configuration could not be used to produce the nuclear material for weapons. The North Koreans also agreed to allow international monitoring of their nuclear facilities to ensure Western governments of their decommissioning. The U.S. government was to provide a subsidy of oil while this was being completed.

32. Jane Shapiro Zacek, "Russia in North Korean Foreign Policy," in *North Korean Foreign Relations in the Post–Cold War Era*, ed. Samuel S. Kim (Oxford: Oxford University Press, 1998), 77.

33. "North Korea's Defense Industry Buckles under Economic Crisis," *Agence France-Presse*, August 30, 1998.

34. David E. Kaplan, "The Wiseguy Regime Has Embarked on a Global Crime Spree," *U.S. News & World Report*, February 15, 1999.

35. Raphael Perl, *North Korean Drug Trafficking: Allegations and Issues for Congress*, Congressional Research Service Report for Congress (Washington, D.C.: Library of Congress, February 8, 1999).

36. State Department sources.

37. North Korean defector to Seoul, interview by author, September 1998.

38. Sue Lautze, "North Korea Food Aid Assessment" (paper prepared for the U.S. Office of Foreign Disaster Assistance, U.S. Agency for International Development, June 6, 1996).

39. Merchants along the Chinese border with North Korea, interviews by author, September 1998.

40. Marcus Noland, "Why North Korea Will Muddle Through," *Foreign Affairs* 76, no. 4 (July-August 1997), 108.

41. NGO aid workers who had visited the zone, interviews by author in Washington, D.C., July 1998.

42. Scalapino, *North Korea at a Crossroads*, 4–5.

43. This story was told to an NGO worker in the Najin–Sonbong Trade Zone; interview by author in Washington, D.C., July 1998.

2. INSIDE NORTH KOREA

1. See Hwang Jong Yop, *North Korea: Truth or Lies?* (Seoul: Institute for Reunification Policy Studies, 1998), chap. 2.

2. Frederick C. Cuny (with Richard Hill), *Famine, Conflict, and Response: A Basic Guide* (West Hartford, Conn.: Kumarian Press, 1999), 37.

3. Ibid., 35–37.

4. Korean Buddhist Sharing Movement (KBSM), *The Food Crisis in North Korea Witnessed by 605 Food Refugees, 30 September 1997–3 March 1998* (Seoul: KBSM, 1998), 12.

5. Report cited on condition of anonymity.

3. THE HIDDEN FAMINE

1. Oberdorfer, *The Two Koreas*, 234.

2. Center for Nonproliferation Studies (CNS) and the Moscow Institute for Contemporary International Problems (ICIP), "The DPRK Report," no. 13 (June–August 1998), a bimonthly analysis written by CNS and ICIP scholars and published by the Monterey Institute of International Studies, online at http://cns.miis.edu/pubs/dprkrprt/98junaug.htm (available as of May 2001).

3. NGO humanitarian aid worker, interview by author in Washington, D.C., June 1998.

4. KBSM refugee interview no. 371. (KBSM allowed me to see the text of sixteen hundred interviews they conducted with refugees. The interviews have never been published. Each interview is numbered.)

5. "Kim Jong Il Berates Cadres for Food Anarchy" (in Korean), *Wolgan Chosun* [Chosun monthly] (Seoul), March 20, 1997, 306–317; trans. as "Kim Jong Il, Speech at Kim Il Sung University, December 1996" *British Broadcasting Corporation*, March 21, 1997. Dan Oberdorfer discovered that Hwang Jang Yop was the source of the text of Kim's speech published in *Wolgan Chosun.*

6. Kevin King, "North Korea Trip Report, April 22–May 9, 1998" (Mennonite Central Committee, nd).

7. United Nations, "UN Consolidated Inter-Agency Appeal for the DPRK, January–December 1999" (appeal issued in December 1998 by the Office for the Coordination of Humanitarian Affairs).

8. Suh Dae Sook, *Kim Il Sung: The North Korean Leader* (New York: Columbia University Press, 1988), 303–331; and Cumings, *Korea's Place in the Sun*, 402.

9. Cumings, *Korea's Place in the Sun*, 76–77.

10. Ibid., 96–97.

11. Nicholas Eberstadt and Judith Banister, *The Population of North Korea* (Berkeley: University of California Press, 1992), 1–2.

12. Charles Armstrong, "State and Social Transformation in North Korea 1945–50" (Ph.D. diss., University of Chicago, 1994), 221, 225.

13. Ibid., 227.

14. Scalapino and Lee, *Communism in Korea*, 819.

15. Interview of an ethnic Chinese Korean retiree who was visiting relatives in North Korea, conducted by a Korean American NGO worker along the North Korean–Chinese border.

16. Interview videotaped by Mark Kirk of the U.S. House Foreign Affairs Committee; copy in file of the committee.

17. North Korean refugee in Jilin, China, interview by author, September 1998. Unless otherwise noted, all author interviews with refugees were conducted in Jilin in September 1998.

18. John Pomfret, "Starving North Koreans Who Reach China Describe a Slowly Dying Country," *Washington Post*, February 12, 1999, A1.

19. Mark Kirk, "Staff Delegation Final Report to Benjamin Gilman on Their Mission to North Korea and China, August 11–23, 1998" (unpublished photocopy), 7.

20. Robert Conquest, *The Harvest of Sorrow: Soviet Collectivization and the Terror-Famine* (Oxford: Oxford University Press, 1986), 314.

21. *Pravda*, September 13, 1933.

22. Conquest, *Harvest of Sorrow*, 314.

23. Ibid., 316.

24. Jasper Becker, *Hungry Ghosts: Mao's Secret Famine* (New York: Henry Holt, 1998), 70.

25. Ibid., 291.

26. Ibid., 121–122.

27. Ibid., 126.

28. Robert D. Kaplan, *Surrender or Starve: The Wars behind the Famine* (Boulder, Colo.: Westview, 1988), 107.

29. Ibid., 110.

30. Sichan Siv is now a U.S. citizen; he served on the White House staff under former president George Bush. After the ouster of Pol Pot, Twining was appointed the first U.S. ambassador to Cambodia.

31. Sichan Siv, interview by author.

32. William Shawcross, *The Quality of Mercy: Cambodia, Holocaust, and the Modern Conscience* (New York: Simon and Schuster, 1984), 55–56.

4. Surviving the Famine

1. Médecins Sans Frontières, *North Korea: Testimonies of Famine—Refugee Interviews from the Sino–Korean Border, Special Report* (New York: Doctors Without Borders/Médecins Sans Frontières, August 1998); posted on-line at http://www.doctorswithoutborders.org/publications/reports/before1999/korea_1998.shtm.

2. John Pomfret, "Portrait of a Famine," *Washington Post*, February 12, 1999, A1.

3. NGO worker, interview by author in Washington, D.C., September 1998.

4. Ibid.

5. For a full treatment of these coping mechanisms and famine indicators I have used Jindra Cekan's "Listening to One's Clients: A Case Study of Mali's Famine Early Warning System and Rural Producers" (Ph.D. diss., Tufts University, 1994); and Cuny, *Famine, Conflict, and Response.*

6. WFP, "North Korea Special Alert," no. 275, June 3, 1997.

7. W. Courtland Robinson, Myung Ken Lee, Kenneth Hill, and Gilbert M. Burnham, "Mortality in North Korean Migrant Households: A Retrospective Study," *Lancet* 354, no. 9175 (July 1999).

8. As a woman grows more malnourished, she becomes correspondingly more infertile. While it is true that in former Eastern bloc countries, especially in the former Soviet Union and Eastern Europe, birth rates were below maintenance levels in areas not experiencing food shortages, this was not true in Asian communist societies, where tradition puts heavy emphasis on producing descendents to continue the family line.

9. Robinson et al., "Mortality in North Korean Migrant Households."

10. Eberstadt and Banister, *The Population of North Korea.*

11. For a fuller treatment of this, see Martina Deuchler, *The Confucian Transformation of Korea: A Study of Society and Ideology* (Cambridge, Mass.: Harvard University Press, 1992).

12. North Korean refugee, interview by author.

13. North Korean refugee in Changbai, China, interview by author, September 1998.

14. David Arnold, *Famine: Social Crisis and Historical Change* (Oxford: Basil Blackwell Press, 1988), 89–91.

15. Dreze and Sen, *Hunger and Public Action*, 216–218.

16. See KBSM/Good Friends, *Report on Daily Life and Human Rights of North Korean Food Refugees in China* (Seoul: Good Friends [formerly the Korean Buddhist Sharing Movement], June 1999).

17. Ibid.

18. Ibid., section 4.3.4.

19. Ibid.

20. Mr. Kwon of KBSM, interview by author in Nampyong, China, September 1998.

21. Moon, interview by author in Changbai, China, September 1998.

22. Reuters, Beijing, December 28, 1998.

23. Conquest, *Harvest of Sorrow*, 257.

24. KBSM refugee interview no. 635.

25. Arnold, *Famine: Social Crisis and Historical Change*, 18.

26. Leonard Berry and Thomas Downing, "Drought and Famine in Africa, 1981–86: A Comparison of Impacts and Responses in Six Countries," in *The Challenge of Famine: Recent Experience and Lessons Learned*, ed. John Osgood Field (West Hartford, Conn.: Kumarian Press, 1993), 42.

27. See Andrew Natsios, "Humanitarian Relief Intervention in Somalia: The Economics of Chaos," in *Learning from Somalia: The Lessons of Armed Humanitarian Intervention*, ed. Jeffrey Herbst and Walter Clarke (Boulder, Colo.: Westview, 1997), 77–95.

28. *Report on Daily Life and Human Rights*, 83.

29. See Eberstadt and Banister, *The Population of North Korea*, for a full discussion of population migration.

30. Médecins Sans Frontières, *North Korea: Testimonies of Famine*.

31. We have evidence for this from Kirk, "Staff Delegation Final Report"; KBSM interviews; and my own interviews.

32. Press conference held in Seoul in March 1997.

33. Pomnyun, KBSM executive director, interview by author in Washington, D.C., November 1999.

34. NGO worker, interview by author in Washington, D.C., June 1998.

35. Stephen Linton, "Life after Death in North Korea," in *Korea Briefing: Towards Reunification*, ed. David McCann (Armonk, N.Y.: East Gate Books, 1997), 92.

36. North Korean refugee in Changbai, China, interview by author, September 1998.

37. "Kim Jong Il Berates Cadres for Food Anarchy," trans. in *FBIS* as "Kim Jong Il, Speech at Kim Il Sung University."

38. Papallion, interview by author.

39. Refugee woman from North Hamgyong province, interview by author.

40. Jasper Becker, "Famine Refugee Tells of Mass Destitution and Death in North Korea," *South China Morning Post*, February 11, 1998, 1.

41. North Korean merchant and retired teacher, interviews by author.

42. Noland, "Why North Korea Will Muddle Through," 108.

43. FAO/WFP, *Crop and Food Supply Assessment Mission to DPRK: Special Report* (World Food Program, December 1996), 9.

44. WFP nutritionist, interview by author, January 1999.

45. Lola Nathanail, "Food and Nutrition Assessment, Democratic People's Republic of Korea, 16 March–24 April 1996" (assessment conducted by Save the Children UK for the World Food Program, Pyongyang office), 23; in World Food Program files, Rome.

46. *Reminiscences of Kim Il Sung* (Pyongyang: Foreign Languages Publishing House, 1996), 7:146.

47. Pomnyun, interview by author in Seoul, September 1998.

48. Médecins Sans Frontières, *North Korea: Testimonies of Famine.*

49. Lautze, "North Korea Food Aid Assessment."

50. Hilary Mackenzie, interview by author, November 1998.

51. Ibid.

52. UNDP, "Thematic Roundtable on Agricultural Recovery and Environmental Protection," 17.

53. Kwon of KBSM, interview by author in Nampyong, China, September 1998.

54. "Ex-POW Says N. Koreans Selling Blood for Food," Reuters, October 28, 1998, from Relief Web, online at http://www.reliefweb.int/w/rwb.nsf/s/7A5BB56CF8EC31F1C12566AB00551A03 (as of May 2001).

55. Weingartner e-mail report; copy in author's files.

56. Ibid.

5. The Economics of the Famine

1. Jung Chang, *Wild Swans* (New York: Doubleday, 1991), 234.

2. Amartya Sen, *Poverty and Famines: An Essay on Entitlement and Deprivation* (Oxford: Clarendon Press, 1992), 1–8.

3. See Cuny, *Famine, Conflict, and Response.* This book was published after Cuny's murder in Chechnya.

4. Fred Cuny, "An Emergency Field Assessment of the Russian Republic, January 17–February 29, 1992" (prepared for USAID by the U.S. Food and Humanitarian Assistance Assessment Team in the New Independent States, April 1992).

5. Thomas Henriksen and Jongryn Mo, eds., *North Korea after Kim Il Sung: Continuity or Change?* (Stanford, Calif.: Hoover Institution Press, 1997), 29–30.

6. Isaac Deutscher, *Stalin: A Political Biography* (Oxford: Oxford University Press, 1969), 338.

7. Henriksen and Mo, *North Korea after Kim Il Sung*, 138.

8. Ibid., appendix 2-1.

9. Ibid., 128.

10. Ibid., 190.

11. North Korean refugees, interviews by W. Courtland, May 1999.

12. Richard Kagan, Matthew Oh, and David Weissbrodt, *Human Rights in the Democratic People's Republic of Korea* (Minneapolis: Minnesota Lawyers International Human Rights Committee; Washington, D.C.: Asia Watch, 1988), 39.

13. Ibid., 43.

14. Ibid., 192–193.

15. Jasper Becker, "The Starvation of a Nation," *South China Morning Post*, February 4, 1996.

16. Kagan, Oh, and Weissbrodt, *Human Rights in the Democratic People's Republic of Korea*, 193.

17. Eberstadt, *Korea Approaches Reunification.*

18. KBSM, *The Food Crisis in North Korea Witnessed by Food Refugees* (Seoul: KBSM, June 23, 1998), 16.

19. E-mail from the KBSM's Jenny Jihyun Park, assistant to the Venerable Pomnyun, dated January 20, 1999. There is a great disparity between the grain prices reported by the WFP and those reported by the KBSM. It appears that the UN agency confused the won with the chon. One won equals 100 chon. Lola Nathanail reports a third variation of grain prices. It is possible that prices varied from year to year or region to region, which would explain the difference. See "Food and Nutrition Assessment," 23.

20. Kagan, Oh, and Weissbrodt, *Human Rights in the Democratic People's Republic of Korea.*

21. KBSM, *The Food Crisis in North Korea Witnessed by Food Refugees,* 13.

22. "Farmers Markets Increase in NK," *Digital Chosun Ilbo* (a Korean Internet newspaper), January 4, 1999, 18:55. The study on which this report is based was conducted by the South Korean Institute of Peace and Unification.

23. Taken from Kim Il Sung's collected works, *On Some Theoretical Problems of the Socialist Economy* (Pyongyang: Foreign Languages Publications House, March 1969), quoted in UNDP, "Thematic Roundtable on Agricultural Recovery and Environmental Protection," 20.

24. North Korean defector, interview by author in Seoul, September 1998; and Mark Kirk, "Trip Report of the House International Relations Committee, August 13–30, 1997" (unpublished photocopy, September 2, 1997), 24.

25. North Korean defectors in China, interviews by author, September 1998.

26. "Kim Jong Il, Speech at Kim Il Sung University," 5–6.

27. Korean Institute of Peace and Unification, *Farmers Markets in North Korea: Assessment and Prospects* (Seoul: Korean Institute of Peace and Unification), 3.

28. Yang, *Calamity and Reform in China*, 32.

29. North Korean refugee, interview by author.

30. Interview with author, June 18, 1998.

31. UNDP, "Thematic Roundtable on Agricultural Recovery and Environmental Protection," 20.

32. U.S. government sources.

33. FAO/WFP, *Crop and Food Supply Assessment Mission to DPRK: Special Report*, Special Alert no. 276 (World Food Program, June 3, 1997), 4.

34. This important comparative data is taken from KBSM refugee interviews reported to me by the Venerable Pomnyun in several conversations, confirmed by interviews I conducted with refugees. The data on the price of staple grains in the PDS was taken from interviews with WFP officials.

35. Oberdorfer, *The Two Koreas*, 372.

36. *Nutritional Survey of the Democratic People's Republic of Korea: Report by the EU, UNICEF, and WFP of a Study Undertaken in Partnership with the Government of DPRK* (Rome: United Nations World Food Program, November 1998), 4–5.

37. I said that "the central government appears to have decided . . . to practice a form of regional triage by cutting off rations earlier this year entirely to focus what little food is left in the capital, its suburbs, some industrial cities and the western part of the country in general." See "Statement on the North Korean Famine by Andrew S. Natsios, Vice President, World Vision, to the Senate Foreign Relations Committee Subcommittee on east Asian and Pacific Affairs, July 8, 1997," 3.

Humanitarian relief managers frequently avoid placing doctors in charge of triage procedures, preferring instead nurses or public health specialists, as doctors steeped in the medical ethics of the Hippocratic Oath find it nearly impossible to let any patient die without great effort to save them. They work without sleep for days trying to save everyone until they collapse and have to be removed from the disaster area. See Shawcross, *Quality of Mercy*, 245.

38. North Korean refugees, interviews by the author, September 1998.

39. Kirk, "Trip Report of the House International Relations Committee, August 13–30, 1997," 8.

40. "Gist of Hwang Jong-yop Work," *FBIS Monthly Report*, FBIS-EAS-98-227, August 15, 1998.

41. Copy of report in author's files.

42. See WFP News Update, "WFP to Deliver First Food Aid Directly to Hard-Hit Northeast of North Korea," July 1, 1997.

43. WFP shipping manifests and shipping records of bilateral imports; copies in author's files.

44. Ibid.

45. Nathanail, "Food and Nutrition Assessment, Democratic People's Republic of Korea."

46. Lautze, "North Korea Food Aid Assessment," 5.

47. FAO/WFP, *Crop and Food Supply Assessment Mission to DPRK: Special Report* (World Food Program, December 1995).

48. Cuny, *Famine, Conflict, and Response*, 25–26.

49. See FAO/WFP, *Crop and Food Supply Assessment Mission to DPRK: Special Reports* for 1995, 1996, and 1997.

50. Lautze, "North Korea Food Aid Assessment," 5.

51. Confidential report of Tun Myat to WFP, May 7, 1997.

52. Tun Myat, WFP official, interview by author in Rome, January 1999.

53. Lautze, "North Korea Food Aid Assessment," 5.

54. Stephen Devereux, *Theories of Famine* (New York: Harvester, Wheatsheaf, 1993), 90–91.

55. Ibid., 94.

56. "Kim Jong Il, Speech at Kim Il Sung University," 8.

57. FAO/WFP, *Crop and Food Supply Assessment Mission to DPRK: Special Report* (World Food Program, December 1996), 5.

58. Devereux, *Theories of Famine*, 94.

59. Nathanail, "Food and Nutrition Assessment," 25.

60. FAO/WFP, *Crop and Food Supply Assessment Mission to DPRK: Special Report* (World Food Program, November 1997), 13.

61. "Kim Jong Il, Speech at Kim Il Sung University," 8.

62. FAO/WFP, *Crop and Food Supply Assessment Mission to DPRK: Special Report* (December 1996), 5.

63. Robert Hauser, WFP country director in 1996, interview by author, January 1999.

64. North Korean defector, interview by author in Seoul, September 1998.

65. Merchant in Jilin, interview by author, September 1998; and "DPRK Farmers Markets" (South Korean Institute of Peace and Unification, January 1999).

66. This data comes from an informal NGO survey of farmers conducted by an NGO agricultural economist, interview by author in Washington, D.C., May 1998.

67. Refugees gave similar accounts to Jasper Becker. See Becker, *Hungry Ghosts*, 330.

68. Tun Myat, interview by author, Rome, January 1999.

69. North Korean refugees, interviews by author.

70. Nahm, *Korea: Tradition and Transformation*, 238.

71. Ibid.

72. I chaired the meeting of NGOs at which this comment was made.

73. Interviewed by author in Seoul, September 1998.

74. North Korean refugee from Hamhung City, South Hamgyong province, interview by author in Yanji, China, September 1998.

75. Becker, *Hungry Ghosts*, 322.

76. *Wolgan Chosun*, March 20, 1997, 306–317.

77. John Pomfret, "Portrait of a Famine," *Washington Post*, February 11, 1999; MSF interviews along the border published in *North Korea: Testimonies of Famine* (New York: Doctors Without Borders/Médecins Sans Frontières, August 1998); and author interviews with refugees.

78. North Korean defector in Seoul, interview by author, September 1998.

79. Article by Jee Hae-beom, *Digital Chosun Ilbo*, February 8, 1999, Beijing.

80. Pomnyun, interview by author in Washington, D.C., November 1999.

---

6. THE DIPLOMACY OF THE FAMINE

1. Oberdorfer, *The Two Koreas*, 51–56.

2. Kristin Gustavson and Jinmin Lee-Rudolph, "Political and Economic Human Rights Violations in North Korea," in *North Korea after Kim Il Sung: Continuity or Change*, ed. Thomas Henriksen and Jongryn Mo (Stanford, Calif.: Hoover Institution Press, 1997), 143.

3. Oberdorfer, *The Two Koreas*, 153.

4. This term first proposed and named by Yale professor Paul Bracken in "Nuclear Weapons and State Survival in North Korea," *Survival* 35, no. 3 (autumn 1993).

5. Oberdorfer, *The Two Koreas*, chaps. 9–13.

6. Hong Nack Kim, "Japan in North Korean Foreign Policy," in *North Korean Foreign Relations*, ed. Samuel Kim (Oxford: Oxford University Press, 1998), 132.

7. Ibid.

8. Kirk, "Trip Report of the House International Relations Committee, August 13–30, 1997," 40.

9. See William Drennan, *Mistrust and the Korean Peninsula: Dangers of Miscalculation,* Special Report (Washington, D.C.: United States Institute of Peace, November 1998).

10. Becker, *Hungry Ghosts: Mao's Secret Famine,* 241–243.

11. Jung Chang, *Wild Swans,* 235.

12. Becker, *Hungry Ghosts,* 268.

13. Michael Frank, "PVO Consortium in Pyongyang Final Report to USAID, August 23–November 15, 1997" (Catholic Relief Services, Baltimore, Md., photocopied report).

14. C. Kenneth Quinones, "Food and Political Stability in North Korea," in *Korea's Economy: Annual Report* (Washington, D.C.: Korea Economic Institute, February 1997), 8.

15. Nathanail, "Food and Nutrition Assessment, Democratic People's Republic of Korea," 22.

16. "Cargill Hopes for Quick U.S. OK on N. Korea Deal," *Journal of Commerce,* January 2, 1997.

17. Lautze, "North Korea Food Aid Assessment," annex 7.

18. Chinese merchants in Tumen City and Changbai, China, interviews by author, September 1998.

7. THE POLITICS OF THE FAMINE

1. C. Kenneth Quinones, e-mail interview by author, November 9, 2000.

2. Ibid.

3. Ibid.

4. Ibid.

5. U.S. Department of State, "Daily Press Briefing, July 17, 1997, Briefer: Nicholas Burns"; online at http://secretary.state.gov/www/briefings/9707/970717db.html.

6. Internal UN memorandum, dated July 19, 1996; copy in author's files.

7. Richard Regan, NSC staff, interview by author in Washington, D.C., June 1998.

8. Confidential sources.

9. USAID officials interviewed by author on condition of anonymity, Washington, D.C., June 1998.

10. Brian Atwood, interview by author in Boston, Mass., October 2000.

11. Internal UN memorandum, dated March 1997; copy in author's files.

12. From author's notes taken at meeting with Kartman in January 1997.

13. U.S. Department of State, "Daily Press Briefing, April 14, 1997, Briefer: Nicholas Burns"; online at http://secretary.state.gov/www/briefings/9704/970414.html.

14. The World Vision survey was conducted by Bruskin and Goldring Research, OmniTel, March 28–30, 1997. The sample size of 1,000 interviews was part of a larger survey, so the cost was minimal.

15. Barbara Croesette, "Hunger in North Korea: A Relief Aide's Stark Report," *New York Times,* June 11, 1997, A1.

16. R. Jeffrey Smith, "U.S. Says It Will Double Food Aid to North Korea; Decision Precedes Meeting on Peace Talks," *Washington Post,* July 15, 1997, A15.

17. InterAction Disaster Response Committee (DRC) North Korea e-mail from Jim Bishop, on Cox amendment, dated July 15, 1997.

18. State Department officials Chuck Kartman and Ann Kambara told WFP executive director Catherine Bertini in July 1996 that food distribution monitoring was important for U.S. domestic political reasons.

8. THE INTERNATIONAL AID EFFORT

1. North Korean defectors in Seoul, interviews by author, September 1998.

2. Quoted in B. C. Koh, "Recent Political Developments in North Korea," in *North Korea after Kim Il Sung: Continuity or Change?* ed. Thomas Henriksen and Jongryn Mo (Stanford, Calif.: Hoover Institution Press, 1997), 10.

3. WFP, *Report of the World Food Program Exploratory Mission to the Democratic People's Republic of Korea, March 5–23, 1991* (Rome: World Food Program, April 10, 1991), 10.

4. Ibid., 12.

5. North Korean defector in Seoul, interview by author, September 1998.

6. Oberdorfer, *The Two Koreas,* 298.

7. North Korean defector in Seoul, September 1998.

8. Hong Nack Kim, "Japan in North Korean Foreign Policy," in *North Korean Foreign Relations: In the Post–Cold War Era,* ed. Samuel S. Kim (Oxford: Oxford University Press, 1998), 125–126.

9. Letter from Amartya Sen to Nancy Lindborg, Mercy Corps International, November 26, 1997.

10. See chapter 7.

11. Associated Press, Beijing, May 12, 1997.

12. Brent Burkholder, "Status of Public Health: Democratic People's Republic of Korea, April 1997," *MMWR Weekly* 46, no. 24 (June 20, 1997): 561–565.

13. Sue Lautze, "The Famine in North Korea: Humanitarian Responses in Communist Nations" (Feinstein International Famine Center at Tufts University, June 1997).

14. Nathanail, "Food and Nutrition Assessment, Democratic People's Republic of Korea."

15. Lautze, "North Korea Food Aid Assessment," 3 and annex 4.

16. Ibid., 6–7; and Catherine Bertini, executive director of WFP, interview by author in Rome, January 1999.

17. Lautze, "North Korea Food Aid Assessment," 5.

18. Clinton administration official, interview by author on condition of anonymity, Washington, D.C., June 1998.

19. "Canadian Foodgrains Bank Field Assessment of August 27–September 3, 1996," June 1997; copy in author's files.

20. Lautze, "North Korea Food Aid Assessment."

21. Tun Myat, WFP official, interview by author, Rome, January 1999.

22. Bertini, interview by author, January 1999.

23. Ibid.

24. WFP transportation staff, interview by author, January 1999.

25. See John Pomfret, "Portrait of a Famine," *Washington Post*, February 11, 1999.

26. Hwang, *North Korea: Truth or Lies?*

27. FAO/WFP, *Crop and Food Supply Assessment Mission to DPRK: Special Report* (December 1996), 5.

28. December 23, 1998, USDA; online at http://www.fas.usda.gov/pecad/remote/korea/rice.html and http://www.fas.usda.gov/pecad/remote/korea/corn.html

29. Ken Quinones, "North Korean Agricultural Production," in *The Korean Economy in 1996: Annual Report* (Washington, D.C.: Korea Economic Institute, January 1996).

30. Quinones, interview by author, November 9, 2000.

31. See Hwang, *North Korea: Truth or Lies?* 9–10.

32. Scalapino, *North Korea at a Crossroads*, 2078–2079.

33. International Monetary Fund, World Bank, OECD, European Bank for Reconstruction and Development, *A Study of the Soviet Economy* (Washington, D.C.: IMF, February 1991), 3:150.

34. *The Politics of Aristotle*, trans. Benjamin Jowett (New York: Modern Library, 1943), book 2, ch. 3, 83.

35. FAO studies of rice harvest losses; copies in author's files.

36. See *Food Review* 20, no. 1 (January-April 1997): 4.

37. FAO/WFP, *Crop and Food Supply Assessment Mission to DPRK: Special Report* (World Food Program, December 1995), 3–4; FAO/WFP, *Crop and Food Supply Assessment Mission to DPRK: Special Report* (December 1996), 8; FAO/WFP, *Crop and Food Supply Assessment Mission to DPRK: Special Report* (November 1997), 12; FAO/WFP, *Crop and Food Supply Assessment Mission to DPRK: Special Report* (World Food Program, November 1998), 11.

38. FAO/WFP, *Crop and Food Supply Assessment Mission to DPRK: Special Report* (November 1998), 11.

39. Quoted in *People's Korea*, a pro-regime paper in Japan.

40. FAO officials, interviews by author, January 1999.

41. Kim Il Sung, "Revolutionizing the Peasants and Carrying Through the Party Conference Decisions in the Field of Agriculture" (speech delivered at the National Congress of Agricultural Functionaries, February 2, 1967), found in Kim Il Sung, *Selected Works* (Pyongyang: Foreign Languages Publishing House, 1971), 4:491.

42. See Scalapino, *North Korea at a Crossroads*, 1129.

43. Kirk, "Trip Report of the House International Relations Committee, August 13–30, 1997," 28.

44. Letter from Marina Ye Trigubenko to author; see also Marina Ye Trigubenko, "Economic Characteristics and Prospects for Development," in *North Korea: Ideology, Politics, Economy*, ed. Han S. Park (New York: Prentice-Hall, 1996).

45. See Cuny, *Famine, Conflict, and Response.*

46. To keep reduced herds alive during the winter months, another 600,000 to 1,000,000 MT of grain would have been needed.

47. Scott Snyder, *North Korea's Decline and China's Strategic Dilemmas*, Special Report (Washington, D.C.: United States Institute of Peace, October 1997), 2–4.

48. Pyon Chin-il, *Korea Report*, FBIS-EAS-96-034, February 8, 1996.

49. The precise title is "Principles of Conduct for the International Red Cross and Red Crescent Movement and NGOs in Disaster Response Programs."

50. I dissented from the Humanitarian Code because it profoundly misunderstood the role of local and international politics in humanitarian aid efforts.

51. See Michael Frank, "PVO Consortium in Pyongyang Final Report to USAID, August 23–November 15, 1997" (photocopy, Catholic Relief Services, Baltimore, Md., November 1997).

52. See Kagan, Oh, and Weissbrodt, *Human Rights in the Democratic People's Republic of Korea.*

53. The full text of the MSF interviews were available on their Web site at http://www.doctorswithoutborders.org/publications/reports/before1999/korea_1998.shtm.

54. Hilary Mackenzie, interview by author, November 1998.

55. See Fred Cuny, *Disasters and Development* (Dallas: Intertect Press, 1994); and Mary Anderson and Peter Woodrow, *Rising from the Ashes: Development Strategies in Time of Disaster* (Cambridge, Mass.: Harvard University Press, 1989).

56. Omawali made his arguments verbally at meetings.

57. For a full analysis of the public health consequences of famine, see Alex de Waal's classic work, *Famine That Kills: Darfur, Sudan, 1984–1985* (Oxford: Clarendon Press, 1989).

58. Lautze, "North Korea Food Aid Assessment," 10.

59. UNDP, "Thematic Roundtable on Agricultural Recovery and Environmental Protection," 3.

60. Ibid.

61. See Marcus Noland et al., *Rigorous Speculation: The Collapse and Revival of the North Korean Economy* (Washington, D.C.: Institute for International Economics, 1999).

62. See Andrew S. Natsios, *U.S. Foreign Policy and the Four Horsemen of the Apocalypse* (Washington, D.C.: CSIS and Praeger Press, 1997), chap. 7.

63. Herbert C. Hoover, *Famine in Forty-Five Countries: The Battle of the Front Line, 1914–1923*, vol. 3 of *An American Epic* (Chicago: H. Regnery, 1961).

64. Benjamin Weissman, *Herbert Hoover and Famine Relief to Soviet Russia, 1921–1923* (Stanford, Calif.: Hoover Institution, Stanford University, 1974), 22–23.

9. A Great Famine?

1. USAID has two principal accounts from which it can draw food aid during a famine: Title II of P.L. 480, which remained relatively stable during the 1990s, and U.S. Department of Agriculture surpluses through Section 416B. Section 416B has been used as a buffer reserve for famine response when Title II is inadequate.

2. KBSM refugee interview no. 45.

3. "Further on Defector's Speech to Unification Council," *FBIS Daily Report*, FBIS-EAS-97-316, November 13, 1997.

4. Becker, *Hungry Ghosts*, 331; and Jasper Becker, "Famine Refugee Tells of Mass Destitution and Death in North Korea," *South China Morning Post*, February 11, 1998.

5. Hwang, *North Korea: Truth or Lies?* 15.

6. North Korean defector in Seoul, interview by author, September 1998.

7. Hwang, *North Korea: Truth or Lies?* chap. 1.

8. *BBC on the Web*, February 17, 1999, 11:20 GMT.

9. Eberstadt made this point in his review of an earlier draft of this book.

10. Associated Press, "North Korea Says 220,000 Dead in Famine," May 10, 1999.

11. Ibid.

12. Pomnyun, interview by author in Seoul, September 1998. These rates were taken from the notes of his interview with this refugee, whose reliability he believes to be high.

13. WFP official, interview by author in Washington, D.C., July 1998.

14. Milton Amayun, interview by author, September 1997.

15. Eberstadt, *Korea Approaches Reunification*, 61.

16. Interview by author, September 1998.

17. Interview by author, September 1998.

18. UNICEF assessments.

19. Letter from Amartya Sen to Nancy Lindborg, Mercy Corps International, November 26, 1997.

20. Kagan, Oh, and Weissbrodt, *Human Rights in the Democratic People's Republic of Korea*.

21. Ibid.

22. Ibid., 34–40.

23. "Convention Relating to the Status of Refugees of 28 July 1951," Chapter 1, Article I(A), online at http://www.unhcr.ch/refworld/refworld/legal/instrume/asylum/1951eng.htm (as of May 2001)

24. Jung Chang, *Wild Swans*, 234; see also Becker, *Hungry Ghosts*, 103.

25. Conquest, *Harvest of Sorrow*, 115.

26. Taken from a WFP internal memo dated October 6, 1997.

27. EU, UNICEF, and WFP, *Nutritional Survey of the Democratic People's Republic of Korea*, 4–6.

28. Ibid.

29. Johns Hopkins researchers, interview by author in Washington, D.C., June 1999.

30. Robinson et al., "Mortality in North Korean Households."

31. The KBSM data suggest death rates twice those of the Johns Hopkins survey. This may be explained by the fact that the KBSM survey population includes a disproportionately high number of elderly people, at 18 percent, who traditionally experience very high death rates in famines. The Johns Hopkins survey interviews a proportionate number of elderly relative to their percentage of the population of the nation as a whole, or 6 percent. This disparity in base data may be explained by the fact that KBSM conducted its interviews in the homes of elderly Korean Chinese, who probably were more likely to take relatives or friends of the same age group.

32. For a comprehensive review of this phenomenon, see de Waal, *Famine That Kills.*

33. Robinson et al., "Rising Mortality in North Korean Households," 294.

34. KBSM/Good Friends, *Report on Daily Life and Human Rights of North Korean Food Refugees in China* (Seoul: Good Friends, June 1999), 83.

35. USAID, Bureau for Humanitarian Response, Office of Foreign Disaster Assistance, in conjunction with the University of Wisconsin Disaster Management Center, version 1, December 1997, reference no. KN-010.

36. Regional data do not appear in the UN survey of November 1998, but were obtained from interviews in Rome in January 1999 with WFP staff members who conducted further unpublished analysis of the data.

37. Interview by author, September 1998.

10. POLITICAL AND SECURITY CONSEQUENCES OF THE FAMINE

1. Oberdorfer, *The Two Koreas*, 375.

2. North Korean defector, interview by author in Jilin, September 1998.

3. Jasper Becker, "Kim Jong-Il Imposing Martial Law in Purge," *South China Morning Post*, March 26, 1998.

4. Interview by author, September 1998.

5. Kagan, Oh, and Weissbrodt, *Human Rights in the Democratic People's Republic of Korea.*

6. International NGO worker, interview by author in Washington, D.C., July 1998.

7. Korean Buddhist Sharing Movement (KBSM), *The Food Crisis in North Korea Witnessed by 1,019 Food Refugees: The Fifth Phase of Research, 30 September 1997–19 May 1998* (Seoul: KBSM, June 1998), 23.

8. North Korean refugees interviewed by Pomnyun; related to author in interview with Pomnyun in Seoul, September 1998.

9. KBSM refugee interview no. 692.

10. KBSM refugee interview no. 417.

11. KBSM refugee interview no. 445.

12. Suh Dae Sook and Chae-jin Lee, *North Korea after Kim Il Sung* (Boulder, Colo.: Lynne Rienner Publishers, 1998), 90.

13. Kim Jong Il, "On Preserving the Juche Character and National Character of the Revolution and Construction" (speech given in Pyongyang, June 19, 1997).

14. See Bracken's article "Nuclear Weapons and State Survival in North Korea."

15. See Natsios, "Humanitarian Relief Interventions in Somalia."

16. See Médecins Sans Frontières, *North Korea: Testimonies of Famine.*

17. Pomnyun ordered regular surveys of market prices for grain in farmers markets—information that is recorded in his periodic surveys—but the data for this more recent observation was taken from an interview I had with Pomnyun in Seoul, in September 1998. My own survey of refugees confirmed Pomnyun's data on the change of food prices in the farmers markets.

18. Papallion, interview by author, September 1997.

19. KBSM refugee interview no. 356.

20. Interview by KBSM, October 1997.

21. This anecdote was told to me by a member of the delegation; disclosure of the individual's name would compromise the translator.

22. Arnold, *Famine: Social Crisis and Historical Change,* 81–84.

23. Ibid., 108.

24. Ibid., 96–99.

25. Ibid., 86.

26. Papallion, interview by author, September 1998.

27. Becker, *Hungry Ghosts,* 322.

28. Pomnyun, North Korean refugees, interviews by author, September 1998.

29. KBSM refugee interview no. 368.

30. "Kim Jong Il, Speech at Kim Il Sung University," 6.

31. See Nicholas Eberstadt, *The End of North Korea* (Washington, D.C.: American Enterprise Institute, 1999).

32. Noland, "Why North Korea Will Muddle Through," 105–118.

33. Interview by author, September 1998.

34. Interview by author, September 1998.

35. John Osgood Field, *The Challenge of Famine: Recent Experience, Lessons Learned* (West Hartford, Conn.: Kumarian Press, 1993), 23, n. 6.

36. Alex de Waal, *Famine Crimes: Politics and the Disaster Relief Industry in Africa* (Bloomington: Indiana University Press, 1997), 106.

37. "Kim Jong Il, Speech at Kim Il Sung University," 6.

38. See Eberstadt and Banister, *The Population of North Korea.*

39. Becker, *Hungry Ghosts*, 127.

40. See Kagan, Oh, and Weissbrodt, *Human Rights*.

41. Becker, *Hungry Ghosts*, 323.

42. Information supplied on condition of anonymity.

43. Yang, *Calamity and Reform in China*, 14.

44. Ibid., 7.

45. Hisashi Fuji, "Situation on the Koran PeniInsula: This Is the Truth," *Foreign Broadcast Information Service (FBIS) Daily Report* no. 98A29116A; trans. from *Tokyo Gunji Kenkyu*, June 1, 1998.

11. WHAT IS TO BE DONE?

1. Robert A. Manning and James Przystup, "Feed Me or I'll Kill You," *Washington Post*, February 20, 1997.

2. Karen Elliott House, "Let North Korea Collapse," *Wall Street Journal*, February 21, 1997, A14.

3. Charles Krauthammer, "Why Feed a Mortal Enemy?" *Washington Post*, April 25, 1997, A27.

4. Marcus Noland, "North Korea: Present Status and Prospects for Survival to the Year 2000" (statement prepared for hearings by the United States Senate Committee on Foreign Relations, Subcommittee on East Asian and Pacific Affairs, July 8, 1997).

5. Becker, *Hungry Ghosts*, 338.

6. See Noland, "Why North Korea Will Muddle Through," 105–118.

7. Story related to the author by Fred Cuny upon his return from Russia in 1992.

SELECT BIBLIOGRAPHY

Armstrong, Charles K. "'A Socialism of Our Style': North Korean Ideology in a Post-Communist Era." In *North Korean Foreign Relations in the Post–Cold War Era*, edited by Samuel S. Kim. New York: Oxford University Press, 1998.

———. "State and Social Transformation in North Korea, 1945–1950." Ph.D. diss., University of Chicago, 1994.

Arnold, David. *Famines: Social Crisis and Historical Change*. Oxford: Basil Blackwell, 1988.

Becker, Jasper. *Hungry Ghosts: Mao's Secret Famine*. New York: Free Press, 1996; rev. ed., New York: Henry Holt, 1998.

Bracken, Paul. "Nuclear Weapons and State Survival in North Korea." *Survival* 35, no 3 (autumn 1993): 137–153.

Brinton, Crane. *The Anatomy of Revolution*. New York: Vintage Books, 1965.

Buchanan-Smith, Margaret, and Susanna Davies. *Famine Early Warning and Response: The Missing Link*. London: Intermediate Technology Development Group Publications, 1995.

Bunge, Frederica M. *North Korea: A Country Study*. Washington, D.C.: American University, Foreign Area Studies, 1981.

Burkholder, Brent. "Status of Public Health: Democratic People's Republic of Korea, April 1997." *MMWR Weekly*, June 20, 1997, 561–565.

Carnegie Endowment for International Peace. *Dialogue with North Korea*. Washington, D.C.: Carnegie Endowment for International Peace, 1989.

Cekan, Jindra Monique. "Listening to One's Clients: A Case Study of Mali's Famine Early Warning System and Rural Producers." Ph.D. diss., Tufts University, 1994.

Chang, Jung. *Wild Swans: Three Daughters of China*. New York: Doubleday, 1991.

Cho, Yong-Kyun. "Strategies for Economic Reform in North Korea." Paper presented at a conference sponsored by the Brookings Institution and the

Institute for Foreign and National Security (IFANS), Washington, D.C., July 9–10, 1997.

Clark, Lance. *Famine Early Warning Case Study: The 1984–85 Influx of Tigrayans into Eastern Sudan.* Working Paper no. 2, Washington, D.C.: Refugee Policy Group, 1986.

Conquest, Robert. *The Harvest of Sorrow: Soviet Collectivization and the Terror-Famine.* Oxford: Oxford University Press, 1986.

Crumplar, Robert. "A Future U.S. Military Presence on a Unified Korean Peninsula." Paper presented at a conference sponsored by the Brookings Institution and the Institute for Foreign and National Security (IFANS), Washington, D.C., July 9–10, 1997.

Cumings, Bruce. *Korea's Place in the Sun: A Modern History.* New York: W. W. Norton, 1997.

———. "Time to End the Korean War." *Atlantic Monthly*, February 1997, 71–79.

Cuny, Frederick C. *Disasters and Development.* Dallas: Intertect Press, 1994.

Cuny, Frederick C., with Richard Hill. *Famine, Conflict, and Response: A Basic Guide.* West Hartford, Conn.: Kumarian Press, 1999.

de Tocqueville, Alexis. *The Old Regime and the French Revolution.* Garden City, N.Y.: Doubleday, 1955.

De Waal, Alexander. *Famine That Kills: Darfur, Sudan, 1984–1985.* Oxford: Clarendon Press, 1989.

Deng, Francis M., and Larry Minear. *The Challenges of Famine Relief: Emergency Operations in Sudan.* Washington, D.C.: Brookings Institution, 1992.

Deuchler, Martina. *The Confucian Transformation of Korea: A Study of Society and Ideology.* Cambridge, Mass.: Council on East Asian Studies, Harvard University Press, 1992.

Devereux, Stephen. *Theories of Famine.* New York: Harvester, Wheatsheaf, 1993.

Dolot, Miron. *Execution by Hunger.* New York: W. W. Norton, 1985.

Drennan, William. *Mistrust and the Korean Peninsula: Dangers of Miscalculation.* Special Report. Washington, D.C.: United States Institute of Peace, 1998.

Dreze, Jean, and Amartya Sen. *Hunger and Public Action.* Oxford: Clarendon Press, 1989.

Earth Satellite Corporation. *Democratic People's Republic of Korea: Humanitarian Response Planning Map.* Washington, D.C.: U.S. Office of Foreign Disaster Assistance (OFDA), U.S. Agency for International Development (USAID), December 1997.

Eberstadt, Nicholas. "Can the Two Koreas Be One?" *Foreign Affairs* (winter 1992–93): 150–165.

———. *The End of North Korea.* Washington, D.C.: American Enterprise Institute, 1999.

———. "Hastening Korean Reunification," *Foreign Affairs* 76, no. 2 (March-April 1997): 77–92.

———. *Korea Approaches Reunification.* Armonk, N.Y.: M. E. Sharpe, 1995.

Eberstadt, Nicholas, and Judith Banister. *The Population of North Korea.* Berkeley: Institute of East Asian Studies, University of California, Berkeley, 1992.

Edwards, Michael, and David Hulme, eds. *Beyond the Magic Bullet: NGO Performance and Accountability in the Post–Cold War World.* West Hartford, Conn.: Kumarian Press, 1996.

Evans, Paul. "Integrating North Korea: Roles and Dilemmas for the International Community." Paper presented at a conference on "Korea and the Search for Peace in Northeast Asia," Ritsumeikan University, Kyoto, Japan, December 9–11, 1998.

Fairbanks, John, and Edwin Reischauer. *East Asia: The Great Tradition.* Boston: Houghton Mifflin, 1960.

Field, John Osgood. "Drought, the Famine Process, and the Phasing of Interventions." In *Hazards and Disasters: A Series of Definitive Major Works,* edited by Donald A. Wilhite. London: Routledge, 1999.

———. "From Food Security to Food Insecurity: The Case of Iraq, 1990–91." *GeoJournal* 30, no. 2 (1993): 185–194.

———, ed. *The Challenge of Famine.* West Hartford, Conn.: Kumarian Press, 1993.

Giorgis, Dawit Wolde. *Red Tears: War, Famine, and Revolution in Ethiopia.* Trenton, N.J.: Red Sea Press, 1989.

Gleysteen, William H., Jr. "Conference of the Brookings Institution and the Korean Institute for Foreign and National Security Affairs." Paper presented at a conference sponsored by the Brookings Institution and the Institute for Foreign and National Security (IFANS), Washington, D.C., July 9–10, 1997.

Hatada, Takashi. *A History of Korea.* Translated and edited by Warren W. Smith, Jr., and Benjamin H. Hazard. Santa Barbara, Calif.: ABC-Clio, 1969.

Henricksen, Thomas H., and Jongryn Mo, eds. *North Korea after Kim Il Sung: Continuity or Change?* Stanford, Calif.: Hoover Institution Press, 1997.

Hoover, Herbert. *Famine in Forty-five Countries: The Battle of the Front Line, 1914–1923.* Vol. 3 of *An American Epic.* Chicago: Henry Regnery, 1961.

Hughes, Christopher W. "The North Korean Nuclear Crisis and Japanese Security." *Survival* 38, no. 2 (1996): 79–103.

Hwang, Jang Yop. *North Korea: Truth or Lies?* (in Korean). Seoul: Institute for Reunification Policy Studies, 1998.

Jacobs, Dan. *The Brutality of Nations.* New York: Paragon House Publishers, 1988.

Jean, François. "Corée du Nord: un régime de famine." *Esprit,* February 1999.

Johnson, Paul. *Modern Times*. New York: HarperCollins, 1991.

Jordan, William Chester. *The Great Famine: Northern Europe in the Early Fourteenth Century*. Princeton, N.J.: Princeton University Press, 1996.

Kang, Chul Hwan, et al. "Voices from the North Korean Gulag." *Journal of Democracy* 9, no. 3 (1998): 82–96.

Kaplan, Robert D. *Surrender or Starve: The Wars behind the Famine*. Boulder, Colo.: Westview Press, 1988.

Kennedy, Scott. "Conflicting Logic of Korean Reform: Why the Best Case Scenarios Are Least Likely." Paper presented at a conference sponsored by the Brookings Institution and the Institute for Foreign and National Security (IFANS), Washington, D.C., July 9–10, 1997.

Kihl, Young Whan. *Korea and the World: Beyond the Cold War*. Boulder, Colo.: Westview Press, 1994.

Kim, Il Sung. *For the Independent Peaceful Reunification of Korea*. New York: Guardian Associates, 1976.

———. *Kim Il Sung: Selected Works* (in English). Pyongyang: Foreign Languages Publishing House, 1971.

Kim, Jong Il. *Let Us Exalt . . .* (in English). Pyongyang: Foreign Languages Publishing House, 1996.

———. *On the Juche Idea* (in English). Pyongyang: Foreign Languages Publishing House, 1982.

Kim, Kook-Chin. "Crisis Management on the Korean Peninsula: A Korean View." Paper presented at a conference sponsored by the Brookings Institution and the Institute for Foreign and National Security (IFANS), Washington, D.C., July 9–10, 1997.

Kim, Myong Chol. "Farewell to the Agreed Framework!" Northeast Asia Peace and Security Network, November 24, 1998. Online at http://www.nautilus.org/fora/security/23C_Kim.html (as of April 2001).

Kim, Samuel S. *North Korean Foreign Relations in the Post–Cold War Era*. Hong Kong: Oxford University Press, 1998.

Kim, Sung-Han. "Korea-U.S. Relations." Paper presented at a conference sponsored by the Brookings Institution and the Institute for Foreign and National Security (IFANS), Washington, D.C., July 9–10, 1997.

Korean Buddhist Sharing Movement (KBSM). *The Food Crisis of North Korea Witnessed by Food Refugees*. Reported in five issues, on February 23, 1998; March 23, 1998; May 23, 1998; June 23, 1998; and November 23, 1998.

———. *Report on Daily Life and Human Rights of North Korean Food Refugees in China: Based on Field Survey in 2,479 Villages in Three Northeast States in China*. Seoul: KBSM, June 1999.

Kyung, Yi Sun. *Inside the Hermit Kingdom: A Memoir*. Toronto: Key Porter Books, 1997.

Lautze, Sue. *The Famine in North Korea: Humanitarian Responses in Communist Nations.* Cambridge, Mass.: Feinstein International Famine Center, Tufts University, June 1997.

——. "North Korea Food Aid Assessment." Conducted for the U.S. OFDA, USAID, June 6, 1996.

Lee, Hy-Sang. "Supply and Demand for Grains in North Korea: A Historical Movement Model for 1966–1993." *Korea and World Affairs* 18, no. 3 (1994): 509–553.

Lee, Ki-Baik. *A New History of Korea.* Cambridge, Mass.: Harvard University Press, 1984.

Lee, Peter H., ed., et al. *Sourcebook of Korean Civilization.* New York: Columbia University Press, 1993–1996.

Lee, Seo-Hang. "Arms Control on the Korean Peninsula: Background and Issues." Paper presented at a conference sponsored by the Brookings Institution and the Institute for Foreign and National Security (IFANS), Washington, D.C., July 9–10, 1997.

Levin, Norman D. "What If North Korea Survives?" *Survival* 39, no. 4 (1998): 156–174.

Mariam, Mesfin Wolde. *Rural Vulnerability to Famine in Ethiopia, 1958–1977.* New Delhi: Vikas Publishing House, 1984.

Médecins Sans Frontières (MSF). *North Korea: Testimonies of Famine, Refugee Interviews from the Sino-Korean Border.* New York: Doctors Without Borders/ Médicins Sans Frontières, August 1998. Posted to their website, http: //www.doctorswithoutborders.org/publications/reports/before1999/ korea_1998.shtm on October 2, 1998.

Michishita, Narushige. "Regional Aspects of Korean Reunification: Focusing on Strategic Issues." Paper presented at the European Union (EU) Policy Seminar, "North Korean Scenarios and EU Responses, 1998–2003," 1998.

——. "Role of Force in North Korean Diplomacy." *Korea and World Affairs* (1997): 217–235.

Minnesota Lawyers International Human Rights Committee and Asia Watch. *Human Rights in the Democratic People's Republic of Korea (North Korea).* Minneapolis and Washington, D.C.: Minnesota Lawyers International Human Rights Committee and Asia Watch, December 1988.

Nahm, Andrew C. *Korea: Tradition and Transformation.* Elizabeth, N.J.: Hollym International, 1988.

Nathan, Andrew James. *A History of the China Internal Famine Relief Commission.* Cambridge, Mass.: Harvard East Asia Monographs, 1965.

Nathanail, Lola. *Food and Nutritional Assessment, Democratic People's Republic of Korea, 16 March–24 April 1996.* Rome: UN World Food Program, 1996.

Natsios, Andrew S. "Humanitarian Relief Interventions in Somalia: The Economics of Chaos." In *Learning from Somalia: The Lessons of Armed Humanitarian Intervention*, edited by Walter Clarke and Jeffrey Herbst, 77–95. Boulder, Colo.: Westview Press, 1997.

——. *U.S. Foreign Policy and the Four Horsemen of the Apocalypse: Humanitarian Relief in Complex Emergencies*. Washington, D.C.: Center for Strategic and International Studies, 1997.

Niksch, Larry A. "North Korea's Negotiating Behavior." In *North Korean Foreign Relations in the Post–Cold War Era*, edited by Samuel S. Kim. Hong Kong: Oxford University Press, 1998.

Noland, Marcus. "North Korea: Present Status and Prospects for Survival to the Year 2000." Statement prepared for hearings by the United States Senate Committee on Foreign Relations, Subcommittee on East Asian and Pacific Affairs, July 8, 1997.

——. "Why North Korea Will Muddle Through." *Foreign Affairs* 26, no. 4 (July-August 1997): 105–118.

Noland, Marcus, Sherman Robinson, and Tao Wang. *Famine in North Korea: Causes and Cures*. Working Paper 99-2. Washington, D.C.: Institute for International Economics, 1999.

——. *Rigorous Speculation: The Collapse and Revival of the North Korean Economy*. Working Paper 99-1. Washington, D.C.: Institute for International Economics, 1999.

Nutritional Survey of the Democratic People's Republic of Korea: Report by the EU, UNICEF, and WFP of a Study Undertaken in Partnership with the Government of DPRK. Rome: UN World Food Program, November 1998.

Oberdorfer, Don. *The Two Koreas: A Contemporary History*. Reading, Mass.: Addison-Wesley, 1997.

O'Hanlon, Michael. "A Military Assessment of the Korean Balance and Its Implications for Arms Control and ROK–U.S. Defense Planning." Paper presented at a conference sponsored by the Brookings Institution and the Institute for Foreign and National Security (IFANS), Washington, D.C., July 9–10, 1997.

——. "One Possible Security Contingency: North Korean Collapse." Paper presented at a conference sponsored by the Brookings Institution and the Institute for Foreign and National Security (IFANS), Washington, D.C., July 9–10, 1997.

Park, S. Han, ed. *North Korea: Ideology, Politics, and Economy*. Englewood Cliffs, N.J.: Prentice-Hall, 1996.

Perl, Raphael. *North Korean Drug Trafficking: Allegations and Issues for Congress*. Congressional Research Service Report for Congress. Washington, D.C.: Library of Congress, February 8, 1999.

Pryor, Frederic L. *The Red and the Green: The Rise and Fall of Collectivized Agriculture in Marxist Regimes*. Princeton, N.J.: Princeton University Press, 1992.

Quinones, C. Kenneth. "North Korea: From Containment to Engagement." In *North Korea after Kim Il Sung*, edited by Dae-Sook Suh and Chae-Jin Lee. Boulder, Colo.: Lynne Rienner, 1998.

———. "North Korean Agricultural Production." In *The Korean Economy in 1996: Annual Report*. Washington, D.C.: Korea Economic Institute, January 1996.

———. "North Korean Agricultural Production." In *The Korean Economy in 1998: Annual Report*. Washington, D.C.: Korea Economic Institute, January 1998.

Reese, David. *The Prospects for North Korea's Survival*. London: Oxford University Press, 1998.

Reischauer, Edwin O., and John K. Fairbank. *East Asia: The Great Tradition*. Boston: Houghton Mifflin, 1958.

Rhodes, Chris. "The Juche Idea and Its Role in the North Korean Political Economy." In *North Korea in the New World Order*, edited by Hazel Smith et al. New York: St. Martin's Press, 1996.

Robinson, W. Courtland, et al. "Mortality in North Korean Migrant Households: A Retrospective Study." *Lancet* 354, no. 9175 (July 24, 1999).

Rony, Denny. "North Korea as an Alienated State," *Survival* 38, no. 4 (winter 1997): 22–36.

Scalapino, Robert A. *North Korea at a Crossroads*. Stanford, Calif.: Hoover Institution Press, Stanford University, 1997.

Scalapino, Robert A., and Chong-Sik Lee. *Communism in Korea*. Berkeley: University of California Press, 1972.

Sen, Amartya. *Poverty and Famines: An Essay on Entitlement and Deprivation*. Oxford: Clarendon Press, 1992.

Smith, Heather. "Discussion Paper in International Economics," no. 133. Washington, D.C.: Brookings Institution, July 1997.

Smith, Hazel, et al. *North Korea in the New World Order*. New York: St. Martin's Press, 1996.

Smith, Hedrick. *The Russians*. New York: Ballantine Books, 1976.

Snyder, Scott. *Challenges of Building a Korean Peace Process: Political and Economic Transition on the Korean Peninsula*. Special Report. Washington, D.C.: United States Institute of Peace, 1998.

———. *A Coming Crisis on the Korean Peninsula?* Special Report. Washington, D.C.: United States Institute of Peace, 1996.

———. *Negotiating on the Edge: North Korean Negotiating Behavior*. Washington, D.C.: United States Institute of Peace Press, 1999.

————. *The North Korean Nuclear Challenge: The Post–Kim Il Sung Phase Begins.* Special Report. Washington, D.C.: United States Institute of Peace, 1994.

————. *North Korea's Decline and China's Strategic Dilemmas.* Special Report. Washington, D.C.: United States Institute of Peace, 1997.

————. *North Korea's Nuclear Program: Challenge and Opportunity for American Policy.* Special Report. Washington, D.C.: United States Institute of Peace, 1994.

Snyder, Scott, and Richard H. Solomon. *Beyond the Financial Crisis: Challenges and Opportunities for U.S. Leadership.* Special Report. Washington, D.C.: United States Institute of Peace, 1998.

Storry, Richard. *The Double Patriots: A Study of Japanese Nationalism.* London: Chatto and Windus, 1957.

Suh, Dae-Sook. *Kim Il Sung: The North Korean Leader.* New York: Columbia University Press, 1988.

————. "Kim Jong Il and New Leadership in North Korea." In *North Korea after Kim Il Sung,* edited by Dae-Sook Suh and Chae-Jin Lee. Boulder, Colo.: Lynne Rienner, 1998.

Suh, Dae-Sook, and Chae-jin Lee. *North Korea after Kim Il Sung.* Boulder, Colo.: Lynne Rienner, 1998.

Thompson, Kenneth W. *Korea: A World in Change.* Lanham, Md.: University Press of America, 1996.

Timmer, C. Peter, Walter P. Falcon, and Scott R. Pearson. *Food Policy Analysis.* Baltimore: World Bank with Johns Hopkins University Press, 1983.

Vreeland, Nena, and Rinn-Sup Shinn. *Area Handbook for North Korea.* Washington, D.C.: U.S. Government Printing Office, 1976.

Watkins, Susan Cotts, and Jane Menken. "Famines in Historical Perspective." *Population and Development Review* 11, no. 4 (December 1985).

Weissman, Benjamin M. *Herbert Hoover and Famine Relief to Soviet Russia, 1921–1923.* Stanford, Calif.: Hoover Institution Press, Stanford University, 1974.

Woodham-Smith, Cecil. *The Great Hunger: Ireland, 1845–49.* New York: Old Town Books, 1989.

World Food Program and Food and Agriculture Organization of the United Nations. *Crop and Food Supply Assessment Mission to the Democratic People's Republic of Korea. Special Reports,* issued December 1995; December 1996; November 1997; November 1998; November 1999.

Yang, Dali L. *Calamity and Reform in China: State Rural Society and Institutional Change since the Great Leap Forward Famine.* Stanford, Calif.: Stanford University Press, 1996.

INDEX

access, as barrier to information
gathering, 28
Africa
drought in, 182
famines in, 7
Agreed Framework, 127–128, 198
American Relief Administration
(ARA), 199–200
Anderson, Sara, 153
ARA. *See* American Relief Adminis-
tration (ARA)
Arnold, David, 226–227
Asia, famines in, 7, 50–51, 52–53
Asian Watch, 37–38
Association of Evangelical Relief
and Development Organi-
zations, 153
Atwood, Brian, 147

Bangladesh, famine in, (1974), 7
Banister, Judith, 232
Becker, Jasper, 46–47, 51, 55–56,
79–80, 137–138, 203, 218,
220, 239
begging, as survival strategy, 83
Bertini, Catherine, 54, 84, 146,
170–171, 175, 189–190
Beureter, Doug, 154
Bishop, Jim, 31, 196

blood, cross-border trade in as
famine survival strategy, 85
border surveys on North Korean
famine, 55–56, 56–57, 58–59,
79–80
criticism of, 86–88
Brown, Kathleen, 153
Bureau of Intelligence and Research
(U.S.), 141
Burns, Nicholas, 143, 147, 152

Cambodia
famine in (1970s), 7
Khmer Rouge in, 52–53
"killing fields" of, 52–53
capitalist systems, effect of on
famines, 93–94
Cargill, barter of grain for zinc from
North Korea, 139
Carter Center, 153
Carter, Jimmy, 149
intervention in North Korea, 126
cash remittances, from Korean
diaspora, 80–81
Ceausescu, Nicolae, 231, 239
Central Intelligence Agency (CIA),
142
Chagang province, famine in, 106,
160, 174

283

Andrew S. Natsios has held high office both in government and in the non-governmental sector. In 2001 he was appointed administrator of the U.S. Agency for International Development, where he had served as assistant administrator of the Bureau of Food and Humanitarian Assistance in 1991–93, and as director of the Office of Foreign Disaster Assistance in 1989–91. Natsios served in the Massachusetts House of Representatives for the 8th Middlesex District between 1975 and 1987. From 1980 until 1987 he was chair of the Massachusetts Republican Party. Between 1999 and 2001 Natsios served as the secretary of administration and finance for the Commonwealth of Massachusetts and as chairman of the Massachusetts Turnpike Authority, where he managed Boston's Big Dig.

Within the NGO world, Natsios served as vice president of World Vision from 1993 to 1998 and as a member of the executive committee of InterAction, a consortium of 150 U.S. NGOs, from 1994 until 1998.

A senior fellow at the United States Institute of Peace in 1998–99, Natsios is a retired lieutenant colonel in the U.S. Army Reserves and a veteran of the Gulf War. He holds a B.A. in history from Georgetown University and an M.P.A. from the Kennedy School of Government, Harvard University. He is the author of numerous publications, including *American Foreign Policy and the Four Horsemen of the Apocalypse;* "An NGO Perspective on Conflict Resolution" in *Peacemaking in International Conflict: Methods and Techniques* (published by the United States Institute of Peace Press); and "Humanitarian Relief Intervention in Somalia: The Economics of Chaos," in *Learning from Somalia: The Lessons of Armed Humanitarian Intervention.*

United States Institute of Peace

The United States Institute of Peace is an independent, nonpartisan federal institution created by Congress to promote research, education, and training on the peaceful management and resolution of international conflicts. Established in 1984, the Institute meets its congressional mandate through an array of programs, including research grants, fellowships, professional training, education programs from high school through graduate school, conferences and workshops, library services, and publications. The Institute's Board of Directors is appointed by the President of the United States and confirmed by the Senate.

Chairman of the Board: Chester A. Crocker
Vice Chairman: Seymour Martin Lipset
President: Richard H. Solomon
Executive Vice President: Harriet Hentges

Board of Directors

Chester A. Crocker (Chairman), James R. Schlesinger Professor of Strategic Studies, School of Foreign Service, Georgetown University

Seymour Martin Lipset (Vice Chairman), Hazel Professor of Public Policy, George Mason University

Betty F. Bumpers, President, Peace Links, Washington, D.C.

Holly J. Burkhalter, Advocacy Director, Physicians for Human Rights, Washington, D.C.

Marc E. Leland, Esq., President, Marc E. Leland & Associates, Arlington, Va.

Mora L. McLean, Esq., President, Africa-America Institute, New York, N.Y.

María Otero, President, ACCION International, Somerville, Mass.

Barbara W. Snelling, State Senator and former Lieutenant Governor, Shelburne, Vt.

Shibley Telhami, Anwar Sadat Chair for Peace and Development, University of Maryland

Harriet Zimmerman, Vice President, American Israel Public Affairs Committee, Washington, D.C.

Members ex officio

Lorne W. Craner, Assistant Secretary of State for Democracy, Human Rights, and Labor

Paul G. Gaffney II, Vice Admiral, U.S. Navy; President, National Defense University

Donald H. Rumsfeld, Secretary of Defense

Richard H. Solomon, President, United States Institute of Peace (nonvoting)

Jennings Randolph Program for International Peace

This book is a fine example of the work produced by senior fellows in the Jennings Randolph fellowship program of the United States Institute of Peace. As part of the statute establishing the Institute, Congress envisioned a program that would appoint "scholars and leaders of peace from the United States and abroad to pursue scholarly inquiry and other appropriate forms of communication on international peace and conflict resolution." The program was named after Senator Jennings Randolph of West Virginia, whose efforts over four decades helped to establish the Institute.

Since 1987, the Jennings Randolph Program has played a key role in the Institute's effort to build a national center of research, dialogue, and education on critical problems of conflict and peace. More than a hundred senior fellows from some thirty nations have carried out projects on the sources and nature of violent international conflict and the ways such conflict can be peacefully managed or resolved. Fellows come from a wide variety of academic and other professional backgrounds. They conduct research at the Institute and participate in the Institute's outreach activities to policymakers, the academic community, and the American public.

Each year approximately fifteen senior fellows are in residence at the Institute. Fellowship recipients are selected by the Institute's board of directors in a competitive process. For further information on the program, or to receive an application form, please contact the program staff at (202) 457-1700.

Joseph Klaits
Director

The Great North Korean Famine

This book is set in Janson; the display type is Janson Bold. Hasten Design Studio designed the book's cover, and Mike Chase designed the interior. Pages were made up by Helene Y. Redmond. Monica Hertzman copyedited the text, which was proofread by Karen Stough. The index was prepared by Sonsie Conroy.